RIDERS IN THE SKY

Riders posing with the Sons of the Pioneers album that inspired the band's name. Photograph by Erick Anderson, used by permission.

ROMANCING THE WEST WITH MUSIC AND HUMOR

BOBBIE MALONE AND **BILL C. MALONE**

TEXAS A&M UNIVERSITY PRESS | COLLEGE STATION

Copyright © 2025 by Bobbie and Bill C. Malone
All rights reserved
First edition

∞ This paper meets the requirements of ANSI/NISO Z39.48-1992 (Permanence of Paper).
Binding materials have been chosen for durability.

LIBRARY OF CONGRESS CATALOGING-IN-PUBLICATION DATA

NAMES: Malone, Bobbie, 1944– author. | Malone, Bill C., author.
TITLE: Riders in the Sky: romancing the West with music and humor / Bobbie Malone and Bill C. Malone.
DESCRIPTION: First edition. | College Station: Texas A&M University Press, [2025] | Includes bibliographical references and index.
IDENTIFIERS: LCCN 2024053894 (print) | LCCN 2024053895 (ebook) | ISBN 9781648432859 (paperback) | ISBN 9781648432866 (ebook)
SUBJECTS: LCSH: Riders in the Sky. | Country musicians—West (U.S.)—Biography. | Western swing (Music)—History and criticism. | Cowboys—Songs and music—History and criticism.
CLASSIFICATION: LCC ML421.R5 M35 2025 (print) | LCC ML421.R5 (ebook) | DDC 782.421642092/2 [B]—dc23/eng/20241113
LC record available at https://lccn.loc.gov/2024053894
LC ebook record available at https://lccn.loc.gov/2024053895

For our grandson,

Theo Sontheimer,

and for "Cowboy Kyle" Nelson,

whose souls are filled with the love and joy of music

CONTENTS

Preface
Riders on Our Minds   ix

Acknowledgments   xiii

Introduction
When Riders In The Sky First Rode onto the Country Music Scene   1

CHAPTER ONE
Doug Green
From Boyhood to Bluegrass to Western Music   15

CHAPTER TWO
Fred LaBour
That's Entertainment!   39

CHAPTER THREE
Three on the Trail   64

CHAPTER FOUR
The Cowboy Way   93

CHAPTER FIVE
The Winning of the West   132

CHAPTER SIX
Band of Brothers   167

Notes   207

Discography   233

General Index   235

Song and Album Index   245

PREFACE
Riders on Our Minds

The authors grew up much influenced by Hollywood cowboy culture. Being ten years older than Bobbie, Bill's introduction to the Grade B western movies goes back to the years of the Great Depression and World War II, while Bobbie's immersion in the westerns came in the 1950s. During those decades of hard times, war, and Cold War fears, Americans had ample reasons to embrace the man on horseback who embodied courage and rugged individualism. For Bill and Bobbie, though, such concerns had little or no relevance. They exhibited their debt to Western culture in various ways. Bill grew up on a cotton tenant farm in East Texas, where mules, not horses, provided the basic means of labor and transportation. His days as a little cowboy were characterized by flights of imagination or by hours spent with a little cap pistol, a bandanna, and a stick horse. He pursued outlaws over hundreds of imaginary miles on his imaginary steed. Western music, of course, was almost a constant companion, heard from the radio cowboys during the day or from the movies on many weekends. He even had an imaginary group, which he called the McLemore Brothers, who captured bad guys and locked them in their private prison, and then sang cowboy songs in their spare time with beautiful harmony—uncannily similar to that of the Sons of the Pioneers.

A decade later, Bobbie dreamed her own cowgirl dreams in her upper middle-class home in San Antonio. To ride horses in Brackenridge Park or at Dixie Dude Ranch in nearby Bandera, Bobbie had a red felt cowboy hat, red boots, "frontier" pants, and embroidered cowboy shirt, all manufactured locally. She remembers that "Home on the Range" was the first song that she sang completely, that she looked for Vaughn Monroe's "Ghost Riders in the Sky" on any cloudy, windy day in elementary school and loved Frankie Laine's rendition of songs like "Mule Train." And at Saturday matinees, she heard cowboy songs sung by Roy Rogers and Gene Autry at neighborhood theaters she attended with her friends. A few years later at Heart of the Hills Camp in Hunt, Texas, horseback riding was her favorite activity (along with editing the camp newspaper), but with her boots, she now just wore jeans and a straw cowboy hat.

Although he had no immediate way of knowing it at the time, the music that Bill heard during those early childhood days both anticipated and shaped the career that he later fashioned as a country music scholar. He made no distinctions between the music made by people like Gene Autry, Roy Acuff, Bill Monroe, and Bob Wills—all radically dissimilar stylists—yet all part of a fabric of downhome styles that emerged from and represented the working-class world of his parents. In early 1961, when he embarked on his doctoral dissertation on the history of country music at the University of Texas in Austin, songs like "Riding Down the Canyon" and "Empty Cot in the Bunkhouse" played as large a role in the cultural capital he had stored as did the songs from bluegrass, honky tonk, gospel, and other subgenres.

When her classical music–loving mother first met Bill, she told him that she enjoyed hearing cowboy songs at dude ranches, but "who would ever have thought of listening to them at home?" Bobbie felt that was not the right thing to have said to her fiancé, whose dissertation had become *Country Music USA*. Bill and Bobbie married in 1977, the same year that Riders In The Sky came on the scene in Nashville. But Bill had worked with Doug Green before he and Bobbie had even met. Sometime in the mid-1970s, when both were historians of country music, Doug was the oral historian at the Country Music Foundation in Nashville and Bill was teaching in the history department at Tulane University. Bill and Judy McCulloh had co-edited *Stars of Country Music*, a book of essays to which Doug contributed a fine piece on Gene Autry. Bill was intrigued and bemused when he soon learned that Doug had organized a trio called Riders In The Sky, a little group that would revive the songs of the Saturday morning matinees. A nice little diversion, he thought, for a country music historian! But the group lasted. Doug's day job at the Country Music Hall of Fame (CMHOF) went by the wayside. Bill remembers talking about Doug's transformation with some of his country music colleagues, "He's actually doing it!" When Bill and Bobbie first saw the Riders performing in Cincinnati in the early 1990s, where she was working on her dissertation research, the Riders were already into their second decade. They're still "doing it" over three decades later, and we're hoping they keep right on doing it!

ACKNOWLEDGMENTS

Research is usually much more fun than writing, but working with the Riders turned out to be more fun in both categories. They provided us with a host of wonderful folks to talk to, and talk they did, sharing their stories and memories and giving us insights into the lives and times of Doug, Fred, Woody, and Joey that proved essential in helping us develop our group biography.

In addition to the many wonderful conversations and emails with the Riders themselves, we'd like to thank their family members, friends, and coworkers who shared their childhood, young adult, early professional and pre-Riders years. These include in alphabetical, not chronological, order: Jay Cassidy, Bob Chambers, Marshall Chapman, Arch Copeland, Mike DeVriendt, the late Nolan Faulkner, Herschel Freeman, Connie Green, Jim Green, George Gruhn, Janet Hendriksen, Bill Ivey, Chris LaBour, Dickey Lee, Peter Lorch, Billy Maxwell, Jim McQuaid, Marcie LaBour Merritt, Sharon Millimaki, the late Rod Moag, Sandy Peterson-Fisher, Andy Sacks, Lisa Silver, and Tina Walker. We also are grateful to have talked with Rider wives, former wives, adult children, and other family members: Sally Green Angeli, Lily LaBour Catalano, Lisa Reed Chrisman, Alice LaBour Fair, Carolyn Gann, Annie Green, Dezarria Donzella "Desi" Smith Green, Grace Green, James Green, George LaBour, Patti Miskulin, Liza Jane Green Parnell, Ned Ramage, Cindy Turner, and Sandy Wilkerson. Folks with whom the Riders played and worked were equally generous with their time and memories, and we so appreciate them: the late Steve Arwood, Ray Benson, Sandy Brokaw, Teena Camp, Hal Cannon, Gary Cook, Sharon Cruse, Manuel Cuevas, Don Cusic, Devin Dawson, Virgil Dickinson, Norton Dill, Pete Fisher, Orin Friesen, Karen Gogolick, Dick Goodman, Tommy Goldsmith, Lisa Miles Harris, Ken Irwin, Ken Jones, Paul Lohr, Gary McMahan, Gloria Gene Moore, Bruce Nemerov, Robert K. Oermann, Jay Peterson, Andy Riess, Dan Rogers, Rick Roltgen, Alan Sacks, David Symington, Jeff Taylor, Brett Truett, the late Johnny Western, and Richard Wiegel. The Riders' fans are a completely devoted and passionate group, and interviewing them was a pleasure: Jamie Amos, Carin Joy Condon, Mary Flanagan, Jayna Henderson, Steve Jacobs (Mr. Wizard IV), Donna Jagodzinski, Ed Jagodzinski, Dr. Tom John, Dr. Michael Lichtenstein, Mike Mahaney, Mary Masteller, Alan McNeely, Butch Nelson, "Cowboy Kyle" Nelson, Susan Nelson, Bill Nye the Science Guy, and Jerry West. We also enjoyed talking and working with others who helped with our research: Jerry Dowling; Kathleen Campbell, Senior Archivist, Reference and Print Collection Country Music Hall of Fame and Museum; Kevin Fleming, Director of Library and Archival Collections, Country Music Hall of Fame and Museum; Tim Davis and Christina Mitchell, Grand Ole Opry Archives; Josh Norton, Getty Images; Michele Beacham, Los Angeles Philharmonic Archives; Hank Edenborn; Matt Fox; Stacy Harris; and Christine Sposari.

Special thanks to all those at Texas A&M University Press, who transformed our manuscript into the book in your hands, beginning with acquisitions editor Thom Lemmons who enthusiastically presented it to the A&M Faculty Advisory Committee, and TAMUP staff members: Katie Duelm as managing and project editor, editorial intern Madison Brown for coding for typesetting, Kyle Littlefield for handling all the metadata, Christine Brown for publicity, including the catalog and awards, Kathryn Lloyd for working with vendors, Laura Forward Long as design production head, Ahagail Chartier for writing and editing copy for the catalog and book jacket and transmitting page proofs to us. Beyond the TAMUP staff, we want to thank Dawn Hall for copyediting, David K. Kessler for his handsome cover design, Melissa Tandysh for designing the interior, Sheridan for handling the printing, and the two anonymous peer reviewers for their early praise.

RIDERS IN THE SKY

INTRODUCTION

WHEN RIDERS IN THE SKY FIRST RODE ONTO THE COUNTRY MUSIC SCENE

GAZING ON THE AMERICAN MUSICAL SCENE IN 1977, ONE FOUND little available evidence that the Singing Cowboy would ever again be a factor in American entertainment. The once-popular figure now seemed too romantic and utterly irrelevant for that era's cynical world. Rex Allen had delivered the valedictory for the Hollywood Singing Cowboy in 1954 in his last movie, *The Phantom Stallion*, and the once-ubiquitous Saturday morning television shows of Gene Autry and Roy Rogers went off the air soon after. Their demise suggested that they had become little more than childhood memories that baby boomers had finally outgrown. The cowboy, of course, in numerous guises, still retained a visual presence in both country music and American culture. Cowboy regalia, for example, remained omnipresent in the gaudy Nudie costumes that many singers still sported, while others typically wore cowboy hats, boots, belts, and jeans. The term "hat act," used none too charitably, soon described many of these performers who dressed like cowboys but rarely sang cowboy songs.

Songs of the West, though, had never totally disappeared from American popular culture. The choral groups, the Norman Luboff Choir and the Roger Wagner Chorale, released beautiful renditions of cowboy songs in 1955 and 1956 for major record labels. Prominent country music stars, including Johnny Cash, occasionally introduced their own western-themed, cowboy, or Indian songs or performed classic ballads on LPs.[1] A few tradition-oriented singers such as Glenn Ohrlin, a longtime performer on the rodeo circuit, kept the flame kindled by including songs like "Strawberry Roan" and "The Old Chisholm Trail" in his sets at folk festivals and similar venues. Then, from time to time, someone like Marty Robbins, with his popular album of 1959, *Gun Fighter Ballads and Trail Songs*, and his number one single, "El Paso," demonstrated that a vast audience could still be won over to such material. It is also impossible to exaggerate the influence exerted by the kiddie cowboy shows that appeared on television in cities around the country. Roger Miller poked good-natured fun at such shows, while demonstrating their relevance, in his hit recording of 1965, "Kansas City Star." The protagonist of the song is so popular in Kansas City that he rejects higher-paying alternatives in other cities. Millions of children throughout America had been reminded of the cowboy heritage, while also picking up snippets of traditional lore and songs from their trusted cowboy hosts. The kiddie cowboy shows date back to at least 1925 when the pioneer cowboy singer, Harry McClintock, hosted such a show on KFRC radio in San Francisco.[2]

Cowboy-oriented songs also became ingrained in the public consciousness as themes introducing popular radio and television series in the 1950s and 1960s. Almost everyone at the time could hum, or maybe sing a few lines from, the themes of such prime time television shows as *Gunsmoke*, *Rawhide*, *Bonanza*, or *Have Gun Will Travel*. As an immensely plastic symbol, the cowboy had never outlived his appeal—with writers, popular culture makers, and politicians continually finding ways to exploit images of the West and its most alluring representative. The Marlboro Man, Coca-Cola Cowboys, Midnight Cowboys, Cosmic Cowboys, Urban Cowboys, and Rhinestone Cowboys, to name only a few, populated the decades of the 1960s and '70s. While visions of rugged independence remained linked to the cowboy, the image was so often manipulated to convey the themes of angst, alienation, rebellion, aggressive masculinity, outlawry, or even downright scruffiness that a couple of songwriters, Ed and Patsy Bruce, could even be moved to advise, "Mamas, Don't Let Your Babies Grow Up to Be Cowboys." In country music videos and other advertisements, the cowboy appeared more often in a pickup truck than on a horse. Only a year or so after the Bruce composition, in 1975, Willie Nelson launched his fabulous singing career with his concept album *Red Headed Stranger*, which presented a more menacing image of the cowboy as a desperado. Writers and singers sometimes did fashion very good material out of their cowboy preoccupation, and they showed that they could be up to date with songs like Ian Tyson's "Someday Soon," a bittersweet chronicle of rodeo life, while Terry Stafford's "Amarillo by Morning," cowritten with Paul Fraser, depicted an even scruffier side of rodeo exploits. Michael Burton's "Night Rider's Lament," on the other hand, beautifully defended a lonely cowboy life lived amid western grandeur. Musicians as a whole, though, tended merely to sporadically adopt cowboy idioms, exploiting them for their commercial appeal before moving on to some other theme. Indeed, by the late 1970s, the idea seemed remote that a cowboy music genre—and one employing old-fashioned themes of virtue and romance and using basically acoustic instrumentation—could thrive.[3]

Then along came the trio, Riders In The Sky. No member of the group had been alive during the heyday of the Singing Cowboy, but they had caught much of the flavor of that era by watching Autry's and Rogers's shows on Saturday morning television, by hearing recordings made by entertainers like Marty Robbins or the Sons of the Pioneers, or by watching cowboy kiddie shows on their local TV stations. Douglas B. Green—soon to be "Ranger Doug"—in fact, had turned his childhood interest into a historical obsession and had become the nation's leading authority of the western musical tradition. Born far away from cattle country—Doug in Great Lakes, Illinois; Fred "Too Slim" LaBour in Grand Rapids, Michigan, and Paul Woodrow "Woody" Chrisman in Nashville, Tennessee—they nevertheless understood that the fading of the Singing Cowboy from American popular culture meant more than the disappearance of a significant symbol for American youth. Above all, they regretted the loss of the beautiful music made by Gene Autry, Roy Rogers, Tex Ritter, the Sons of the Pioneers, and other Singing Cowboys.

The Hollywood Singing Cowboy phenomenon valued by the Riders was not the first manifestation of America's fascination with the West and the cowboy. The West itself was memorialized before the cowboy even came on the scene. Late nineteenth-century landscape painters such as Albert Bierstadt extolled the grandeur of the vistas of this wild and seemingly unsettled region, while Fredric Remington and Charles Russell's paintings documented various aspects of western life, including frontiersmen, mountain men, and Indians.

The famous cattle drives that initially ran from Texas to Missouri and Kansas brought the cowboy into public consciousness and spotlighted the supposedly rugged independence of those hardy souls as they plied their trade out on the lonely prairie (although herding remained a *group* enterprise). This image grew in the late nineteenth century, as dime novelists began building a romantic portrait of America's West that anticipated the twentieth-century explosion promoted by mass media culture. Ned Buntline (Edward Zane Carroll Judson), beginning in the mid-1840s, authored at least 400 dime novels containing fanciful, and often lurid, stories about every conceivable type of adventurer. Buntline did the most to create the legend of Buffalo Bill Cody, whom he had met in Nebraska in 1869. His first depiction of Cody, *Buffalo Bill: The King of Border Men*, appeared that year in a New York weekly. He demonstrated that a vast audience, made up principally of young men, was ready to gobble up books about this mythical West.[4]

But for popularizing the rough-and-ready image of the West, one need look no further than Cody himself, who took his Wild West Shows around the world at the end of the nineteenth and the beginning of the twentieth centuries. Cody's entrepreneurship propelled this mythology forward when he debuted his first Wild West Show in Omaha, Nebraska, in 1883. The show had a thirty-year run and became a major attraction in Europe, where it first toured in 1887, as well as in the United States. Cody presented a romantic vision of the West to highly receptive audiences by featuring parading cowboys and their trick roping, shooting, and riding, and Indians in full battle dress, including the famous Sitting Bull. The Wild West Show did much to replace the older vision of James Fenimore Cooper's Natty Bumppo as the quintessential western hero with the newer depiction of the cowboy. Interestingly, although Cody's shows used music, they did not feature cowboy songs; they instead presented a sixteen-piece group called Buffalo Bill's Cowboy Band that played marches and the popular songs of the day.[5]

Also prominent in promulgating his devotion to the West was Owen Wister, born on July 14, 1860, in Philadelphia. As an educated Easterner, graduate of Harvard Law School, and friend of Teddy Roosevelt, Wister did his part to make Americans conscious of western majesty and uniqueness. Between 1885 and 1900, he visited the West fifteen times, with Wyoming as the place that really opened his eyes to the pristine beauty of the region and its characters. In 1902, he wrote *The Virginian*, a novel dedicated to Roosevelt, that introduced the stereotypical cowboy as a taciturn but brave individualist—nothing less than a personification of the Anglo-Saxon knight. Wister turned the novel into a play that opened on Broadway in January 1904, and he wrote a song, "Ten Thousand Cattle Straying," for the villain, "possibly to lighten up the rather heavy stage proceedings, which include a hanging and two shootings."[6]

Although the cattle drives only lasted from the late 1860s through the 1880s, they fostered images that endured in American popular culture, particularly in western movies like *Red River* (1948). The vision of rugged and seemingly independent horseback-riding heroes and their herds quickened the appetites of people back East, and around the world, who hungered for more. British historian Eric Hobsbawm, among others, has presented us with a more nuanced way to consider this aspect of American popular culture. He critically excoriated this "invented cowboy ... a late romantic creation" who served "a double function: he represented the ideal of individualist freedom pushed into a sort of inescapable jail by the closing of the frontier and the coming of the big corporations." The cowboys were, in fact, low-paid wage workers who toiled long hours at dangerous and dirty tasks—working-class agents or representatives of the capitalistic transformation of the West.[7]

Despite the reality of cowboy life, the perceived romance of the cowboy's existence won the day in the American imagination. Cowboys themselves were not immune to this fantasy. It infiltrated and affected their lives, as Jane Kramer demonstrated in a highly influential *New Yorker* article, later published as *The Last Cowboy* (1977). She explored the life of Henry Blanton, a third-generation, forty-year-old Texas Panhandle cowboy. Although he had honed his skills at roping, riding, mending fences, or keeping up with a herd of twenty-two hundred cows, he felt dissatisfied. In an era where fences and feedlots had replaced the open range, Blanton felt frustrated at his inability to embody the aura of the cowboy of the silver screen, especially that projected by the popular actor Glenn Ford, who "lived by codes, not rules—codes of calm, solitude, and honor—and the belief that a cowboy had a special arrangement with nature and, with his horse under him and the range spread out around him, knew a truth and a freedom and a satisfaction the ordinary men did not." Blanton may have been able to dress like Ford, but he could not live the imaginary life depicted in his favorite western movies.[8]

Racially, cowboys were a diverse body of workers; about 25 percent of the men who made the long drive were Black, while others were of Mexican or Anglo descent. Their ability to work in a protected environment could also be attributed, in part, to a racially mixed security force. After the Civil War, Black or Buffalo Soldiers had been sent to the West to protect settlements, railroad building, and other business investments. The irony of Black men fighting Red men in order to secure the West as a haven for White men suggests another facet of the reality fractured by the lens of popular culture. Unfortunately, realities such as this were too long lost in the perception that the West was preponderantly white, as Hobsbawm also noted when he stated that the cowboy could be used to defend a "more dangerous ideal: the defense of the native waspish American ways against the millions of immigrants from lower [sic] races." Too often, cowboy music has reinforced this perception.[9]

In 1908 and 1910 the collectors Nathan Howard Thorp and John Lomax issued America's first collections of cowboy songs—garnered from working cowboys and people associated with them—and by 1919, a vaudeville singer, Bentley Ball, with his stilted delivery and trilled *r*s, even recorded a couple of authentic cowboy songs learned from the Lomax collection, "The Dying Cowboy" and "Jesse James." As early as 1923, Oscar Fox, a German American musician, choirmaster, and composer from near Marble Falls, Texas, began arranging and composing melodies from the Lomax book. He enjoyed setting poetry to music even though he never wrote lyrics himself. Among the most enduring of those he arranged included "Cowboy's Lament" ("The Streets of Laredo") in 1923, "The Old Chisholm Trail" (1924), and "Old Paint" (1927). Woodward Maurice "Tex" Ritter, from Panola County, Texas, studied at the University of Texas in the early 1920s and learned cowboy music from three outstanding scholars of the West—John Lomax, Oscar Fox, and folklorist and collector, J. Frank Dobie—and Ritter sometimes worked with Fox, singing ballads to illustrate the scholar's lectures. Only later in the decade did he perform on radio before gaining prominence as a Hollywood cowboy singer in the 1930s and 1940s.[10]

When he was a young man David Guion, a classically trained musician and composer from Ballinger, Texas, had worked as a cowboy. Later, he began arranging folk songs for classical performance, including the well-known "O Bury Me Not on the Lone Prairie" (1931) and "Little Joe, the Wrangler" (1933). Guion's chief claim to fame, though, came from his arrangement of "Home on the Range," also taken from the Lomax collection, which was used in one of his New York productions. Litigation over the song's authorship, and the perhaps spurious claim that it was Franklin Roosevelt's favorite song, contributed to making "Home on the Range" one of the most famous western songs of all time.[11]

Even before the appearance of the songs collected by Thorp and Lomax, Tin Pan Alley songwriters had begun turning out their own melodic interpretations of western life, often romantic or lighthearted depictions of Indian maidens or cowboys and cowgirls that took the country by storm when they appeared on piano sheet music or on cylinder or disc recordings. Songs like "Red Wing," "Snow Deer," and "San Antonio," couched in the popular or ragtime melodies of the day, circulated widely. Some of these songs differed little from the pop love ballads of the 1920s but were made distinctive by their use of western contexts. "Where the Silvery Colorado Wends Its Way" (1922) and "When It's Springtime in the Rockies" (1929), for example, moved into the repertories of minstrel and vaudeville entertainers as well as dance bands and vocal quartets.[12]

The nascent country music industry, which began to take shape in the early 1920s, seized often on the image and songs of the cowboy. Some early recording performers, such as Harry McClintock and Jules Verne Allen, had cowboyed themselves; Carl Sprague grew up on a ranch near Alvin, Texas; and the Cartwright Brothers (Bernard and Jack) spent their childhood in Boerne, "directly on the route of the 'long drive' that proceeded on to Kansas." These singers recorded a bevy of classic cowboy songs such as "When the Work's All Done This Fall," "The Old Chisholm Trail," and "Utah Carroll," that reflected the actual *work* of the cowboy, but the romantic *image* of the cowboy ultimately won the day in country music. It, in fact, became one of the defining themes of this emerging idiom, a way to assert respectability for a music made principally by working people. So-called cowboy singers appeared everywhere during the 1930s, as soloists and as groups, on radio stations from Nova Scotia to New York to Texas to California, on record labels, and in personal appearances. They even appeared on Broadway in 1931 in a musical called *Green Grow the Lilacs*, the forerunner of *Oklahoma*.

Jimmie Rodgers's cowboy songs, recorded between 1927 and 1933, marked a distinctive departure from those performed by earlier singers such as the Cartwright Brothers. Ultimately known as the "father of country music," because of his popular renditions of blues, railroad, hobo, and sentimental tunes, Rodgers also recorded a handful of cowboy songs that reflected the influence of Tin Pan Alley. His residence in Kerrville and

San Antonio, Texas, at the end of his life, may have made him more conscious of the cowboy's prominence in American culture. Even though Rodgers recorded only seven cowboy-themed songs, such as "When the Cactus Is in Bloom" and "The Yodeling Cowboy," those few songs extolled the supposed, shackles-free virtues associated with cowboy life. The lyrics of "The Yodeling Cowboy" assert that "My cowboy life is so happy and free, out west where the laws don't bother me." While Rodgers's cowboy songs could embody nostalgia, as in "Land of My Boyhood Dreams," a tribute to his adopted state, Texas, his western songs generally portrayed the cowboy as a lighthearted and carefree individual who was nevertheless brave and fearless. Such recordings were the progenitors of a spate of Hollywood and Tin Pan Alley cowboy songs that flourished in the United States during the 1930s. Before his death from tuberculosis on May 26, 1933, the force of his unique yodel, charisma, and popularity created an alleged link between yodeling and cowboy music in the emerging country genre. After Rodgers posed in cowboy regalia in a publicity photo, and largely because of him, country singers by the dozens donned cowboy boots and hats and began singing and yodeling cowboy songs. During the two decades that followed, cowboys appeared everywhere in American popular culture. In fact, they had moved into the popular culture of other lands, anywhere that Jimmie Rodgers's records circulated (in the British Isles and elsewhere in the English-speaking world, such as New Zealand and Australia, and even East Africa). Rodgers was not alone in spreading American country music with a western flavor abroad. Kansas-born, New York pioneer recording artist Carson Robison played a major role, as both singer and songwriter, in introducing cowboy songs to mainstream American culture and to the rest of the world. In 1935 opera singer James Melton recorded Robison's "Carry Me Back to the Lone Prairie" for the Columbia label, and saw it achieve great popularity throughout the world. Many people assumed that the song was a traditional cowboy ballad. Robison also took his band and music to England for extended stays in 1932, 1936, and 1938, performing with the Pioneers (later, the Buckaroos), dressed as cowboys and singing mostly western songs. He also performed on Radio Luxembourg in that principality on the European continent.[13]

Following Jimmie Rodgers, cowboy music became omnipresent in American entertainment. Furnished by professional songwriters on Tin Pan Alley and elsewhere, songs were featured on radio, on Broadway, on recordings, and the genre exploded once singing cowboys appeared in films. One of Rodgers's most affecting songs, "Prairie Lullaby," was written by a New York tunesmith named Billy Hill, one of many non-Western writers who found musical gold in the materials of the West. Billy Hill (born William Joseph Hill) was the most popular of these writers but lived to be only forty years old. While trained at the New England Conservatory of Music, he fell in love with the West after a trip to the region where he worked part-time as a cowboy. Although he wrote a wide array of songs, such as "Have You Ever Been Lonely," "They Cut Down the Old Pine Tree," "The Old Spinning Wheel," and "The Glory of Love," his many western songs became his best sellers, including "Empty Saddles," "Wagon Wheels," and "The Last Roundup," a huge hit from 1933. "The Last Roundup," and "Empty Saddles" both appeared in the Ziegfeld Follies of 1934. Hill was part of a contingent of writers and arrangers who supplied cowboy and western songs for the growing chorus of radio cowboys. These writers included the Happy Chappies (Fred Howard and Nat Vincent), who, while working mostly on the West Coast, contributed songs like "When the Bloom Is on the Sage," and Johnny Mercer and Cole Porter, who even got into the act with "I'm an Old Cowhand" and "Don't Fence Me In." In the 1940s Fred Rose and Cindy Walker used western songs as their entrée into the songwriting business, and as preludes to their successful careers as country songwriters. Walker's "Blue Canadian Rockies" was written for Gene Autry in 1950 but has been recorded a multitude of times, including a version by the country-rock band, the Byrds.

Billy Hill's "The Last Roundup" proved to be one of the giant hits of 1933. Not yet a Hollywood sensation, Gene Autry recorded it that year as "Oklahoma's Singing Cowboy," and the song was soon on its way to becoming part of every cowboy singer's repertory. Autry, of course, was the chief embodiment of the Hollywood Singing Cowboy. Born in Texas and reared in Oklahoma, Autry built an early recording career that drew heavily on the songs of Jimmie Rodgers. His early repertory of risqué blues tunes might come as a surprise to people who know him only through his many western songs. His career changed dramatically after 1934, when he signed with Mascot Pictures and made the first of ninety-three films that eventually established his reputation as America's Favorite Singing Cowboy and one of Hollywood's leading box office attractions. Drawn by his success, a host of other movie singing cowboys such as Roy Rogers, Tex Ritter, Jimmy

Wakely, Carolina Cotton, Herb Jeffries (the only African American among the group), and the Sons of the Pioneers, soon followed. As Bill C. Malone wrote in *Singing Cowboys and Musical Mountaineers*, Autry

> became one of Hollywood's most popular and commercially successful personalities with a style that combined music, personal heroism, and Victorian morality. With his songs and Sears, Roebuck merchandised guitars, he did more than simply attract people to his performance and music; he also lent to that music the prestige and respectability of the American cowboy.... As Douglas B. Green noted, "no youngster in the thirties and forties ever wanted to grow up to be a hillbilly, but thousands upon thousands wanted to be cowboys, and by treating the country song with dignity and respect Autry made it part of the shining good deeds and character of the cowboy."

Not only did Douglas Green write the essay on Autry from which the above quote comes—in the 1975 publication *Stars of Country Music*—he deliberately chose Autry as one of his models when, a few years after he authored the essay, he became Ranger Doug. While Gene Autry was at the center of the Singing Cowboy phenomenon, Doug and the other Riders borrowed most heavily from the Sons of the Pioneers when they built their winning commercial formula.[14]

The Sons of the Pioneers came into existence in the same year that Gene Autry recorded "The Last Roundup," when Bob Nolan (Robert Nobles), Tim Spencer, and Roy Rogers (Leonard Slye) created their close harmony trio. By 1935, after brothers Hugh and Karl Farr joined them, with fiddle and guitar, they assumed their historic posture. The Farr Brothers, from Texas, were accomplished jazz musicians. The Sons initiated their career on radio in California but attained national notoriety after 1936 when they performed at the Texas Centennial, as part of a Gene Autry movie, *The Big Show*. Canadian-born Bob Nolan drew inspiration from Billy Hill and similar musical chroniclers of the West, but his reverence for the desert and other scenes of the western landscape had inspired his song- and poetry-making long before he became acquainted with Hill's creations. The songs that Nolan and Tim Spencer wrote—like "Blue Prairie," "That Pioneer Mother of Mine," and "The Rainbow's End"—sometimes assumed mystical and spiritual dimensions. In addition to their evocative songs, they fashioned unforgettable harmonies. The Pioneers inspired the enduring perception that smooth singing and yodeling, sophisticated instrumentation, and cowboy and western images somehow went together. Radio transcriptions in the mid-1930s presented their music to a much larger audience, as did their appearances in western movies. They dressed like cowboys; they harmonized beautifully; they yodeled; they introduced outstanding songs like "Cool Water," "Tumbling Tumbleweeds," "Way Out There," "Timber Trail," "The Everlasting Hills of Oklahoma," and "Blue Shadows on the Trail," mostly written by Nolan and Spencer. And they featured "hot" instrumentation, provided by the Farr Brothers. The Sons of the Pioneers provided the whole package of traits later employed by the Riders. Only in their song selections did they differ. While the Sons of the Pioneers did sing many outstanding "cowboy" and "western" songs, they also sang a wide array of other material, including Stephen Foster compositions, mountain, sacred, and country songs. Despite his spiritual inclinations, Tim Spencer could also write a song like "Cigarettes, Whiskey, and Wild, Wild Women." His "Room Full of Roses," first recorded in 1949, had no western ingredients, but was the Pioneers' biggest hit, performed by both pop and country singers. As their disciples, Riders In The Sky even more zealously promoted their strictly *western* identity.[15]

The Riders combined all of the elements expected of a western group, but enlarged that template to include the humor and outlandish antics traditionally conveyed by such cowboy movie sidekicks as Smiley Burnette and Gabby Hayes, tinged with the edgier humor of more recent vintage such as that of the Smothers Brothers, Mike Nicholls and Elaine May, and *Mad Magazine*.[16] But when Too Slim (Fred LaBour), Ranger Doug, and Windy Bill Collins joined their talents in their first performance on November 11, 1977, at Herr Harry Phranks and Steins, complete with a 100-pound cactus, a saddle, and a fake campfire, they could have had little inkling that their western songs and comedy shtick could be the basis for a professional performing career.[17] The initial audience response, however, quickly informed them that a hunger for their brand of cowboy music cum humor was still very much alive in the United States. Although few people could have anticipated western music's rebirth at the end of the 1970s, in retrospect, we know that parallel rediscoveries of tradition were underway during those years. The Riders had tapped into that peculiar blend of nostalgia and camp that in 1974 had nourished the beginning of Garrison Keillor's long-running National Public Radio program, *Prairie Home Companion*. Musicians like Ray Benson and Asleep at the Wheel were reviving western swing, coaxing older performers like Leon McAuliffe, Jesse Ashlock, Floyd Tillman, and Cliff Bruner out of retirement. Pete Wernick, Tim O'Brien, Charles Sawtelle, and Nick Forster—professionally known as Hot Rize—were transforming the formality of bluegrass music into a more savory and humorous offering with their alter egos, Red Knuckles and the Trailblazers, who also presented an appealing version of honky-tonk/western swing. With its heavy use of longhorns, armadillos, and other southwestern metaphors and symbols, the Austin musical scene in the mid-1970s certainly inspired a renewed look at cowboy culture. This was the scene that lured Willie Nelson as he contemplated a renewed commercial life after his failure to achieve success as an entertainer in Nashville. Still, the broken-hearted, but dangerous, cowboy of the *Red Headed Stranger* was a far cry from the singing cowboy that the Riders would celebrate just a couple of years later.

Although the time may have been ripe for cowboy revivalism, Riders In The Sky did not simply seize a historic moment. They created the moment. Two of their early members, Windy Bill Collins and Tommy Goldsmith, soon rejected complete identification as singing cowboys, but the master fiddler Woody Paul Chrisman in 1978 became a lasting mainstay and defining component of the Riders trio. The trio accomplished something rare. They translated lifelong memories and personal dreams into an enduring commercial reality, enhanced when accordionist Joey Miskulin joined the group in 1988 at the beginning of their second decade and became a full partner several years later. As Ranger Doug told us, "Separately we would have had interesting lives, together we made magic."[18]

In the multitude of performances that they have given since 1977, the Riders have built a complete entertainment package that, while exhibiting an indebtedness to the Sons of the Pioneers, is very much their own. While their recordings are almost universally stellar, Riders In The Sky can only be fully appreciated in a live context, in a stage show, or on a television or computer screen. They are consummate performers with a sense of timing, spontaneity, and pacing rare in today's popular music.

From the time the impish Too Slim ambles onstage with his walrus mustache and oversize chaps, and then adjusts the stand-up bass that is bigger than he is, the audience is completely drawn into the Riders' circle of illusion. No act in country or western music so completely establishes rapport with an audience in the same way the Riders do. And certainly, no act has an audience with as wide a range of ages, with children constantly discovering the romance of the range for the first time, old folks rediscovering their childhood fantasies, and still others merely marveling at the musicianship and humor being displayed.

What is witnessed onstage is the loving recreation and perpetuation of a myth. We can be sure that no real cowboys ever sang, harmonized, yodeled or played instruments as skillfully as these musicians. The Riders' instrumental sound centers on the combination of the hot fiddling of Woody Paul, "The King of Cowboy Fiddlers," and the masterfully eclectic accordion playing of Joey, "The Cowpolka King." Too Slim and Ranger Doug provide them a compelling rhythm and drive. Known as "the Idol of American Youth," Ranger Doug not only builds a solid, jazz-inflected rhythm on his big archtop guitar, but also takes the lead on most of the trio's numbers, while never failing to astound his listeners with his supple and deceptively effortless yodeling.

The group's off-the-wall humor—described by Slim as "Monty Python meets the Sons of the Pioneers"[19]—surely does not approximate the kind one might have encountered in the bunkhouse or around the campfires on those long trail drives, even if cowboy life was hard and lonesome, with long spells of boredom that somehow had to be broken. On the other hand, we can be confident that real cowboys didn't roll tumbleweeds across the range, or plug in mechanical campfires to warm their hands, or wear "Cacties," or give trail traffic reports. It's not implausible to think, though, that bored cowboys might have talked to cow skulls or played tunes by slapping their faces, the way that Too Slim does. The Riders' humor can be irreverent, particularly when Woody Paul does his "Mr. Sincere" routine, a satirical interpretation of country superstars, but they never condescend or ridicule the tradition of which they are a part. Performing with an abiding love and respect for the western past (intensely mythicized though it might be), they have fun with the tradition, but never make fun of it. Even better, they have become part of the tradition that they so lovingly preserve. When you see or hear Riders In The Sky, you do not step back into a period piece or a re-created segment of history. You will always hear them pay tribute to the western musical greats of the past, with songs like "Cool Water," "The Texas Plains," and "Cattle Call," but you will also hear them do their own compositions, like "Desert Serenade," "Here Comes the Santa Fe," and "The Shelter of the Wildwood," which fittingly take their place alongside the classics. Riders In The Sky long ago moved well beyond revivalism; they have made the music vital by putting their own personal stamp on a distinct tradition of American music. Even more strikingly, they have remained together for nearly half a century, that is, evolving from young men to septuagenarians and still delighting themselves and their audiences by ad-libbing even their frequently performed routines and forever pushing their musicianship forward.

How did they create such magic? We're setting out to tell you that story.

CHAPTER ONE

DOUG GREEN

From Boyhood to Bluegrass to Cowboy Music

SUBURBAN MICHIGAN SEEMS AN UNLIKELY PLACE TO INCUBATE A Singing Cowboy revival. But the incessant bombardment of radio, television, musical recording, and movies directed toward American baby boomers in the late 1950s and early 1960s nurtured two highly intelligent, inquisitive, and creative young men—Doug Green and Fred LaBour—with the sustenance needed to initiate career paths that careened far beyond their upper-middle-class upbringing and parental aspirations. Like many young men of their era—including Elvis Presley a few years earlier—they were children of America's vibrant pop culture. And music was in their blood. Their not dissimilar but independently forged dreams led them to Nashville after undergraduate degrees earned at the University of Michigan. Once their paths converged in Music City several years later, magic ensued.

Douglas Bruce Green, son of James Donald Green and Hilda Maria Peterson, was born on March 20, 1946, at the Great Lakes Naval Training Center in Lake County, Illinois, some nine months after his parents married the previous June. Before serving in the navy, Doug's father was a physician in general practice in Detroit, while before her marriage, Hilda Peterson was a nurse in the city. He, the handsome doctor, she the beautiful nurse. Their backgrounds and upbringings completely differed, but their careers had brought them together. James (born 1921 in Detroit) was a third-generation son of Michigan. His grandfather, James Charles Green, and wife, Elizabeth Sarah Field, had emigrated from England directly to the state sometime before 1888. Doug's paternal grandmother, Anna Isabelle Fraser, was born in Detroit, but her parents had moved there from Scotland and Ontario. His paternal grandfather was a carpenter who remodeled houses to rent to others, but the Great Depression had destroyed his real estate ambitions.

Hilda (born 1917) was from Ishpeming in the state's Upper Peninsula (UP), and like many of those from that part of the state, her parents were Finnish immigrants. Doug once told an interviewer that all one could find in the UP was "a bunch of wild Finlanders and timber wolves and jack pines and nothing much else." Hilda's father, Charles Jacob Moilanen, was born in Suomusaaimi, and he and his wife, Sophia, lived in the UP with four children when she became deathly ill. He sent to Finland for a nanny, Maria Latvala who worked for the family. One of the four children died from diphtheria, and Sophia died as well. Soon after, Maria and Charles were married. Charles, Doug said, was a jack-of-all-trades: a timber inspector in the mines and a truck-driving door-to-door salesman for Jewel Tea. Maria and Charles had an additional ten children, with Doug's mother, Hilda, being the third from this union. At some point, like many of his Scandinavian immigrant contemporaries, Charles Moilanen changed his surname to the more Americanized Peterson, a logical choice because his father's name was Peter. Doug's mother; her brother, Hank; and her half brother, Arvid, played important roles in implanting their love of music in the impressionable young boy who would ultimately make it his profession.[1]

Because of the changing circumstances of his father's career, Doug spent the first years of his life in the Midwest, the West, and the Northeast, perhaps presaging his delight in being on the road and getting a feel for different folks in different climes. After the stint in the navy, the family returned to the Detroit area, where his father set up his practice in the suburb of Birmingham, and where Doug's younger siblings, Jim and Constance, were born. Doug began school at Quarton Elementary and still has his second-grade graduation card. His memories from that time include his teacher reading Greek myths to the class as they sat outside under a shady tree, and a field trip taken to Cranbrook, the private and prestigious prep school (at that time, only for boys) he would later attend.[2]

Doug with his parents, Hilda Peterson and James Green. Collection of Doug Green, used by permission.

Doug's younger brother, Jim, recalled that their paternal grandparents had moved to St. Petersburg by the time the Green siblings were growing up, so they saw them less frequently than they did their mother's relatives. When Hilda and Don went on vacation a couple of times, their paternal grandmother came to stay with the children. But, Jim said, "a big rivalry existed

From Boyhood to Bluegrass to Western Music   17

between my grandmother and my mother," so family visits had to have been uncomfortable for both parents and grandparents. Don Green's two sisters, Edith and Olive Elizabeth, also lived in the Detroit area, and the families got together periodically. The extended Finnish family in the UP nevertheless offered the children their most memorable experiences, undoubtedly enhanced by occurring in such a rustically exotic environment.[3]

While the family lived in suburban Detroit, they always spent some time each summer visiting the Finnish relatives at the relatively primitive summer cottage or "camp"—with outdoor plumbing (old-fashioned pump and outhouse, but also a sauna) on the Little Dead River, some ten miles from Ishpeming. Doug's grandfather and Arvid, the oldest of Hilda's siblings, got wood from old logging camps, from which they built the beautiful log cabin. It was at the camp that young Doug first admired, then learned to play, the guitar that both his uncles played and that hung on one of the camp's walls. His mother had enjoyed singing with Hank and Arvid when they were growing up: folk songs like "The Spanish Cavalier" and country songs like "Worried Mind" and "Have I Told You Lately That I Love You?" Doug's cousin, Janet Hendricksen, reminisced, "Everyone was musical." Hank and Arvid would sing and play, sitting around the campfire. "My father [Arvid] and Hilda were the closest," Janet continued, since both siblings were "very artistic. She would draw beautiful pictures on the fireplace on birchbark. . . . My father could sketch beautiful drawings. He and Hank saved money to send Hilda to nursing school." Doug loved listening to his uncles sing and play but doesn't recall hearing Arvid yodel, a talent that the family claimed he possessed. When Doug began yodeling, mostly Jimmie Rodgers style, while still in high school, he drove around in his folks' car with the windows up, so he wouldn't drive everyone crazy at home with his practicing.[4]

Because Don Green had not served abroad during World War II, when the Korean War broke out, he was once again called into active duty (1955–57). While he served overseas, Hilda and the children lived in Costa Mesa, California. Doug attended Lincoln School for third and, perhaps, part of the fourth grade while his father was gone. Prior to his California residence, Doug had never paid much attention to western or hillbilly music except at the family camp in Ishpeming, and listening to his childhood favorites, "(Ghost) Riders in the Sky" and "Cool Water," heard on the radio while lying on the carpet at home. He loved these two songs for their rich descriptiveness, which stimulated his ability to visually imagine them. Doug's musical horizons were similarly widened by the abundance of western music on TV in Costa Mesa:

> not only Roy and Gene's TV shows and reruns of their old films, but also Doye O'Dell's *Western Varieties*, *The Spade Cooley Show* and, of course, *Town Hall Party*. And I always ran home to watch *Sheriff John's Cartoon Time*, which although it was not a musical show per se, had a memorable theme song, "Laugh and Be Happy," and a birthday song, "Put Another Candle on the Birthday Cake." . . . In addition, in the days before Disneyland, Knott's Berry Farm (a throwback to the Old West) was the big attraction, and I saw the Wagon Masters there, playing around the campfire.[5]

Just as indelibly etched in his memory are Doug's recollections of his father's return after his year overseas:

> My mom bought us all new corduroy outfits and we trooped up to Long Beach to board the USS *Algol*. I recall it was not berthed next to the dock, but we had to cross a whole other ship to get to it, and I recall being so excited to walk two gangplanks over open water. And then to see my Dad! Oh, the joy! . . . Being on board a Navy ship was unbearably cool for a kid of 8 or 9, probably 9. The day was bright and sunny, and we were beyond excited. He brought us all splendid jackets with painted dragons and the like back from Korea or Japan, and we thought those were marvels of nature![6]

When his naval service was completed, Don Green decided that he wanted to specialize in internal medicine and did a residency at the Peter Bent Brigham Hospital in Boston. The family moved to the suburb of Newton Centre, and Doug completed the fourth and part of fifth grades at Mason-Rice School. Although his parents encouraged him to take piano lessons while they lived in Costa Mesa and in Newton Centre, Doug claimed that he "'washed out'" in both locations because he hated practicing. But already an admirer of good-looking women when he was in upper elementary school, he retains a "vibrant, memory" of an outstanding teacher during his time there. He described her as a voluptuous Jewish lady with abundant and quite beautiful auburn hair. She brought her violin to class one day and played it, and I thought it was the most astonishing, moving, sensual sound I'd ever heard. I raved about it so much that somehow the word got to a neighbor there in Newton Centre, a sweet, ancient lady named Mrs. Ulmer, who simply gave me an old violin, a family heirloom. I took lessons sporadically but had no feel for the instrument as a player, much more so as an appreciator.[7]

As Doug wrote, years earlier, "Like every other kid, I wanted to play ball and read comics and go swimming and goof around with my brother [instead of practicing piano or violin]. I've wished a thousand times since then that I'd learned to play that fiddle when I was a kid. But it never occurred to me to play notes off the written page on it." Yet showing his early and enduring penchant for holding on to musical possessions that mattered, he kept the fiddle. He gave it to his young granddaughter Sofia who was taking violin lessons, hoping that she would demonstrate more interest and talent at playing it than her grandfather ever displayed.[8]

After the Boston sojourn, the family moved back to Michigan so that Don Green could begin his new career in internal medicine with an office in Birmingham, and in time for Doug to finish the fifth grade at Quarton. The following year, he attended sixth grade at the then-brand-new Midvale School. Now that they were back in Michigan to stay, the summer visits to the Finnish relatives at the camp on the Dead River resumed with pleasing regularity. Doug's younger brother, Jim, recalls that they'd spend a couple of weeks there at a time. Hilda and seven of her siblings all lived to adulthood, and the children enjoyed being with them and their cousins. Communicating with the Green siblings' Finnish grandmother was another matter. Although she made "fantastic bread," she spoke very little English, which made her less accessible to her grandchildren. As Doug's cousin, Sandy Peterson-Fisher, recalled, "Doug and his siblings were like celebrities because they lived in the lower peninsula, and that carried on for Doug, even in adulthood." All the cousins wanted to be "Doug's best friend" when his family visited. She felt that "Aunt Hilda and Constance were more 'city people,'" while she found Doug and Jim "always down-to-earth, and they're still that way." Doug feels that his "real interest in playing music" truly began shortly after the family returned to Michigan when they were visiting the UP. Doug spent as much time as he could with his beloved uncles, Hank and Arvid. Because he was so enthusiastic about singing and learning to play guitar, his uncles were equally drawn to him.[9]

> At our summer cabin, I hauled that old guitar—a 1937 Montgomery Ward—off the wall and began banging on it, although it was missing some strings. I harangued my mother to drive into Ishpeming in our new 1958 Chevy convertible to get new strings—and the transmission blew on that trip. But I got the new strings, and once I got them on I realized I had no clue how to tune it. So, I tuned it to an open chord by ear and just slid my finger up the neck to make the next chord. I spent hours with that thing and finally learned how to tune it. It was so liberating—I could play any dang note I wanted and didn't have to read it off a printed page. I could sing along with full chords—a whole band on one instrument. I'll never forget that enchanted summer I discovered the guitar.[10]

Hilda, the "musical 'soul'" of the family, had a beautiful voice, and though shy about using it, she was "always singing and humming around the house," back at home in the suburbs. However, she remained ambivalent about the old songs she'd learned as a child, principally from the *National Barn Dance* on powerful station WLS in Chicago. Like many who rose to middle- and upper-middle-class status, she seemed embarrassed by her working-class background and its concomitant taste in music. Doug believed that she played a bit of popular music around the house, but "as she was eager to transcend her working-class roots," she "played a lot of classical music on the radio and on records to make up for it." His father was, as both sons explained, a "workaholic," who, in Jim's words, "was fairly remote, not very involved in our daily lives." True to that description, he "played piano decently, but it was mostly as a physical and intellectual exercise." Consequently, in addition to classical music, the soundtrack of Doug's home contained the mainstream popular music of the early 1950s, with smooth, romantic songs like "Love Is a Many Splendored Thing" and "Be My Love" and those from musicals, especially *South Pacific*. Doug described his extroverted father (loved by patients and the life of the party) as "a natural mimic and famous for being a jokester" who enjoyed listening to comedy albums by the likes of Shelley Berman and Bob Newhart, "and later, the Smothers Brothers. Early on it was Spike Jones, and I remember rolling on the floor, laughing, with my brother, Jim."[11]

For his secondary education, Doug was accepted at Cranbrook School for the seventh grade in 1957, and he remained a student there until he graduated in 1964, with his brother Jim following the same trajectory two years later. Don Green moved his practice to the even more affluent suburb of Bloomfield Hills, and the family relocated once again, this time within walking distance of Cranbrook. Unlike her brothers, Connie attended public schools, in both Birmingham and Bloomfield Hills, from elementary through high school graduation.[12]

Both Doug and Jim found Cranbrook an extremely rigorous academic environment, with a tremendous emphasis placed on writing, which included the choice of a weekly preparation of a poem, a short story, a television script, or a 500- to 1,000-word essay. Doug's fellow classmate Jim McQuaid (from herein, Jim McQ to distinguish him from Doug's younger brother), described the Cranbrook method as "work, study, get ahead, kill," a test, he claimed, that he and Doug both failed. Jim McQ said that he was a very fast reader, which helped but, as bright and verbally gifted as Doug is and would continue to be, according to Jim McQ, "Doug's experience was different. He was made to feel dumb at Cranbrook." Doug read and wrote a lot of poetry during this time, but he was not moved by any specific poet. Although for years he hated the highly "oppressive" competitive nature of his private school's "hoity-toity" education—both athletically and academically—only years later as Doug became a skillfully prolific writer and songwriter did he feel that the Cranbrook experience had produced its desired effect. As he admitted, before his senior year, he'd been a "feckless" student. He had wanted to enroll at the University of Michigan immediately after graduation but hadn't buckled down soon enough to do so. Jim Green, on the other hand, was a much more dedicated and academically successful student, a self-described "grind," even as he averred, "Doug paved the way for me at Cranbrook. He was almost a father figure in high school."[13]

Doug failed to excel as an academic superstar in high school, but academics were not really his top priority. Built tall and strong like his Finnish forbears, he played hockey, football, and track but felt that he only distinguished himself at track, in which he competed at shot put and discus. After graduation, Doug was on the track team at Albion College, a small liberal arts institution in the town of Albion in the southcentral part of the state, before transferring to the University of Michigan for his last two undergraduate years. Beyond track, Doug acted and sang in Cranbrook's production of *Li'l Abner* and *Bye, Bye Birdie*, as well as in the glee club, along with his good friends Bob Chambers and Arch Copeland, his brother, Jim, and Mitt Romney—a year younger than Doug—who attended Cranbrook while his father was governor. Jim told us, "We'd sing in harmony, practicing. We tried to sing duet-style. We were super close as kids and teenagers, who shared the basement. When he [Doug] went off to college, I was heartbroken, because I relied on him so much. I really love him; he may not be the idol of *all* American youth, but he was the idol of *this* American youth."[14]

Although Jim mentioned that their father had specific professional goals in mind for his sons, their more supportive mother always encouraged her sons' interests in music. He and Doug listened to pop and rock and roll, and Doug really liked the "folk" music of Joan Baez, Peter, Paul, and Mary, and similar acts so popular during their middle- and high school years. He also paid attention to country music, as it "spilled over onto the popular music stations," with performers like Conway Twitty and Jim Reeves. "Marty Robbins was, of course, a hero: great western stories, great voice, great harmony singing." In fact, Doug was drawn to harmony singing in many forms, in old time music as well as folk, but he especially appreciated the close harmonies that the Everly Brothers and the Browns—Jim Ed, Bonnie, and Maxine—achieved. While Jim played cello from fourth through the seventh grades and played a ukulele before Doug did, his older brother was "off and running" from the time he took his uncle's 1937 guitar down from the wall at the summer camp. Doug's first new guitar was a Harmony Sovereign, a Christmas gift from his parents during his junior year. The following year he bought a Martin D-28 with the money earned working at Petrol by Murphy gas station. Both brothers gravitated to bluegrass, with Doug on guitar and Jim playing five-string banjo.[15]

Jim McQ, like Doug, began at Cranbrook in 1957, preceded there by a brother, six years older, who had a Martin guitar, a five-string banjo, and Pete Seeger's book, *How to Play the 5-String Banjo*. During Jim's sophomore year, his brother died, and Jim used his brother's banjo "as an emotional crutch," also taking banjo lessons from a fellow student and then-fledgling bluegrass musician, Warren Kennison. Jim McQ got into the music of Bill Monroe, and said, "I was always looking for someone to play guitar with me, and that was Doug." Because he expected Doug to play like Lester Flatt, Doug spent a lot of time practicing guitar and singing.[16]

Doug mentioned that "like 99 percent of Finns my mother was raised Lutheran," but when it came to religion they were "on again, off again: My dad was always off, and my mother was sometimes a devout Lutheran and sometimes wouldn't go close to it." Still, they dutifully sent their children to Sunday school through the elementary school years. Having joined the church youth group, Doug made his first public performance (other than at school musicals) there with his Harmony guitar and high school girlfriend, Nancy Zeis, singing folk songs and harmonizing in the manner of Ian and Sylvia (Ian Tyson and Sylvia Fricker), who were popular at that time. "I found the Lutheran faith heavy on guilt and did not follow the faith in any serious way." Although Cranbrook was "nominally" Episcopal, boys of other Christian, Jewish, and even Muslim faiths were represented, and Christianity "was not shoved down our throats there." Short chapel services occurred on two mornings, while guest speakers from a wide variety of organizations "opened our minds to the world" the other three mornings of the week. Doug did not have any interest in religion or spirituality until about 2000, when he attended a Religious Science meeting, enjoying "the nonjudgmental and nondoctrinaire outlook and welcome" that suited his sensibilities.[17]

While material success blessed the Greens, and all appeared to be ideal, with a prominent and charming paterfamilias and a glamorous, devoted, appreciative mother who "loved to laugh and delighted in her children," daily life within their household did not always live up to that image. Affable Don Green also loved to give everyone nicknames (Doug hated his), and tease, which, at times, turned mean, especially when directed at his daughter, Connie. Although attractive, she tended to be overweight, and her father's constant teasing at the dinner table made her brothers uncomfortable. When Jim McQ came for dinner at the Greens' home, he told us, "It struck me at the time how nasty his father was to Doug's sister," but found Hilda "sweet and submissive, relative to her husband." Now remorseful as adults, Connie's older brothers did not come to her defense and sometimes joined in laughing at her expense. While Cranbrook had a sister school, Kingswood, no attempt was made to send Connie there, and she couldn't help but feel that her parents considered public school to be sufficient for their daughter. Then, too, Doug and Jim were older and closer to each other and, as sons of that generation, experienced more freedom than their sister did. Additionally, as all three of his children mentioned, their father, aside from the nicknames and the teasing, paid little attention to them, and most likely, not nearly enough to his beautiful wife as she would have wished. Tragically, she turned to prescription medications and alcohol to compensate for her frustrations. As the only daughter and the youngest sibling, Connie endured more of her mother's downward spiral than did her brothers, telling us that her mother "was really nice most of the time when she wasn't drunk. I needed to avoid my dad and hope that my mom didn't do anything to hurt herself there in Bloomfield Hills, where everyone thought everything was peachy." After the three children left for college, Don and Hilda divorced. Don Green remarried; Hilda did not. Doug's oldest daughter, Liza Jane, remembers her grandmother fondly for her sweet loving kindness, and Liza Jane's younger sister, Sally, said her own mother thought of her mother-in-law similarly, but Hilda, unfortunately, never overcame her addictions, which contributed to her suicide in 1976.[18]

Doug packed his 1953 MG, earned through summer work at the gas station and delivering for Parmenter Flowers during Christmas vacations, and left Bloomfield Hills in 1964 for Albion College to begin his freshman year. Although he returned home in the summer to work at various odd jobs, such as selling ads for the yellow pages of the local phone book or digging trenches and laying down phone lines, he otherwise never looked back. With Jim McQuaid at the University of Michigan in Ann Arbor just fifty-five miles east of Albion, Doug was on the road every weekend he could get away, playing bluegrass with his old friend. Once he'd begun coursework as an English major at Albion, Doug realized that the academic rigor at Cranbrook was, at last, paying dividends, since it had prepared him well to buckle down to make the good grades he hadn't been ready to work for in high school. He did make a lasting friend at Albion, however, Peter Lorch, who hailed from Litchfield, Connecticut. They met as freshmen and discovered that they had much in common: they lived on the same floor in the dormitory, had Martin guitars, liked to pick and sing together, and enjoyed each other's collections of bluegrass music. The two somehow also connected with a local middle-aged banjo player from the town, Alex Chopper, "a student (via records) of Don Reno, and several of the kids on that small campus played guitar." Doug and Peter also got to know "Ace" (neither recalled his last name), a nice "Mexican American guy who played with his rock and roll band, Ace and the Gay Tones, at a little dive bar." Ace graciously allowed

Doug (self-described as "terrible at the time") to sit in with them two or three times. Their sophomore year, Peter and Doug lived off-campus in a house with four or five other male students. Among Peter's favorite memories from the Albion years were driving to Chicago with Doug to hear Flatt and Scruggs play at the McCormick Place and accompanying Doug on several of those trips to Ann Arbor, which, as Doug recounted, "fired [me] up to transfer." During one or more of those trips, Jim McQ probably introduced Doug to the Herb David Guitar Studio, the gathering center in the area for musicians of all stripes. Herb David had been a wrestler in high school, and Jim McQ described him as "socially clueless" but friendly, "a grousing kind of guy, whose real thing was building and repairing guitars and other musical instruments." By hanging out at the music store, Doug got to know other musicians and Herb's wife, Mary Greenman, both of whom would play significant roles in his life.[19]

On Labor Day weekend of 1966, between Albion and Doug's enrollment at the University of Michigan for his final two undergraduate years, he went with Jim McQ, Mary Greenman, and, possibly, another Ann Arbor fellow bluegrass enthusiast, Miles Sonka, to Carlton Haney's second bluegrass festival, held in Fincastle, outside of Roanoke, Virginia. (The year before on the same weekend, Carlton Haney staged the first multiday bluegrass festival, also at Fincastle.) At the festival, Doug had one of his two major musical epiphanies. Although he'd been playing bluegrass since high school, he had never seen Bill Monroe in person. He found Monroe's delivery "kind of whiney and harsh when I first heard it," and later recounted, "His music had seemed somewhat remote to me up to that point, and I preferred the sunnier sounds of Flatt and Scruggs, Reno and Smiley, and the Dillards." That Fincastle performance was such a complete revelation that from then on, he was determined to learn the entire Monroe playbook. As he told us, "The 1966 festival was transformative for me — meeting so many college kids who were deep into bluegrass as I was," he found there—notably, banjo-playing bluegrass scholar Neil Rosenberg and a then-sixteen-year-old banjo-playing Fred Bartenstein, who later became a freelance bluegrass writer and promoter. Doug laughed when he told an interviewer that, having seen Bill Monroe at the festival, "I became a convert, groveled in the dust, like so many little college kids my age."[20]

Once settled in Ann Arbor when he started his junior year, Doug dived into the larger musical scene that encompassed the university and the community. Jim McQ rented an old house with two other male students, and Doug became the fourth occupant. As Jim recalled, they had a banjo, guitars, and dobro, and their quarters became "an open house for music where they played together many hours a week." Both Jim McQ and Doug had jobs behind the counter at the Herb David Guitar Studio, and Doug got to know Bill Ivey, who taught beginning guitar students there and was a senior at the university. Bill spoke of Herb David as assembling "a creative music center by bringing in different guitar players and banjo players with different musical attributes." Doug and Bill played in jam sessions, singing "Midnight on the Stormy Deep" and other old-time duets. Through their work at Herb David's, Jim McQ and Doug also got acquainted with several southern transplants who had moved to the Detroit area for factory work. They all played music together on weekends: bluegrass until midnight on a Saturday night, then sacred songs as Saturday night became early Sunday morning.[21]

Among the working-class migrants from Appalachian Kentucky, Virginia, and Tennessee who'd come North seeking better-paying jobs, Doug specifically mentioned former Blue Grass Boy Frank Buchanan, "a dear friend who always treated this young Yankee upstart as... an equal, and we remained friends throughout his long life." Doug became even closer to Nolan Faulkner, originally from Wolf County in eastern Kentucky, who became a mainstay of the Herb David scene. He was sometimes described as "Bill Monroe Jr." At the time Doug and Jim McQ got to know him, Nolan was working at American Aggregate, a gravel pit where he'd held many positions, including running a bulldozer. Understanding that "without a union, a working man didn't have any protection at all," he was a committed Teamster who got Doug a job at the pit the following summer driving a truck that pulled sand and gravel. Although Doug, Jim McQ, Bill Ivey, and Warren Kennison were university students from privileged backgrounds, they were not snobs and completely respected Nolan as a master mandolin player who took them under his wing. He performed with his band, The Big Sandy Boys, mostly on weekends, and had been playing since he was eight or ten, having learned from his half brothers. While Bill Monroe was his "hero," Nolan could play his own complicated style, "done by feel, most of it, Monroe-style," which, he claimed, he'd already figured out before he ever heard Bill Monroe. Nolan explained that "Doug would come to our gigs in Ann Arbor, at the old Heidelberg Restaurant, the Halfway Inn, and the Ark

From Boyhood to Bluegrass to Western Music   27

[a performance venue on the University of Michigan campus]. I'd probably been playing with another college student, and I let them all play." While Jim wasn't interested in joining The Big Sandy Boys, Doug was ready, as were fellow Michigan students Rod Wolf, as the bass player, and Ron Kay, on banjo. Besides Nolan on mandolin, the other member of the band, whom Doug called a "highland genuine bluegrasser," was Shorty Patrick, on fiddle. Doug's playing with The Big Sandy Boys was his first experience with any kind of traveling and semiprofessional music-making, the first actual money he made playing music. Nolan said that he and Doug "got along pretty good," and, likewise, Doug found Nolan "a great teacher and a great guy." He and Nolan became close friends, and Nolan told us, "I took Doug [and Jim McQ] with me down to the old homeplace [Winchester, Kentucky] one time or another. They especially liked the rich, home-cooked meal my mom and sisters would make. They showed a lot of respect for that music." Pete Goble, "Snake" Chapman, and old-timey banjo player Wade Mainer and his wife Julia were other Southerners around Detroit who Doug got to know and appreciate through his work at the music studio. Beyond music-making and singing, bluegrass launched Doug into strengthening his extraordinary ability to connect to all kinds of people and to maintain many of those relationships over a lifetime.[22]

In addition to working for Herb David, Doug drove a campus bus, and he and Jim McQ revived the moribund university folklore society, with Doug serving as president. Jim McQ said, "We reregistered the Folklore Society so that we could sponsor the Bill Monroe concert" in March 1967. While Doug was the "driver" of the event, Jim had been active in the organization before Doug matriculated on campus, and Jim had suggested resuscitating the Folklore Society by enlisting a critical number of members. Doug made the arrangements to get Bill Monroe and his band to campus (for $600) by contacting Bill's ex-wife, Carolyn, who was still doing his bookings. Doug and Jim McQ publicized the event by putting posters "everywhere," which ensured a good turnout in the Frieze Auditorium. Doug had written the name of one of Bill Monroe's songs on the back of every ticket sold, and if someone held a ticket with the last song performed, that individual got a Bill Monroe album. Doug laughed, "Well, God, the guy got like two encores, because everybody was yelling out all these obscure Bill Monroe songs, you know, stuff he hadn't done in thirty years.... He thought it was just wonderful!" Mary Greenman and Herb David invited

Doug, Jim McQ, and Bill Monroe and the Blue Grass Boys to their home for dinner beforehand. Jim McQ mentioned just how much Mary enjoyed having the young university crowd over. Doug was already demonstrating his ingenuity in accomplishing what he wanted to achieve in the world he was looking forward to occupying.[23]

Doug got friendly with Carolyn Monroe through the arrangements for Bill Monroe's visit, and during one of their chats, she mentioned that Bill was looking for a guitar player, since Red Allen, then playing with him, had suffered a "'case of nerves' brought on by alcohol abuse." Doug's radar went into high alert, and he had Nolan teach him "every key that Bill Monroe used for each song that he played." Doug knew all the words and all the keys by the time he, Mary Greenman, and Jim McQ went down to the Brown County Jamboree at Bean Blossom on April 30. Doug brought along a suit, just in case he had a chance to audition for Bill's rhythm guitar slot. Doug auditioned, playing "Walls of Time," which impressed Bill enough that he got the job. Nolan attended the festival with his wife and one of his daughters. Nolan wistfully recounted that "Doug went on that tour instead of me. Doug got the job instead of me. I knew I wouldn't have taken that job, leaving my wife and little girl. Doug wasn't the best guitar player or the best singer at that time." Doug admitted that knowing Bill's repertoire probably helped him get the job, telling an interviewer that while he may have been the "third-to-worst" singer Bill ever had, "but, boy did I know the material!" Bill hired him on the spot to play guitar and be the lead singer with the Blue Grass Boys for the next three weeks while Bill searched for a full-time musician to join his band. Once Doug climbed onto the bus, he immediately recognized that "the lure of the road was forever in my blood at that moment." Mary and Jim McQ drove back to Ann Arbor by themselves while Doug began to come to terms with the realization that being a professional musician was *definitely* the career he wanted.[24]

In fact, Doug was so excited about being *on* the Blue Grass Special that he stayed on the bus for two days while it was being serviced at the Nashville bus station to ready it for the tour. However, the bus broke down near Dallas en route to the West Coast, forcing Bill and Doug to fly to Washington State for shows on May 5 and 6, while the rest of the band waited for the bus to be repaired. Bill and Doug played with local bands for those dates, then traveled by Trailways bus to Los Angeles to reconnoiter with the rest of the band. At twenty-one, Doug was intimidated, but thrilled, to be working with

Bill Monroe, "who doesn't always tell you what he wants, but you'd better not be lacking." When he saw a photograph from a date on the tour, he said that he "looked scared as a corpse, and I was. But it was great." He told Tom Ewing that it "was a fantasy come true."[25]

Doug was still on the tour when Bill Monroe hired the very talented multi-instrumentalist Roland White to be a full-time Blue Grass Boy in Doug's place, and the two men got along well. After the tour ended in Nashville, Doug secured a ride with Michigander Virginia Stouffer, Bill Monroe's "love interest at the time," who was driving back for a family visit. Doug returned to the University of Michigan for his senior year, "a profoundly changed person." He told John Rumble, "It totally changed my opinion of how I wanted to spend the rest of my life. I certainly didn't want to do teaching knot-headed college students or writing book reviews, you know. This is what I wanted to do. I wanted to get in that bus and go." After touring with Monroe, Ann Arbor must have felt surreal—driving a truck in the gravel pit, working at Herb David's, jamming with friends, and playing with the Big Sandy Boys. Rod Moag, then a doctoral student at the University of Wisconsin and acoustic musician, arrived to attend a summer linguistics institute. He brought a fiddle and mandolin along and soon found a music jam "on the street outside Herb's store" where he met Doug. They got together many times that summer to pick and sing, often with Nolan Faulkner. Rod, who was blind, shared this memory of accompanying Doug to a gig: "We pulled up at the side of the road near the hall where the show was to take place. Doug said, 'Don't step off there, there's a ditch.' 'Oh well, I can jump it,' I replied, to Doug's amazement, and did just that." Then he played mandolin and sang tenor on some songs during the show. Another evening, Mary Greenman, Doug, and Rod went out for a ride to get some root beer floats. Sitting in the back seat alone, he "sensed a certain spark between the front seat passengers." Rod was quite perceptive. While Mary was sixteen years his senior and still married to Herb David, she and Doug had become romantically involved.[26]

During Doug's senior year, he lived with his brother, Jim, then a sophomore. As Doug told us, it was "music all the time!" John W. Morris, who founded Old Homestead Records a few years later, had a bluegrass and old timey show on a radio station out of nearby Ypsilanti. Doug's first radio appearance occurred in 1968 when he and Jim sang a duet of "Weapon of Prayer" on Morris's show, with Doug carrying the melody and Jim the harmony. While Doug was preparing to graduate with a BA in English, he continued to jam with Jim, Nolan, and others, and enjoyed The New Lost City Ramblers and Jim Kweskin & The Jug Band as well when they appeared on campus. Doug was sponging up all the music that appealed to him, letting it soak into his soul while he contemplated his next move postgraduation. While he knew that he wanted to play music professionally, he nevertheless followed the expected route of many English majors: applying to graduate school at Indiana University in its acclaimed department of folklore and ethnomusicology and at Vanderbilt in its esteemed English department. Doug gained acceptance to both. Bloomington, Indiana, may have spoken to his academic inclinations, but it offered no contest to Nashville—the real lure of Vanderbilt, which Doug's father undoubtedly must have realized. A graduate degree nevertheless seemed like a legitimate career for one with Doug's education and parental expectations.[27]

When Doug moved to Nashville in May 1968 to attend Vanderbilt, he rented a duplex on Hilltop Lane in East Nashville right next to Roland White. That worked beautifully for Doug, since it became abundantly easy to play music every night, mostly at jam sessions with Roland and Vic Jordan. He also had some paying jobs at festivals, in coffee houses, and at Bobby Green's Dusty Roads Tavern, "a terrible little place, but the main place for bluegrass at the time" and now the site of the Titans' football field. Doug recalled, "It was an incredible time for me."[28]

Just as Doug's musical life was becoming incredible, his personal life was becoming more complicated. At some point, Mary Greenman and Herb David divorced. In the meantime, she learned that she was pregnant with Doug's child. Doug left for Nashville in May and, on June 1, their daughter, Liza Jane, was born. As Liza Jane Green Parnell succinctly summed it up, "She [Mary] was older, but they got along really well, went to a bluegrass festival, I happened." Mary had always wanted a child and would have been "perfectly fine" with being a single mother, but when she continued to send Doug photos of "this perfect, adorable child . . . I just knew I had to do the right thing." Doug was a young twenty-two-year-old when he and Mary married at the courthouse in Ann Arbor. When Liza was a year old, she and Mary moved to Nashville, joining him in the duplex next door to Roland White. Mary was a devoted schoolteacher, providing the family's main source of income while Doug continued his graduate studies, playing music when he could.[29]

During the summer of 1969, Doug went back on the road with Bill Monroe, replacing James Monroe on bass. At twenty-three, he was more seasoned, as he told us:

> I had *been* a Blue Grass Boy, and Bill welcomed me with big smiles and handshakes and hugs at both the Virginia and his brand-new Bean Blossom festivals. The 1969 festivals I played with both Bill and Jimmy Martin! Big time for a very young, very green, very inexperienced kid, who had enrolled at Vanderbilt that fall [before 1968] in a not very subtle ploy to get to Nashville.

No longer a fill-in while Bill Monroe was looking for someone else, Doug was playing full-time as a Blue Grass Boy for the summer festival season, which began in March and included the Smithsonian Institution's third annual Festival of American Folklife on July 3. Doug's favorite perk as a Blue Grass Boy occurred at night when the band was on the bus traveling. If enough band members were awake, he would try to "instigate" some quartet singing, because he so loved harmony. "Oh man, that to me was heaven ... going down those roads late at night and singing quartets." But on the twelfth of July, he played his last show with Bill. The Blue Grass Boys were on the Grand Ole Opry that night and, similarly to baseball, Doug was "swapped" to Jimmy Martin, whose bass player, Bill Yates, went to Monroe. Although disappointed, Doug had no say in the matter, and he remained a great admirer of Bill Monroe, telling Dan Miller that Monroe's "commitment to his style was irresolute and unwavering, and although [the] Riders work in a different tradition, I drew from the example of his determination to present the music his way ... to keep true to our tradition and style." Doug said that he made almost no money with Jimmy Martin—"$35 a day for three months." As Doug explained, the $35 was only for playing the gig. If it took a day to drive to the venue and a day to return, it was still only $35 for the three days! "Not only was the salary awful, I had to pay for my own food, too." Once, when Doug was playing bass on stage with him at a festival, Jimmy broke a string on his guitar and turned to Doug, handing him the guitar, and saying, "Think you can change that string with that col-lege degree?" But Doug understood that he had gained a great deal that summer, especially realizing the primacy of rhythm and timing as structural elements of a band.[30]

While Doug was still in his bluegrass phase, two small-town DJs, Earl Triggs and Carlton Devon Swafford, approached him with a proposal that he put together a bluegrass gospel album. As Doug explained, they thought that the album would do well advertised on late night television on a "'per inquiry' basis, since that was the era of surprise successes of such albums by Christy Lane, Boxcar Willie, and Slim Whitman." For the projected album, he asked Buck White and his then-teenage daughters and banjo player Vic Jordan to join him. Doug then "plundered the Louvin Brothers repertoire" and borrowed the album's title, *In God's Eyes*, from a song written by Willie Nelson. The album was released in 1972 and turned out to be "a pleasant little affair that didn't make any of us any money," with the bulk of the records ending up in a warehouse down by the Cumberland River that later flooded. However, Doug was not deterred. Attempting to advance his "sputtering bluegrass career," he contacted his old friend from Ann Arbor days, John Morris, who had founded the Old Homestead label, and agreed to create a second album with the same folks who appeared on the first. Doug conceived this record as a traditional bluegrass album and named it for his daughters, *Liza Jane and Sally Anne*, who, in turn, had been named for old-time fiddle tunes. Since, as Doug said, he "was not writing many songs in those days and had very little confidence in my own ability at the time," no originals were included on the Old Homestead recording.[31]

As Doug admitted, marriage, parenting, completing graduate classwork, and picking up paying gigs delayed the completion of his master's thesis (on Anthony Burgess) until 1971. From their duplex, the Greens moved to their own "tiny rental" in Belle Meade. Then Mary and Doug's second daughter, Sarah (Sally) Anne, was born in 1970. Doug capitalized on his having worked on his master's at Vanderbilt to secure a position at Andrew Jackson's historic home, The Hermitage, which offered, in addition to a "miniscule salary," living quarters on site. As the site's historian, he was responsible for training docents. When that job was eliminated the following year, the family moved to Wildwood Avenue in the Belmont Avenue area, and Doug went to work at GTR (later, George Gruhn Guitars), which had opened the year before (1970) in a little shop near the Ryman Auditorium on Fourth, near the corner of Broadway.[32]

Although trained in zoology and animal behavior at the University of Chicago, New York City–born George Gruhn began collecting guitars in 1963 and turned his passionate "compulsive mania" into a thriving business, ultimately *the* place to acquire stellar instruments. He remains fascinated by undomesticated animal behavior, keeping snakes in his office. A multi-instrumentalist himself, George met Doug sometime in 1965 or 1966 at bluegrass festivals before Doug began playing professionally. When George looked at instruments, he realized that he could "organize them in taxonomic order, so it all seemed like the way I saw reptiles." He had jammed with Roland and Doug, but "wasn't much of a player" and was much more interested in collecting and dealing in instruments. After he opened GTR, Doug became one of his first employees and worked for George about two years. He recalled that Doug "wasn't a great salesman, but then none of us were great salesmen at the time. He had great penmanship, and did my inventory by hand, which we would mail out." Working there, Doug met Ron Hillis from Iowa, whose high school nickname was "King Chord," and David Sebring, both of whom liked swing and proved important to the development of his own rhythm guitar style. Doug purchased his first archtop guitar, a 1936 Gibson, then and there. As he explained, a flattop guitar sounds good when playing an open chord, but an archtop projects much more when playing rhythm. George complimented Doug's playing: "There's an art to the kind of rhythm that he does. He plays the notes that other guys aren't playing. It actually fills in a lot better—very different from bluegrass." Aside from these influences and instruments that put him on the road to becoming a proficient and innovative rhythm guitarist, Doug also met many performers at the music store, including the Nitty Gritty Dirt Band. George was fast becoming the "world's leading expert on vintage American guitars and related instruments," and enlisted Doug's help in coauthoring *Roy Acuff's Musical Collection at Opryland*, an opportunity for Doug to use those hard-won writing skills that he had honed at Cranbrook and in undergraduate and graduate work in English. The book, sumptuously photographed by Dean Dixon, contained not only a brief history of the museum housing the collection, but an overview, "String Instruments in America," and a chapter on "musical instrument makers"—a slender, yet substantive publication to be sold as a souvenir at the Roy Acuff Museum. The volume was not published until 1982, George having completed the writing when Doug became too involved with Riders In The Sky to do so. And Doug had already stopped working at GTR after a couple of years. George was a demanding employer, and, ultimately, Doug found it too stressful to work for him, although they've remained good friends ever since.[33]

Doug's personal life at the time he left GTR may have added considerably to the stress he was experiencing. According to his daughter, Liza Jane, Mary "did not want my dad to pursue music full-time, and he played music whenever he could." The conflict over the direction in which Doug wanted to be heading was further complicated by his having met Cynthia Turner, a divorcée with a son, Turner, who taught Liza Jane and Sally Ann at their preschool. Liza told us, "My sister and I told my mom that we saw our dad kissing Cindy, which we knew was wrong. My mom was heartbroken." Doug and Mary divorced in 1974, and he married Cindy the following year. He and Cindy have two children together, Annie Laurie—also named for a song—born in 1980, and James, born in 1982.[34]

In the early spring of 1971, bluegrasser Red Allen asked Doug to play bass with him at Bean Blossom, Indiana, near Bloomington and Indiana University. His old friend Bill Ivey drove to the park to visit Doug. Bill was then wrapping up PhD studies in Folklore at the university, but had no success securing a university teaching job. Doug told him that "the job heading the Country Music Foundation (CMF) Library and Media Center—at the time housed in the basement of the Country Music Hall of Fame building—was 'still open.'" Bill thought, correctly, that his experience as cataloger at the Indiana University Archives of Traditional Music would help in applying for the position. His assumption was correct, and he was hired. Just a few months later, in October, the trustees of the Country Music Foundation promoted Bill to oversee both the CMF Library and the Country Music Hall of Fame. While "the still-new Hall of Fame and Museum had secured a place as a Nashville tourist destination, as a new director of the CMF," Bill sought to make "the nonprofit more 'academic,'" by "developing its reputation as a legitimate research center." This time, it was Bill's chance to return the favor by offering Doug a position at the CMF. Doug had been interested in the history of country music, at least since high school when he tuned in to WCKY in Cincinnati, listening to old hillbillies on Wayne Raney's show, and Bill recognized that Doug combined his drive as a musician with a real scholarly interest in whatever he was doing. Bill also understood that Doug wanted to write about "the legacy that Bill was advancing, the roots of that musical style," and was willing to work hard to do so, just as he worked tirelessly to make himself a good singer, yodeler, and guitar player. With his master's in literature from Vanderbilt, his experience working on the papers of Andrew Jackson at the Hermitage, and his "passionate interest in the roots of country music," he was well-suited for the job Bill was creating. Ultimately, Bill trusted Doug as a "pioneer" who "could find his own way."[35]

And find his own way, Doug did. In 1972, he joined the Country Music Foundation staff, and until 1978, he worked there, where at least part of his mission was publicizing the existence of the organization and doing important work to keep the old timers' music alive. He served as the editor of the *Journal of Country Music*, and, in a separate endeavor in 1976, wrote *Country Roots: The Origins of Country Music*, a trade-oriented history of country music, which included a chapter on country humor that had not been previously stressed. While an oral historian at the CMHOF, he interviewed older country stars, and, as he told Dan Miller, "what a treat and delight that was to sit down with a tape recorder and talk with Roy Acuff, Zeke Clements, Pee Wee King, Art Satherley, and Ray Whitley, for hours." Doug also rekindled his "childhood love for western music" by interviewing many singing cowboys like Eddie Dean, Jimmy Wakely, Frankie Marvin (for many years, Gene Autry's sideman), and cowgirl Rosalie Allen. For a while, the County Music Foundation put on an old timers' show at Nashville's Country Music Fan Fair in the summer where Doug got to know some of the performers he admired, including Foy Willing, Floyd Tillman, and Del Wood. Doug mentioned that Ray and Kay Whitley and Johnny Bond "took this kid in his twenties under their wings and made me feel like family," even inviting him for Easter dinner, after which they "sang and sang." He called Ray and Johnny "godsends," who "were genuine mentors to me as I tried to soak up all the knowledge I could.

> These men and women were a huge inspiration to me, and really gave me the impetus to write *Singing in the Saddle* as well as pursue a career in this style of music, which was becoming relegated to the nostalgia bin in the record stores, thought of as quaint or even campy, while I found it vivid, vibrant, and beautiful . . . Which is to say meeting these men and women helped propel me into western music and my infatuation with it and my determination to keep this style alive and thriving. I hope our humor, and my songwriting, have played a part, I hope a large part, in doing just that.[36]

While Doug was writing the book and devoting an entire chapter to singing cowboys, he may not yet have realized that the style and figures that dominated the genre would play *the* leading role in his professional life within a couple of years after the publication of *Country Roots*. The last paragraph seems to foretell that future, however:

> Though we may prefer to think of the singing cowboy as a rather implausible figure from our mutual pasts (it is human nature that it is difficult to take things so integrally entwined with our childhood seriously), we should spend a bit of time rethinking his importance, for the role the singing cowboy played in bringing country music to a national audience in a manner that gave it worth and dignity cannot be overestimated. Not only did he save the stagecoach from sure disaster, the cattle from stampeding, the mob from lynching an innocent man but he also propped up, fostered, and gave to country music dignity, sympathy, and credence at a time when these were sorely needed. Let us tip our hats to those men with their flashy suits, fancy guitars, and noble stallions. Without them country music might still be a cultural backwater today, if, indeed, there existed sufficient interest in it to sustain the music at all.[37]

Most fortunate for Doug during his time at the CMHOF was falling under the tutelage of Bob Pinson. Bob had been a world-class collector of country music, and in 1971 he sold his collection to the CMHOF and was then hired to oversee and expand it. Because Bob enjoyed sharing his storehouse of information on the recordings and performers he'd collected, he mentored Doug during their "old time disc of the day" music sessions in which they took a break from their separate responsibilities and spent fifteen minutes of great listening and sharing. Partially because of the old-time disc of the day, and listening to Gene Autry and Marty Robbins, Doug became increasingly interested in western music, which, at that point, supplanted bluegrass for him. Then in 1974, the CMF sent Doug to Tulsa to the first Western Swing Festival (there were none following), organized by Guy Logsdon, director of libraries and professor of folklife at the University of Tulsa. This assignment became a turning point in Doug's musical career. There he heard great musicians, including many of the Bob Wills players who were still alive. Guy had also booked the then-current iteration of the Sons of the Pioneers—even though they were not usually associated with western swing, and, Doug told music publicist, historian, and music business professor at Belmont University Don Cusic, "Why they were booked... I'll never know." Doug had earlier considered the group "western, but [they] didn't swing, and if anything, I thought they were a little like a quaint relic, somewhat musty and faintly unhip." But he was "blown away and sat slack-jawed as they sang their standards." Meeting Lloyd Perryman, a long-time member of the Sons of the Pioneers, was another highlight. Doug said to us, "that was *it*! I got so excited. I collected a bunch of tapes.... Seeing these guys live was a revelation: so visual and so literary at the same time." Returning to Nashville, he immediately began absorbing as much information about the Sons of the Pioneers as he could from Bob Pinson and other sources, listening to the Sons' smooth harmonies, and becoming an ardent admirer of the songwriting of band members Bob Nolan and Tim Spencer.[38]

During Doug's CMHOF years, he continued to play music anywhere and with whomever he could, including a gig at Shakey's Pizza Parlor and once a week with a loose group, the Shin Bone Alley All Stars, in which Fred LaBour played. And when Doug performed with any small band or did solo music, he always sang a cowboy song. The experience of playing with Dave Sebring and John Hedgecoth inspired him to get his own band together, and he founded a bluegrass group, the Doug Green Band, joined by Fred LaBour, but they played fewer than ten dates a year. Fortunately, Doug maintained his day job, since he was earning so little money as a musician. But that was all about to change—not so much the money as his commitment to being a full-time musician with a unique band.[39]

CHAPTER TWO

FRED LABOUR

That's Entertainment!

For Fred Labour, like his future "Saddle Pal" Doug Green, the road to the mythical West ran south: it began in Michigan and ran directly toward Nashville. The two men somehow never met in Michigan, but their passion for music-making eventually brought them together in Music City. Frederick Owen "Fred" LaBour was born in Grand Rapids on June 3, 1948, the youngest child of loving and devoted parents, George F. LaBour Jr. and Hazel Fredricka Gotch. The youngest of four children, Fred was preceded by George F. "Jeffy" LaBour III, who was born February 8, 1937, followed by Marcie, who was born December 14, 1939. Tragically, Jeffy died in 1943 before the LaBour's third child, Christine "Chris" was born, December 27, 1944, and Fred arrived three and a half years later.

Until he moved to Ann Arbor in September 1966, to attend the University of Michigan, Fred never lived for extended periods anywhere but Grand Rapids. Those eighteen years, though, were highly formative in shaping the musician who became "Too Slim," the comedic mainstay of Riders In The Sky. Although we might question the meaning of William Wordsworth's famous dictum that the child is father to the man, we can nevertheless argue that the main features of Fred's character had revealed

Christmas with the LaBours: from *left to right*, Chris, Hazel, Fred, and Marcie. Collection of Fred LaBour, used by permission.

themselves well before he left home. First of all, he had developed a healthy love and respect for the outdoors, an affinity inherited from his father but shared by the other members of his family. Grand Rapids was Michigan's second largest city and a vibrant center of heavy industry. It was known, in fact, as "The Furniture Capitol of the World," because of the prominence of that enterprise, which attracted Fred's paternal grandparents, George F. LaBour Senior and Gertrude Craven LaBour, who had moved from Wisconsin Rapids to Grand Rapids in the second decade of the twentieth century. Like so many other promising businesses, George Senior's furniture store failed during the Great Depression, after which he spent most of his time working at the local courthouse as a bankruptcy referee and being active in the Masonic Lodge. Fred has a vivid memory of his grandfather's always having Wrigley's Spearmint gum in his vest pocket and dispensing it to the LaBour children when they visited their grandparents' home, while the oyster stew his grandmother served on Sunday evenings seemed like a "delicacy" to the young boy. George Senior died when Fred was twelve, his first "encounter with death up close and personal." Later, when they went through the little drawers of his grandfather's cabinet in the basement of his home, Fred discovered that they were filled with "jokes, cataloged by subject . . . wives, mothers-in-law, Jews, Polacks, Germans, Black folks." He believed that his grandfather "kept them on file for his speaking engagements at Lodge." Did Fred have any sense then that he, too, would be stashing jokes mentally, if not in little drawers, to use before his own audiences? Although he may not have witnessed his grandfather's talks, the humor gene certainly came down through the family. Fred's grandmother lived on, but suffered from memory loss, now known as Alzheimer's, hardly recognizing her family in later years. Already failing, she attended a high school variety show where Fred served as emcee in the guise of an elderly vaudeville character. He recalled that with his "old-man makeup and hair, she couldn't get over how much I looked like her late husband. I think she might have thought I actually was him."[1]

Fred never had the chance to meet his German maternal grandparents; Emma and Fred Gotch died before he was born. Yet even on his mother's side, one finds another entertainment precedent in the person of Frank Gotch, a great-uncle from Humboldt, Iowa, "the first American professional wrestler to win the World Heavyweight Freestyle Championship," a title he kept from 1908 until he retired from the sport in 1913. He popularized "what would come to be known as sports-entertainment in the United States." After retiring from one form of entertainment, he moved to another: starring in *All About a Bout*, a play that toured internationally. As one of the most popular athletes of his day, he even garnered an invitation to the White House from President Theodore Roosevelt. His niece, Hazel, grew up in Ft. Dodge, Iowa, spending much of her childhood on her relatives' farm. Hazel moved to Grand Rapids with her family when Fred Gotch landed a job as foreman at a gypsum mine.[2]

George LaBour Jr., a University of Michigan graduate, had begun law school, but after only a year dropped out to return to Grand Rapids to help the family. Fred feels that his father always regretted not obtaining his law degree, although he became a successful sales manager and executive vice president for Michigan Wheel Propellers, a product principally designed for outboard motorboats, but employed by the US Navy in World War II for use on torpedoes. Hazel, too, had no opportunity to realize her academic aspirations. As an excellent high school student and writer who graduated as the Depression set in, she hoped to get beyond her two years at Grand Rapids Junior College. But she met George on a double blind date—they were attracted to each other, not to their actual dates that evening—and married in about 1932.[3]

After living in town during the first two years of their marriage, the couple bought a large old house at the edge of the city on two acres surrounded by an additional fifteen acres of swamp, wood, and meadows. Honed by their experience of the Great Depression, the LaBours believed that the family should be as self-sufficient as possible. During the winter months, George had to spend much of his time on the road, traveling to boat shows. Although his job with an industrial product paid the family's bills, George's heart was in the country. As Fred said, "The idea of growing everything that we needed was part of their ethos." The LaBours' home and its lovingly landscaped grounds (Fred's good friend and neighbor, Mike DeVriendt, described it as a "gentleman's place") made an ideal environment to raise children. George spent much of his spare time gardening and farming, and he expected everyone in the family to pitch in to whatever outdoor work needed attention—in the huge apple orchard, for example. Mike helped Hazel with the garden and took care of the swimming pool, telling us that Fred's ambitions did not run in those areas. The LaBour children arose early in the summer to work in the orchard, and Chris fondly remembers how, in the fall, when they'd picked the apples, "the neighbor kids would come over, and we'd make gallons of cider in the cider press on the property. Delicious." Mike DeVriendt remembers being part of the cider-making, and still living in the house where he grew up in Grand Rapids, now has the LaBour's old cider press. In contrast to George's contemporaries who had done well and joined the country club, Fred said, "My dad bought a forty-acre piece of land about ten miles west of us and raised registered Angus cattle. He was really proud of those cattle."[4]

The entire LaBour family enjoyed the rigors and recreation of outdoor life through every season. Marcie loved horses from the time she was three and rode her aunt's horse. She claims, "I've not been without a horse since, getting my first horse at six ... I showed horses, was in 4-H with horses, and my family was supportive of me." Fred spent much of his time building camps and tree houses, while his siblings also shared outdoor experiences, as Chris told us:

> Growing up in Michigan, we were given a whole lot of freedom, and we had this beautiful piece of property with woods, pond, a field, playing outside all the time. Fred and I played together with a whole group of neighborhood kids, playing cowboys and Indians, building a raft for the pond, making fires, cooking our hot dogs there. We ice skated on the pond behind the house. We had the second swimming pool in Grand Rapids, so we had lots of swimming parties. Every year our parents hosted a huge neighborhood picnic on July third, and my father and Fred would set off the fireworks.[5]

Like Doug, Fred's family spent their two-week annual summer vacations in Michigan's Upper Peninsula. The LaBours rented one of the rustic cottages called Epler's Cabins on Lake Manistique. They fished, went to the nearest beach on Lake Superior, or visited Lower Taquahmenon Falls, driving through the deer preserve. As Fred recalled, "The highlight of the trip was visiting the county dump at dusk when the bears came out to eat garbage." The visitors would turn on the headlights of their cars to watch the bears, and, "It was great! Talk about entertainment!" Beginning in 1956, the LaBours had begun driving to the rugged territory of the great American West to visit national parks and dude ranches, staying for a couple of weeks at a time at places like Turpin Meadows Ranch near Jackson Hole, Wyoming, and the 63 Ranch near Livingston, Montana. They spent their daytime horseback riding, and at night listened to singing cowboys entertain around a campfire, a scene that had prescience—one that Fred and the other Riders would humorously re-create.[6]

Hazel LaBour suffered from severe asthma and, when the leaves began falling, she nearly died from her allergic reaction to leaf mold. She had to leave Grand Rapids each year for the Southwest in early October, returning for Thanksgiving and staying through Christmas, then leaving again to spend the rest of the winter in Arizona. With George on the road during those same months, Fred recalled that, when he was in lower elementary school, the family sometimes had "several housekeeping older ladies," who

That's Entertainment! 43

stayed with the children when both parents were away, a less than happy situation for him. But at other times, his Aunt Alice came and stayed and he found her "just great. Aunt Allie was so smart, so funny and so kind to us. She came up with all kinds of diversions to get us through those long, depressing Michigan winters. Movie night on Friday, visits to restaurants we'd never even heard of, cribbage tournaments." When they were older, each child took turns staying in Arizona with Hazel, bringing their school work along with them. When Fred was in third grade, he went with her to Tucson on the train, and they stayed at Tanque Verde Dude Ranch, "rode horses into the Santa Catalina Mountains, played pool, built a fire every morning in our little bungalow, and generally had a great time. I was out of school for three weeks, but my teacher had given me homework for the whole trip [and] my class wrote me letters." The West was already insinuating itself into his life.[7]

Music, another delight that Fred imbibed during childhood, was a constant in the LaBour household. On their long car trips to the UP or out West, the family sang snippets of classical pieces, Broadway show tunes, pop songs (learned from the 45 rpm records that Hazel brought home from the supermarket), folk revival pieces, rock and roll and country. Fred credits his mother for giving him her "'love of words." She also wrote poems and, on Christmas Eve, loved to recite a long narrative ballad by Frank Desprez called "Lasca," the story of a Mexican girl and her cowboy sweetheart who were killed in a cattle stampede. Fred has continued this annual ritual holiday recitation.

Country music came into the LaBours' consciousness, whether welcomed or not, through Marcie, whose music preference was strictly country. Fred loved to accompany Marcie to a diner in Grand Rapids that sported a jukebox with the largest collection of country recordings in the city, and he learned to sing harmony "driving along with her in her Willys jeep in about 1955" as they listened to singers like Carl Smith or Faron Young. Marcie also avidly listened to WJEF in Grand Rapids, which supplied a daily assortment of songs by people like Johnny Cash, Marty Robbins, and Marcie's favorite singer, Ferlin Husky. This powerful station could be heard throughout much of the upper Midwest and was a particular favorite among transplanted Southerners who had come north to find industrial jobs. Marcie and Fred also listened to WMAX, where its most popular personality, Pat Boyd, had southern roots and was one of the few women disc jockeys in the country. Remembered for her closing remarks each day—"Put on the coffeepot, Mama, I'm A-Coming Home"—she was sometimes described as "Michigan's Sweetheart of Country Music." Many years later, she attended the Grand Ole Opry as a special guest, and Slim, who by that time was a member of that institution, was able to thank her for what she had done to shape his career.[8]

Although cowboy songs were only an incidental facet of the programming heard on country radio, Fred did receive some exposure to cowboy music and humor on a local television kiddie show. Like Doug Green, who listened excitedly to Sheriff John during the family's brief sojourn in California, Fred heard and loved the yodeling and storytelling of a television favorite, Buck Barry (whose real name was Chester Burry). Barry hosted a popular show, *The Buckaroo Rodeo*, which ran from 1955 to 1969 on WOOD-TV in Grand Rapids. The Buck Barry show was Fred's first vivid introduction to the world of media cowboys, and a taste of the glittering, though imaginary, realm of show business that he would one day embrace. Barry had been a member of Tim McCoy's Wild West show in 1938 and had done bit parts in a few Gene Autry movies. Wearing fringe and sequins, Buck often opened his show with a yodel song, backed by his guitar. More important, though, he told stories that captivated both adults and children in his audience, and sometimes featured films by Popeye or the Three Stooges (but always with the caveat that kids should not emulate the violence seen in those comedy series). Buck was a longtime fixture on radio and television in western Michigan and was almost always the marshal in the Christmas parade in Grand Rapids. Fred was an enrapt viewer of the show, which contained many of the ingredients later featured by Riders In The Sky, and a sometime member of "the peanut gallery" in the radio studio. When Buck's horse died in a fire that destroyed his barn, Fred said that he was "devastated." He gained lasting impressions that stayed with him during his adult years. In many ways, Riders In The Sky were Buck Barry and *The Buckaroo Rodeo* writ large.[9]

Two more aspects of Fred's Riders In The Sky persona showed up early in life. He described himself as "always the entertainer and clown of the family—and of the classes at school." As Too Slim in Riders, Fred plays tunes on his face by slapping his cheeks to achieve a hollow effect, a talent he'd already acquired in elementary school. He described the origin and evolution of this "talent" to us:

I've played my face my entire life. I remember even in first grade my habit of tapping my cheek with a pencil while I worked at my desk. I noticed if I changed the shape of my mouth I could alter the pitch. From there it was a short jump to slapping my face gently and picking out a tune. When I found out people liked it, I started to hit harder so people could hear it. I was pleased years later to read about a spa in New York City which advertised "Gentle Face Slapping" as a means of toning up skin and imparting a "glowing sense of health." They charged $325 for 30 minutes and I thought "Man. I'm in the wrong business." Kids especially love it. If you want to connect with an audience of kids, you can't go wrong with face playing. They sit up, they laugh, they start slapping along and I've seen countless young face players leave our show tap tap tapping on their way out.

Fred's first appearance on stage occurred in about the fifth grade, when he acted in a school play as a butler, but he elaborated on the role: "I got this idea to come out as Groucho Marx, so I went and got a cigar, got a mustache, got some big glasses. No one knew I was going to do this, and the place just erupted... I remember the applause and the excitement I felt from doing something that really worked on stage... it was my idea and... [it] delighted the audience. I was kinda hooked from that point." Savoring that moment, Fred became the class clown, and he exhibited a facility for clever puns, wordplay, and practical jokes. Along with his keen sense of humor, Fred always liked to sell things. "I always had an egg route, and I had about fifteen chickens, and a regular route delivering eggs to folks around the area, and in summer, I grew strawberries. I always liked to make money. I sold greeting cards, delivered donuts." He told Don Cusic, "The lady down the street used to see me coming up her driveway, and she'd yell, 'I don't care what it is, I don't want it.'" The seeds of running the band's mercantile were planted when Fred was that young. Later, when he earned money for the first time by working in a bookstore, his job was "mostly mailing out stuff," and, as the Riders partner in charge of merchandise, he claims that mailing out albums, t-shirts, and other items from the mercantile remains a central part of the job.[10]

The hard work George advocated for his children shaped their future career choices in various ways. Chris described Marcie as the family "rebel," because her love of horses surmounted all else—even her college education. On the family's first trip to a Montana dude ranch, Marcie saw a sign that said, "Come back to Montana." And she did. She enrolled at Michigan State University for a year, then returned home to announce at the dinner table that she refused to return. After a short stay with an aunt in Jackson, Michigan, she moved out West—with her horse—to wrangle horses at Judson School in Paradise Valley, just north of Scottsdale, Arizona, where she met her husband, Alvin Merritt, who was a guide and packer. Marcie became a camp cook in the wilderness. The two of them bought a ranch in 1961, near Polson, Montana, where they raised cattle and quarter horses. The LaBours had provided their children with a strong work ethic and nurtured their independence. Even so, it seems incredible that, in 1961, when Chris was sixteen and Fred thirteen, their parents allowed them to drive from Grand Rapids to Montana, in order to help Marcie and Alvin on their ranch. Fred continued to go West for five or six weeks every summer during his pre-college years. The Merritts' ranch stretched his work skills, since he spent those weeks "painting barns, mowing, bailing and stacking hay, moving irrigation pipe, helping brand, and doing other ranch chores." Part of the time he worked with Fred Sunkel, "an Indian guy," driving a truck and picking up bales, sometimes working all night. Sunkel, Fred said, had the loudest truck in Montana. During these lengthy and arduous evenings, he began writing country songs in his head. As Marcie said, "Fred was more into the whole cowboy way of life than the horses," and, unlike the other Riders, he has actually been a part-time working cowboy.[11]

    Marcie and Alvin divorced after their children grew up, and then, motivated as she had not been as a college freshman, Marcie returned to earn her degree in Outdoor Studies and Education at the University of Oregon and taught third grade until she retired. She moved to Arizona in about 1980 and now lives on three and a half acres in Picture Rocks near the Saguaro National Park West where she works on horseback as a volunteer ranger. The positive associations with the Southwest eventually attracted Fred's sister, Chris, as well. She had majored in education at the University of Michigan, taught everything from preschool to college, and moved west to the Tucson area, supervising student teachers at the University of Arizona. After George died, Hazel went back to college at Michigan State, finished her degree in education, and taught for a year in the inner city. When Fred graduated from college, Hazel asked him if he ever intended to come back to Grand Rapids, because, if so, she was saving the house for him. When he told her he was never returning, she put the house on the market, sold it in three days, and moved out to Polson to be near Marcie and the grandchildren, then eventually moved to Tucson, where she spent the rest of her life. Fred alone still lives east of the Mississippi, on thirty acres outside Nashville, but he continues to call forth the imagery of the West several nights each week as a Rider.[12]

Fred described his father's brother, Uncle Bob, and Mike DeVriendt, his good friend, neighbor, and classmate of Chris's, as "cornerstones of his comedic sensibility." Fred took to calling Mike, "Uncle Mike," and he, in turn, dubbed Fred, "Cousin Fred." In addition to writing for the *Grand Rapids Press*, Uncle Bob had been a writer and theatrical director in Chicago and New York and had been both a director and writer in the early 1960s for radio's *Garry Moore Show*. Although he was a serious writer, Uncle Bob seems never to have outgrown his boyhood. He enjoyed practical jokes and verbal wordplay and loved the companionship of younger people, especially Uncle Mike and Cousin Fred. They, in turn, couldn't get enough of Uncle Bob's company. Fred thought of him as a second dad and fully appreciated, and even basked in, Uncle Bob's praise, telling us, "He thought I was funny, and I remember feeling very validated by that." The three spent much time together at Bob's farm in Sand Lake, north of Grand Rapids. In the winter, they'd ski all day, then play charades and board games like Scrabble. Uncle Bob had a classic Volkswagen beetle with no backseat, so he could transport grain, and when the three drove to the local diner, one of the boys had to hold on as best he could in the bumpy back space. At the diner, Uncle Bob would try "to score another piece of pie from the waitresses he knew there." In the summer, they played golf at one of the local courses, laughing so much that Fred remembers lying on the green, unable to get up.[13]

Buck Barry, whom Fred would sometimes "parody" in school plays, was merely one of the many television performers who piqued his interest. Mike speculated that Fred may have gotten his face-playing—something his mother found annoying—from watching Buck Barry. Fred and Mike were also influenced by Rem Wall, a longtime performer on WKZO TV, Kalamazoo, who performed with his Green Valley Boys on the Green Valley Jamboree, whom Mike recalled, kept his shows lively with subtle jokes, and a double entendre kind of humor. As Fred grew older, television became a source for more sophisticated and "adult" humor, particularly through the antics of comedians like Groucho Marx and Jack Benny and the whole retinue of Borscht Belt entertainers like Henny Youngman who had discovered a new venue for their comic genius. Fred told Don Cusic that he adored Stan Freberg—comedian, songwriter, and singer (among other talents)—and that the Smothers Brothers were yet another of his comedic influences.[14]

Fred's most indispensable inspiration, however, shared by all three of the original Riders and other members of their generation, was that of *Mad Magazine* and the culture it embodied, then spawned. The magazine had been launched in 1952 by Harvey Kurtzman and Maxwell Gaines as a comic book, but it evolved quickly as an irreverent critique of mainstream values and authority. Like the humor featured by many of the comedians of radio and television, *Mad Magazine* provided yet another vehicle for an underlying Jewish sensibility. Fred affirms that analysis, telling us, "What we think of as comedy would not exist without bedrock Jewish humor. Sarcasm, wordplay, lampooning powerful figures and cultural stuffiness—catnip for smart, funny Jews and their 'outsider' identity, thanks to millennia of surviving prejudice and hate." *The Simpsons*, *The Smothers Brothers Comedy Hour*, *The Daily Show*, *Saturday Night Live*, and *The Colbert Report* are only a few of the television favorites that emerged in the wake of *Mad Magazine*'s comedic reign. All three of the original Riders In The Sky have acknowledged the influence of the humor found in the magazine's pages.[15]

In addition to this urban style of humor, Fred learned much from the Roy Rogers television shows of his youth, finding the cowboy sidekick comedy completely captivating. Fred borrowed heavily from the sidekick archetype when he impersonated the curmudgeon cook/sidekick, Side Meat, in Riders' skits. Of all the sidekicks featured in the western movies, George "Gabby" Hayes was his special favorite, whom Fred called "such a kind and avuncular character." Like the Riders themselves, Hayes was not a cowboy, but was instead a highly trained actor from the East—born in Stannards, New York—who had never been on a horse until he was in his forties. However, he learned to embody the role of a crusty, cantankerous curmudgeon, which he played to perfection in scores of movies with such leading actors as John Wayne, Gene Autry, and Roy Rogers. Impressed with Gabby's lovable irascibility and his use of nonsensical language, Fred, as a Rider, somehow managed to combine the humor of *Mad Magazine* with the cowboy antics of Hayes and other western sidekicks. When an interviewer said to Fred, "You're the sidekick on stage, right?" Fred proudly declared, "Yeah, I have the turned-up hat, and I speak fluent gibberish."[16]

While reveling in his role as a madcap humorist, Fred, nevertheless, took his religion seriously. He and his mother, unlike his father and sisters, enjoyed going to St. Mark's Episcopal Church in Grand Rapids. Founded in 1836, the magnificent edifice is the "oldest standing building" in the city. Fred detailed what he liked about being a part of the congregation:

> I liked the poetry of the liturgy, and I loved the music, especially the big pipe organ when the organist pulled out those thunderous bass stops. I can still hear when he kicked it wide open on the last chorus of "Oh, Come All Ye Faithful!" Talk about the voice of God! I was an acolyte for six years and even thought I'd be interested in studying in a seminary. My Mom jokingly referred to me sometimes as The Bishop.
>
> In high school I developed a crush on a girl who sang in the choir, and when I found out she attended the Sunday night Youth Group, I signed up. We dated for two years. Sweet girl. Never underestimate the power of sex in getting people to church.[17]

Fred also learned early on that music was not only a means of self-expression but also a way to command attention and attract girlfriends. Fred took piano lessons from the nuns at the local convent but lost interest when his preference for Fats Domino riffs over Chopin motifs drew censure from his teachers. One of Fred's earliest displays of musical talent came when he was in the sixth grade, at a Boy Scout camp at Camp Ottawa in Northern Michigan, having written funny verses to the tune of "It Ain't Gonna Rain No More." According to Fred, his rendition "brought down the house." He received his first string instrument at about the age of twelve when Uncle Mike gave him a ukulele, but his musical development really advanced in the ninth grade when he bought a Supro guitar (a hollow-back electric instrument) from a girl up the street. His sister Chris said that he serenaded the family constantly with repeated versions of "Shortenin' Bread." Fred played all kinds of songs during these early years of musical discovery, but, like a multitude of people from his generation, he experienced a major artistic awakening on the evening of February 9, 1964, when the Beatles appeared on Ed Sullivan's television show in New York. Soon, Fred and a close friend,

Ricky Steketee, along with drummer Rich Grigas—playing two guitars and drums "because we didn't know what a bass was"—organized their own band. The Sneakers (so-called because Fred often slipped around to make music) bought matching suits and began playing at "school shows and little teenage clubs around town." Uncle Mike arranged a few gigs for them, and working mostly on Friday and Saturday nights, they sometimes made as much as $200, and "the dance floor was always full." While his school counselor, envisioning lofty horizons for the promising student, asked Fred about his aspirations, he shocked the counselor by responding, "I want to be in a band and play in bars." His parents, though, were not as impressed. Seeing a decline in his grades, they told him that while music was a great hobby, he needed to prepare for something more important in life, like doctor or lawyer. Fred then quit the band, and working largely under the sway of Bob Dylan, tried to content himself with playing acoustic music alone in his room.[18]

Fred enrolled at the University of Michigan in September 1966. He temporarily placed his musical interests on hold and embarked on a program designed to satisfy his parents: premed studies. His academic work was interrupted on January 6, 1968, though, during his sophomore year when his father suddenly died of a cerebral hemorrhage just months before retiring. Fred was devastated because he had not had the opportunity to tell his father goodbye. He dropped out of school and went home to help his mother through this depressing period. When he returned to Ann Arbor at the end of the spring semester, he found the premed curriculum too difficult and soon began piling up a mass of credits in English. Ultimately, a major in English also proved unfulfilling because he felt that too many of the courses were pretentious and overreaching in their efforts to find "meaning." He told us that, in looking for something "more real world than English" he went into the School of Natural Resources but found that he was alone in approaching the major with much more of a Thoreau-type perspective than that of a hunter or fisherman. His counselor told him about a new associate's degree in the field, which he gladly pursued, and he graduated six weeks later with an associate degree in wildlife management. In 2008, when asked about his college education, he joked that he was the only member of the Riders currently using his degree. Being educated in wildlife management, he told the interviewer, "has given me insight into the nocturnal behavior, migration patterns, and mating rituals of the fiddle player." He also quipped to us that the degree has been useful because his thirty-acre property outside Nashville was teeming with wildlife. "My wildlife management style is to provide them sanctuary and leave them the hell alone."[19]

Fred had still not embarked on his ultimate path to music. Like many other students of his generation, he was sometimes drawn to pressing political and social issues. The University of Michigan, after all, was a hotbed of the radicalism that flourished on many American colleges and universities during the Vietnam era. Fred became involved in a variety of issues: for example, he "felt very strongly that the Vietnam War was an indefensible war crime," and he consequently burned his draft card and made plans to go to Canada. In September 1968, he sat in with two hundred others at the Washtenaw County Building in Ann Arbor in support of some welfare mothers he believed had been victimized by racism and mistreated by the city government. He was arrested and eventually sentenced to community service cutting brush along the county roads. Many years later, while flying with the Riders to a gig in Canada, he was pulled out of line in a Canadian airport and questioned for two hours about this earlier act of "civil disobedience" in Michigan.[20]

The two enterprises, though, that most fully captured his energies were reporting for the college paper, the *Michigan Daily*, and filmmaking. The *Michigan Daily*, printed in broadsheet form, had been one of the most important student-run publications in the United States since its founding in 1890. Tom Hayden, the founder of the Students for a Democratic Society (SDS), in fact had been editor in his junior year, 1960–61. One of Fred's close friends, Jay Cassidy, also an alumnus of the paper, said that "working for it was a quite intense experience. In retrospect, you wasted a good education working for the newspaper." As a film and sports writer for the journal, Fred probably never envisioned that a seemingly innocuous bit of pranksterism on his part would circulate around the world, decades before anything went "viral." Assigned to write a review of the recently released Beatles album, *Abbey Road*, he was pondering how a "natural resources student with a very devious and creative mind" could make the piece unique. While driving one Sunday afternoon from Ann Arbor to Lansing, Michigan, Fred heard a talk show hosted by Russ Gibb on Detroit WKNR-FM. A caller had suggested that certain "signs" on the *Abbey Road* cover and in the album's songs indicated that Paul McCartney had died and had been replaced by a look-alike. That evening, while laughing about the caller's ideas with his friend, Jay, Fred speculated, "Suppose it's true . . ." The next morning, with his many Beatles albums lined up on his desk, Fred concocted a satirical "news" story alleging that McCartney had been killed, and that "clues" about the incident had been disclosed in the Beatles' music and album covers. He even supplied the name of a man in Scotland who had supposedly taken McCartney's place.[21]

With the *Daily*'s night editor, John Gray, supplying a title—"McCartney Dead: New Evidence Brought to Life"—the story appeared the next day, October 12, 1969, on page two, but readers pounced on it. Fred remembered that "the *Daily* sold out and ran an entire extra press run, which I think was unprecedented." The campus drugstore sold out of beer and Beatles records. The story was picked up by newspapers around the country, and in fact made its way to Scotland where McCartney was asked, "Are you alive?" Fred was even flown to Los Angeles, along with Russ Gibb, to appear on a television special hosted by the famous attorney, F. Lee Bailey, that explored the "clues" found in the Beatles' music. At this point, Fred admitted that he had manufactured the story. He later said, "Yep, I had my fifteen minutes of fame, which I've managed to stretch into seventeen." While Fred has never hesitated to talk about his harmless McCartney prank, he nevertheless has said that he regrets contributing to the American propensity for conspiracy thinking.[22]

While Fred was exercising his imaginative talents as a music critic, he was also experimenting with filmmaking, an art that would later prove to be very useful during his days as a Rider. He and Jay Cassidy worked at the Cinema Guild on campus, a venue that featured classic and avant-garde movies. Jay often worked as a projectionist, while Fred introduced the films and took up tickets, a task that earned him the sobriquet of "Ticket Fred." Some of Fred's brief ticket-taking monologues were filmed as movie shorts shown before the main events. Fred and Jay also collaborated on a series of short films—some quite irreverent—that ran principally at a film festival organized by a professor and sponsored by the Cinema Guild. In 1971, working with another of their colleagues from the *Michigan Daily*, photo editor Andy Sacks, they filmed one of their movies, *Her Big Heart*, on Marcie's ranch near Polson, Montana, in the Flathead Lake area. Fred and Jay and Fred's then-girlfriend, Sarah Krulwich—who later became a *New York Times* Arts and Broadway photographer—spent several days in the area with a small film crew and employed both local talent and some of Marcie's horses to make a dramatic film about ranchers. As Andy recalled, the three were all involved with the Cinema Guild and "into deep films." Fred rented

That's Entertainment! 53

a documentary film camera for the gig. They picked Gretchen Milloch as an actress; she later had a career in public radio in Lansing. Andy and his girlfriend wanted to get into the production aspects, but Andy ended up cooking for the other "staff" members. Although they had a lot of fun and learned a great deal about the challenges of filmmaking on the fly, as Andy succinctly commented, "The film never really congealed completely."[23]

When Fred graduated in May 1971, he completely severed his ties with academia and became fully committed to music. He later remarked that his chief interests after getting out of college were "baseball, girls, and music." Remaining in Ann Arbor for several months, he bought an electric bass and began making music with anyone who was available. The same Andy Sacks who collaborated with Fred on his Montana movie project, and later parlayed photographic skills into a prestigious career as a visual chronicler of American popular culture, also broadened Fred's musical horizons after they both graduated. Andy was a first-class pianist who organized a band called The Continentals, a trio that played jazz and vintage pop songs, and he told us how Fred joined the band and moved from playing guitar to playing the bass. The band's personnel included Andy on piano, Fred on guitar, Tom Toothacker on bass, Jerry Hopkins on sax and clarinet, and Jane Hassinger as the "girl singer." Andy explained, "One night we were rehearsing, and Tom hadn't shown up, so Fred picked up Tom's electric bass, and Fred took to it. We went on without Tom." Fred became the bass player. As The Continentals, they played Kales Waterfall Supper Club, which Andy described as being "decorated kind of like a grotto. We worked six nights a week there for two weeks, and that got us worked up and 'in the pocket,' four sets a night. We did tunes out of the American Songbook such as 'The Lady Is a Tramp.' The other [club] was Nick's Place in downtown Ann Arbor, more of a black crowd, so they weren't into Fred's playing 'Your Cheatin' Heart,'" which, as Fred said, he had enjoyed singing to "the supper club crowd." Once Fred found his way around the bass, Andy described him as both "versatile and adept." These were Fred's first professional gigs since high school.[24]

The road that ultimately led to country music beckoned a short time later when Fred joined two Detroit natives and University of Michigan graduates, Lisa Silver, a classically trained violinist and music major, and Herschel Freeman, a guitar player whom Fred knew from the Department of Natural Resources, to form the Honky Tonk Angels. Fred played electric bass, and Lisa's then-boyfriend, Jeff Wikle, played guitar. Herschel, who claimed that Hank Williams's "Lovesick Blues" changed his life, played rhythm guitar. Lisa had a lovely voice and served as a vocalist, covering songs by Patsy Cline and Loretta Lynn. As Lisa recalled, "We learned about half a dozen songs and went to a place called the Huron Lounge in Ypsilanti and worked there for a while, then worked at the Star Lounge, then the Pretzel Bell in Ann Arbor, maybe for about a year and a half or two years." Herschel told us that at the Pretzel Bar, the Angels performed "twice a week for a 75-cent cover charge." They became locally famous, Fred told us, for their renditions of the "classic" country songs of people like Buck Owens, Hank Williams, Porter Wagoner, and Dolly Parton. He remembers that the Hank Williams standard, "Jambalaya," was the first song he played with the band. Lisa recalled that Fred's "whole shtick was taking off already" with "comedic ramps ... sometimes in the middle of a song. Those were some of my most fun times ever, and we were pretty good for a college bar band. We did country standards with a little twist on it ... an eclectic mix of '70s country music, earlier hits, a fun and unusual combination. The humor really set it apart." Herschel and Fred had also begun performing their own compositions. Herschel said that "Fred could really turn out great songs" and was "a gifted writer," recalling that Fred had at least one particularly affecting song, "Father's Day," "the story of a divorced dad spending a day at the zoo with his son."[25]

Herschel, however, was the first Honky Tonk Angel who got the "bug" to try his luck in Nashville. "We made a demo tape in the living room, sometime in January 1972," Fred said, "and he and I went up and down Music Row into publishing offices." As they made the rounds on Sixteenth Avenue, the center of publishing houses where dreams either faded or soared, Fred accompanied Herschel as a "journalist," writing for a small counterculture-oriented magazine called *YES*. This writing gig paid Fred's way by documenting Herschel's experience in an essay that portrayed the efforts of a local Michigan boy trying to break into the songwriting business in Nashville. The city was a culture shock for the two young men. They had left Michigan in a snowstorm but found warm weather in Music City. The pleasant weather, combined with a profusion of blooming daffodils and "lovely receptionists speaking with a soft southern twang," made them think, "Man, we can get used to this." Herschel did sign with a publishing division of Capitol Records. When Fred saw this happening, he told us,

"I thought 'Hell's bells, if Herschel can do this, so can I,' and the two of us went back a couple months later, each with our own tapes." At a publishing company upstairs from Quadraphonic Studio, Troy Seals liked the second song on the tape Fred brought him. Back in Ann Arbor months later, Fred got a phone call from Troy telling him that "our song, 'The World's Most Broken Heart,' had a hold on it." Fred's first reaction was "Wait. *Our* song?" Eventually, when Tammy Wynette recorded it, he learned that Troy had rewritten the melody so that both shared songwriting credits. "Troy made the song work melodically," Fred said later. "He certainly deserved to split it." The song's fate was a realistic lesson about the way the music business actually works, but that is a later story. After their second trip, both Herschel and Fred believed they could see a future in songwriting in Nashville, and Lisa, who wanted to be "the next Linda Ronstadt," decided that she, too, would move to Music City. Herschel knew Lynn Kushner, who, in Fred's words, was "a woman who had a writing deal, and we moved into her apartment: four people living in a tiny space with a golden retriever and her ten puppies." They survived the congested arrangement, and on New Year's Eve 1973, they moved into a larger house on Wildwood, "the four of us," Fred reiterated, "and the eleven dogs." As fate would have it, Doug Green lived next door.[26]

All three of the Honky Tonk Angels achieved varying degrees of success in the music business. Herschel got fed up with his mediocre luck in Nashville, returned to Michigan and worked in a music store, but eventually became a promoter and booking agent in Memphis, specializing in international traditional musicians. Lisa became a protégé of the fiddler Buddy Spicher, recorded with him, but won her greatest success as a sessions musician and backup singer. She was also one-third of the Cherry Sisters, "some of the most sought-after background singers from the mid-'70s through the mid-'90s and beyond"; cowrote the great tribute to workers, "Forty Hour Week for a Living," recorded with great success by the group Alabama; and eventually became the music director and cantorial soloist of Congregation Micah in Nashville. Fred, of course, became the inimitable Too Slim, contributing mightily to the revitalization of the Singing Cowboy.[27]

Fred's path to the Singing Cowboy began within weeks after his moving into the house on Wildwood, when he saw his next-door neighbor, Doug Green, pitching a softball to his very young daughters, Liza Jane and Sally Anne, in the front yard of their house. Doug wasn't strumming a guitar or yodeling, but he was doing something that immediately won Fred's heart: he was wearing a Detroit Tigers baseball cap. Fred quickly found that he and Doug had grown up in Michigan and had both been at the University of Michigan at the same time, even living on the same street, but, strangely, had never met there. The two also shared a fondness for the same baseball team and revered the Tigers' Hall of Famer, Al Kaline. Even better, Fred discovered that they were both passionate about music. Like Doug, Fred was trying to play music anywhere and everywhere he could, and they began playing together "in a loose association of acoustic musicians who were all interested in swing and bluegrass."[28]

Fred was still hoping to make it as a songwriter, but he didn't become a serious writer until he moved into a place by himself a few months later in an apartment behind Acuff-Rose Publishing House on Eighth Avenue. Then he got a publishing deal with Paul Tannen at Screen Gems. He recorded five songs that met with little success, realizing, "I was writing what I thought would sell, rather than what I really liked to hear, playing this Music Row game." So, he quit trying to play that game. When he visited a friend at Cornell whom he'd known when both were in the Natural Resources Department at Michigan, Fred found a washtub bass in the corner and found he could actually play it. This was in late 1974 or early 1975. "When I got back to Nashville," he told us, "I bought a Juzcek bass from W. F. Crafton who sold instruments from his barn/shop. He dealt with the Nashville Symphony and always had Ella Fitzgerald on in his workshop." Fred started concentrating on playing the upright bass. "The 'energy crisis' was in the news and I figured if the power got shut off, I'd be all right if I played acoustic. Musically, I was inspired big time by David Ball and Uncle Walt's Band, as well as Ron Carter, and Paul Chambers on Miles Davis's *Kind of Blue* album."

He jammed with Peter Hoyle, a good musician and Vanderbilt student who lived downstairs, and they began playing in a little bar down the street called Bishop's Pub. Fred said that during that era,

> I discovered swing and Django and played with a trio doing the Django songbook. My goal was to play seven nights a week, a different kind of music every night. Bluegrass, blues, rock and roll, swing, jazz, country, standards, whatever. My ears were wide open. Good thing, too, because it led me to a pickup bluegrass gig in

Clarksville one night, and Ranger Doug and I were both on it. He did a Bob Nolan song as a solo, "Song of the Prairie," and I was trying to follow the changes on bass, and it was going all over the place, way outside standard bluegrass and country chord changes. After he was done, I asked him where that song came from. He said it was written by this guy, Bob Nolan. I asked if Bob Nolan had written any other songs, and Doug told me that yes, he had, about 1,200 of them. "Whoa," I thought. I knew a lot of songs but here was something great I didn't even know existed. Sometime around then he called me up, and we talked about starting a western swing band à la Asleep at the Wheel, a band we both loved. We thought we could do something like that in Nashville, but it never got beyond the two of us.[29]

Doug organized the Doug Green Bluegrass Band where Fred again played electric bass. Doug played rhythm guitar and sang lead vocals, while the rest of the band included a varying number of musicians that often consisted of Bruce Nemerov on banjo, James Bryan on fiddle, and Bob Fowler on guitar and vocals. Fred learned that Doug sometimes added cowboy songs to the mix of the hard-driving bluegrass numbers. Fred even added a couple of western songs to the repertory, "Git Along Little Dogies" and "I'm Gonna Leave Old Texas Now." He also discovered that he could yodel, and he and Doug started doing a duet version of "Yodel Blues," a song written by the pop songwriters Johnny Mercer and Robert E. Dolan, and popularized by Rosalie Allen and Elton Britt.[30]

Sometime in 1974 Fred received a call from Larry Ballard, who had found Fred's name through the local musicians' union. Ballard had a new album out—*Young Blood and Sweet Country Music*, for the Elektra label—and needed a bass player for the band that he and his brother Bobby were organizing. Larry came out of a rock background but was a good country singer, and was being managed by Pete Drake, the famous promoter and steel guitar player. Fred successfully auditioned for the job in his apartment, and it was only when the Ballards packed up to leave that he learned that they were from Grand Rapids, too! Fred played in the band at several gigs around Nashville, but he also traveled with them as far as Helena, Montana, where they played in a giant Quonset hut turned honky-tonk called Wong's Silver Spur. The crowd preferred older country music, and Larry knew enough Conway Twitty songs to satisfy the patrons. After a later gig in Billings, Montana, Fred sent Doug Green a postcard saying, "Hot licks, fast chicks, old dogs, new tricks." The band did not play many shows; he remembered that they "rehearsed a lot and played sporadically." Fred nevertheless gained invaluable experience playing the honky-tonk circuit. After his largely unsuccessful foray in Nashville, Larry Ballard went back to Michigan. Fred continued to play for a short time with Bobby Ballard and his wife in an all-acoustic trio called the Hartz Mountain Travelers, singing mostly country-rock songs from the repertories of people like the Eagles and Gram Parsons. By this time Fred had begun to experiment even more with the standup bass, finding that he liked the tone and feel of this instrument much more than the electric version.[31]

The birth of Riders In The Sky, however, was still a few years away. Fred played any and all kinds of music before he chose "the cowboy way," and he struggled to survive in Nashville playing music when possible and working at various day jobs, including as a janitor at Vanderbilt. His struggle for economic survival intensified in May 1976 when he married the then-pregnant Peggy Young, an ICU nurse at Vanderbilt, whom he had met at the Station Inn. Doug Green conjured up a license as a marriage officiant and married them in the boardroom at the old Country Music Hall of Fame with office workers and secretaries as witnesses. They married at noon, and then went immediately back to work: she to the ICU unit, and he to his janitor's job on the third floor of the Vanderbilt School of Engineering. They had two children, Frank, born in October 1976, and Lily, born in November 1978. After Frank's birth, Peggy chose to quit her job in order to care for him. The family now depended completely on Fred as the breadwinner, which added another layer of stress.[32]

Before riding off into the West with Riders In The Sky, Fred had a last fling with a commercial country band, once again playing an electric bass, this time with Dickey Lee. Dickey, a well-known veteran Nashville singer-songwriter, had learned about Fred from his bandleader, Bill Collins, and had gone to hear him play with the Ballard band. Bill was actually a boyhood chum of Doug Green's brother, Jim, and a frequent guest in the Green household. Doug's father had dubbed Bill "Cool" Collins, when he saw him playing "air guitar" with his sons while they listened to music. Doug later told a journalist that as he and Bill were growing up and playing together as kids, "We were really better at blowing up toy battleships and small plastic airplanes than we were at music." Bill got a degree in English from the University of Wisconsin but followed the lure of music to the West Coast and elsewhere before he landed in Nashville and got reacquainted with Doug when he ran into him at GTR. One evening, Bill and Dickey went to see Larry Ballard's band, and, for some reason that he cannot now explain, Fred was smoking a cigar and wearing a string undershirt. Dickey said, "The first thing that struck me about Fred was that he had a cigar sticking out at the bottom of his electric bass," which, along with Fred's musical competence, convinced a bemused Lee to invite him to audition. Fred said, "Dickey asked me to come over and sing at the house, '9 Million, 999 Thousand Tears to Go,' and I got the job."[33]

Dickey Lee was born Dickey Royden Lee on September 26, 1936, in Memphis and, at the time we interviewed him, he claimed to be the only survivor of the fabled Sun Studios where he had performed mainstream country and teen-oriented music. When Dickey left for Nashville to become a songwriter, he told us, "I was a rock 'n' roller with a country heart." As a protégé of Cowboy Jack Clement, one of his biggest hits was "Patches," a teenage suicide song. Dickey was a fine honky-tonk singer, however, and an accomplished songwriter. His hits gained him admission to the Nashville Songwriters Association in 1995. One of his songs, cowritten with Steve Duffy, was "She Thinks I Still Care," recorded by many singers but with the definitive version by George Jones. The affiliation with Dickey Lee, then, was a major coup for Fred, and certainly the most important connection that he had yet made in Nashville. While Dickey appreciated Fred's sense of humor, he noted that his lead—and excellent—guitar player, Bill, was also really funny. With Fred, Bill fashioned a style of harmony that beautifully complemented the lead singing of Dickey Lee. Dickey appreciated that they all had a good time together and recounted an evening following a show in Pittsburgh. It was snowing as they drove home right after the gig. Fred was driving. "About 4:00 a.m.," Dickey said, "I am looking out through the snow and see a sign saying 'Cleveland, Ohio, 10 miles.'" Obviously, Fred had missed a sign somewhere and had gotten them well off track.[34]

Peggy's pregnancy with Frank presented complications for Fred who wanted to honor his commitment to Dickey Lee. Fred said that Dickey "had waited three weeks for me while my wife waited to go into labor, and he let me know it was time for me to go with him, or he'd have to find someone else. They induced her, and next morning, I was in a van going up I-81 to my first show." They were on their way to Virginia to open for the country superstar Ronnie Milsap. Like Doug's first wife Mary, Peggy had probably never fully understood the powerful role that music played in the life of her husband. Fred continued to play with Dickey Lee for the next year and a half. Despite the superb musicianship of the Dickey Lee band, Fred soon became tired of the road and the necessity of performing the same set of songs every night. To supplement the gigs with Dickey Lee, he'd also been working for Manpower at a galvanizing plant "where they dipped huge pieces of steel into vats of acid and 900-degree molten zinc. My job was to knock off bits from the ends of the pieces with a hammer." While his day job posed danger, his night job limited his creativity. Even though he valued the experience he'd gained with the Dickey Lee band, Fred said that he "became disillusioned and frustrated with the music and not being able to really entertain and do what I wanted."[35]

Just when Fred felt that he was "done with it" and ready to swear off being a sideman in a country band, fate intervened. As Doug told the story in a 1992 fan-oriented publication:

> I recall a chill November evening in 1977, when Patty Hall, a delightful, lovely, and talented California-transplanted folksinger, called to ask me to fill in for her at Nashville's darkest, dankest folk club/songwriter's showcase. She pleaded illness; I pleaded insanity and said yes, though I knew the money would be miniscule. I'd been doing a solo singing-cowboy act for a while, but I longed to hear the harmony on those songs I heard in my head.

Fred picked up the story from there in a version often repeated, in an email to the authors:

> That's when Ranger Doug called me and said, "Patty Hall is sick and can't play Herr Harry's this weekend. Want to do it and just play cowboy songs?" "Can I play upright bass?" "You *have* to play upright bass." "I don't have a hat." "I have an extra hat. I'll bring you a hat." That hat is the one I'm wearing on the *Three on the Trail* [the Riders' first] album cover.

After Doug asked Fred to join him, Fred suggested that they should invite Bill Collins, with whom they'd perform as a trio. Fred recalled that they rehearsed just once, practicing the few cowboy songs that all of them knew, like "Tumbling Tumbleweeds," "Timber Trail," and "Back in the Saddle Again," and deciding that they'd fill in with some of their favorites that would fit the bill.[36]

On the bitterly cold evening of November 11, 1977, Riders In The Sky (which had not yet been officially named) made their first public appearance in a little basement club, Herr Harry Phranks and Steins, that later became one of the birthplaces of punk rock in Nashville. Located at 1909 West End Avenue, in the basement of what is now St. Mary's Bookstore, Herr Harry's—remembered by one patron as a "cavernous" club—was established and run by Harry Rowan and his wife Joan. Standing at the end of the bar, but not far from the corner where the musicians played (there was no stage), Harry would loudly ring a bell if something particularly pleased him.

Doug, Fred, and Bill arrived at Herr Harry's resolved to put on a show. They wore cowboy hats and any other item that resembled cowboy attire. They also brought Doug's huge Saguaro cactus that was still growing in a washtub, a saddle, and a "campfire" powered by an electric plug—items that would suggest a scene of cowboys on the trail. They had a repertory that could last them through the evening. In addition to the classic cowboy songs that Doug suggested, Fred and Bill each knew some cowboy songs, especially from the Marty Robbins canon, and some old chestnuts like "Red River Valley" and "Home on the Range." But during the evening they also ventured outside the cowboy domain. Doug even sang the Marty Robbins country-pop hit, "Devil Woman," while Fred pulled out "Chattanoogie Shoe Shine Boy," and Bill did "Deep River Blues." Above all, they had great fun, telling jokes and doing their best to crack each other up. All three of these Michigan boys had a *Mad*-inspired sense of humor. As Bill Collins related to Don Cusic, "We spent most of the night sitting around big pitchers of Harry's excellent beer and recounting old *Twilight Zone* episodes to each other. Then when we did play, much hilarity ensued." Fred even did a Louis Armstrong impression. The show presented an opportunity to pull out all the clichés of the kiddie cowboy shows of TV and to cover them with the dross of adult humor. That evening, Herr Harry's provided only a tiny audience—Fred thinks there may have been eight people—many of whom had come to the bar only to find respite from the cold. As he told Cusic, "We had so much fun. There was practically nobody there; we were just playing for ourselves and for the sheer joy of doing it. I remember we made twenty-five bucks—we were working for the door—the first night. We split it three ways—eight dollars each, and we had a dollar left over, so we cut the dollar into three pieces . . . that was the kind of all-for-one and one-for-all spirit that we had."

That democratic spirit that Fred referred to turned out to be a value at the core of the Riders In The Sky: no leader, all equal partners who recognized that the sum of their performances proved greater than any individual strength, and that the band's experience would be a team effort. Such foundational trust, we believe—along with the excellent musicianship, beautiful harmony singing and yodeling, skillfully crafted songs, and off-the-wall humor—sustained the band and ultimately led to its enduring appeal. Doug's third of that dollar bill is pasted on the first page of one of his scrapbooks that he has donated to his collection at the Country Music Hall of Fame and Museum Archive. Two days later, as Fred recalled the humor and musical camaraderie of that first evening, he called Doug and said, "I don't know what happened back there, but America will pay to see that." Like a bucking bronco, the band that became Riders In The Sky had broken out of the chute.[37]

CHAPTER THREE

THREE ON THE TRAIL

AFTER DOUG, FRED, AND "WINDY" BILL PLAYED A SECOND NIGHT at Herr Harry's, with a similar set of cowboy-oriented songs, Doug immediately began looking for other bookings. But first, the band needed a name. Fred was already trying to learn "the catechism of western music" by listening to the hefty supply of Sons of the Pioneers records that Doug had given him. When he saw the title, *Riders in the Sky* on one of the Sons of the Pioneers' albums, a double-LP Camden/Pickwick 1973 reissue, with a cover simulating hand-tooled leather, Fred recalled, "It just jumped out at me that this is the name of the band." Doug agreed, wondering, "Why didn't I think of that?" The band did not play again until December 16, when the Old Time Pickin' Parlor booked them as Riders In The Sky (the first time the band's name was mentioned) for three gigs in a row, and one in mid-January 1978. A trio of dates at the club Mississippi Whiskers followed. The Riders could not yet conceive of giving up their day jobs, because they had no real assurance that this "cowboy thing" would ever provide them with performing careers. As Fred put it, "In Nashville, there was a huge door for country music hopefuls with a line around the block, and at the door for cowboy hopefuls, no one was there, and it had cobwebs over it."[1]

The first iteration of Riders In The Sky: Windy Bill Collins, Too Slim LaDuui, and Ranger Doug Green. Riders In The Sky Archives, courtesy New Frontier Touring.

Windy Bill shared Doug and Fred's comedic sensibilities and was also in sync with them as they immediately began increasing their repertoire of songs, learning more ways to harmonize, and exploring entertaining elements to add to their shows. Windy Bill saw this as "a very creative period for us." Doug recalled that when they began, "We were really playing for

Three on the Trail   65

ourselves, and we were having a great time." The appeal was "as much entertainment as music." After seeing the audience response, it didn't take long before he began writing songs. He didn't want Riders In The Sky to be "just a museum piece," a simulation of what the Sons of the Pioneers did back in 1941. For a former rock 'n' roller, Bill found that songs from the Sons of the Pioneers were "challenging musically" with "sophisticated chord progressions and harmonies." He described what learning "Timber Trail" and "Blue Shadows on the Trail," for example, involved, and how the Riders began to put their act together. "Doug would bring in a lyric for us to learn, but part of it would just say 'yodel.' So, Doug realized he had to start annotating the actual syllabary of the various yodels. We had to learn them phonetically... And then we started yodeling in harmony, which was a whole 'nother trip!" Bill felt that "it all came together" when they opened for the singer-songwriter, Linda Hargrove, at the Old Time Pickin' Parlor. They had their fake fire; he and Doug entered the stage, each with a saddle in one hand and a guitar in the other. Fred carried his bass, and then the trio gathered around the campfire, with Doug blowing on it to get it lit while Fred plugged the hidden light bulb into an amp. The audience was immediately transported into the Riders' western fantasy. Fred shared his perspective about another early set at the Old Time Pickin' Parlor: "We had western shirts, boots, and hats. Word got around pretty fast. We opened for Billy Joe Shaver, and people who came were bemused, thought we were 'campy,' which generated audiences. Then musicians started realizing we were doing what nobody else was doing, and we were good at it. Windy Bill had a hard time playing the song straight. I think he thought it was more of a big joke." A journalist at *Billboard* caught their act that night and commented, "We called 'em 'brilliantly bananas' in the last review and they seem to live up to it—right now they're as tight as a cinch pulled by a lumberjack around a burro's belly and gettin' tighter daily."[2]

Don Cusic, the Riders' first biographer, was the country music editor at *Record World*. He had gotten to know Doug when the two worked at the Country Music Hall of Fame and played on the same softball team (along with Fred), sponsored by the magazine *Country Music*. In 1977, Doug had performed at Don's wedding, before the birth of Riders In The Sky. After Don's introduction to the Riders at the Old Time Pickin' Parlor, he formed with partner Dan Beck, New Horizon Management, and became the Riders' first manager. Although Cusic soon realized that the job did not suit him, he and Dan were initially instrumental in getting the word out around Nashville and beyond about the unique band they'd booked. The Riders' uniqueness, though, made the band a hard sell in a music-industry-oriented community that didn't know what to do with an act that did not easily fit into one of the preordained categories, which limited what New Horizon Management could accomplish. Don and Dan had scheduled a big show at the Exit/In on Tuesday, March 28, 1978, to which they had invited several music-industry people to introduce them to the Riders. As Don related, "Roger Sovine (the then-vice president of Broadcast Music, Inc., BMI) told me afterwards, 'A little bit of this shit goes a long way.' The industry didn't know what to do with them. Riders just were out of that realm." Roger Sovine would be surprised to know that his quick dismissal ultimately turned itself inside-out: the Riders did go a long way, at this writing, over forty-seven years.[3]

Sooner than anyone could have predicted, the cobwebs that Fred had mentioned began to dissipate, through Dan and Don's efforts and Doug's skillful Nashville networking. On February 20, 1978, the Riders were asked to appear on Ralph Emery's early morning show on WSM-TV in Nashville. Fred vividly remembers this appearance as the "beginning of his always introducing me as 'Fred Too Slim LaBeau, from Canada, I believe.'" This popular program also introduced them to their largest audience yet. In a career that lasted sixty years, Emery had become country music's most famous disc jockey and radio personality, with an informal and folksy air that endeared him to the world of entertainers and fans alike. An appearance on one of his many shows ensured wide exposure for an entertainer. Performing for and chatting with Emery and his audience also permitted the Riders to tone down the spicy material that they presented in more hip establishments. They were ready and eager to play for any audience that would pay to see them. They heartily accepted the dictum laid down by Ray Benson, leader of Asleep at the Wheel: "If you've got the dough; we've got the show." That same afternoon of their early morning appearance on Emery's show, for example, they played at the Knowles Senior Citizens Center. The folks at the Center certainly would have been familiar with the music of Gene Autry and the other Hollywood Singing Cowboys. The Riders' first excursions outside of Nashville, on the other hand, occurred at a couple of Tennessee school venues, the Greenbrier Elementary School in Greenbrier and the Pinewood Elementary School in Clarksville, for listeners who were too young to know much about cowboy music but were receptive to goofy and good-natured antics. In short, only a few months after that first performance at Herr Harry's, the Riders had already given evidence of building the kind of diverse following that has remained with them throughout their almost-fifty-year career—even without the help of music company executives.[4]

This early configuration of the Riders played together again at the Old Time Pickin' Parlor on March 30 and 31, and on one of these nights, Woody Paul Chrisman was in attendance. Woody told Don Cusic, "I remember hearing them sing and play, and they were way out of tune.... Willie Collins was playing the guitar with 'em, and they just sounded really bad." Fred added to the story: Woody "listened to us and then came up to us afterward and said, 'You know, I believe I could do you boys a lot of good.'" Doug recalled, "In his suave and tasteful way, Woody approached us after a show and announced that we needed him in the group." It turns out that they did. Just before Woody joined them, Windy Bill quit. He had recently married a woman with two children and bought a home, and the Riders weren't playing often enough to give him a steady income. While Fred and Doug still had their day jobs, Bill was just playing music. He returned to Dickey Lee full time.[5]

Bill was quickly replaced by another highly respected Nashville musician, Thomas "Tommy" Goldsmith. Like Windy Bill, Tommy was a rock-oriented musician who also loved country music. He was born in Raleigh, North Carolina, on February 1, 1952, but spent much time in Nashville and Austin after 1971, building a rock-solid reputation as a guitarist, harmony singer, and producer. After he returned to Nashville, he had played with Doug in the loose group of acoustic musicians who all knew each other. He performed with a rock group named the Contenders, which had broken up well before Doug contacted him about coming to watch the Riders perform. Then Tommy went to Doug's home, and the two of them practiced. The next time they got together, Fred and Woody also joined them, and the four musicians produced a sound they all liked and thus became the new incarnation of Riders In The Sky. Fred told the story this way: "We auditioned Woody, and he played 'Bluebonnet Lady' and 'The Cowboy Song.' I kept telling Ranger Doug, 'He's crazy.' And he'd say, 'But he's such a good musician.' And then I'd say, 'But he's crazy,' and he'd repeat, 'But he's such a good musician.'" Fred had to admit that "the energy was right."[6]

When Paul Woodrow Chrisman Jr., better known as Woody Paul—soon to be dubbed "the King of the Cowboy Fiddlers"—joined the Riders, he had already earned the description of a talented, but eccentric, fiddler. Noted music journalist Robert K. Oermann described him as "a long, lean, lanky, loonie cowhand from, Triune, Tennessee who feels this group offers him the most musical variety he has ever had in a band." Born in a Nashville hospital on August 23, 1949, but raised near tiny Triune, thirty miles south of Nashville, Woody Paul was the son of Minnie Katherine Douglas and Paul Woodrow Chrisman. The Chrismans, longtime residents of central Tennessee, since at least 1812, seem to have been of German extraction, having emigrated from Pennsylvania via Virginia and North Carolina. They, and the Douglases, were part of that large contingent of migrants—German and Scotch Irish—who came south from Pennsylvania through the valley of Virginia and on into the backcountry of the South. Woody's mother, Katherine (known to all as Mama Kat), was only fifteen when she married thirty-two-year-old Paul (who liked being called Old Man). Woody told us that she "was raised poor on a farm, but became a stenographer, and my dad wanted to get into farming, and she did different jobs: post office worker, seamstress. She was basically a housewife, but by the time I got to be ten or eleven, she was working pretty much full time." Woody was an only child; his mother lost two babies after his birth. The family moved around "a bit" when Woody was a baby, but very soon after, "pretty much settled into our house in Triune between Arrington and Murfreesboro" on family land where his father was a dairy farmer. Both parents, but especially Mama Kat, doted on their only child, and she made all of Woody's clothes.[7]

    As those who knew Old Man have mentioned, Woody, quite literally, was tailored from the same cloth. Billy Maxwell, who began kindergarten with Woody and then went to middle and high school with him, told us that Old Man epitomized eccentricity—and intelligence. Unlike his young wife, he had gone to Middle Tennessee State in Murfreesboro, had taught in a one-room school, and was a highly skilled cabinet maker who also loved and played down-home music. Eight years before Woody's birth, Old Man had a hunting accident and shot himself in the foot. The injury led to infection, and he had to have his lower leg amputated, after which he hand-carved his own wooden prosthetic. Teaching in a one-room school, he sometimes took his banjo and played for his students. When Woody was young, his father often took him along. Old Man wanted his students to learn to play music, too, so he spent his own money buying instruments

Woodward Paul Chrisman before he became Woody Paul. Collection of Woody Paul Chrisman, used by permission.

for them. When the school administration found out that Woody's father was spending so much time teaching music—and perhaps ignoring some of the basic curriculum—the superintendent told him that it would not be allowed. Upon hearing that dictum, Woody's father punched the administrator, promptly got fired, and concentrated on being a dairy farmer and cabinet maker—and kept playing banjo. One of the instruments he had purchased for his students was a fiddle. Allen McNeely, a big Riders' fan in Boise, got to know Woody well and told us that to get the fiddle ready for Woody, his father had made a new tailpiece from an old dog-watering bowl, and then he carved a new bridge for the instrument. By the time Woody turned eleven years old, he took up the fiddle and learned harmonica, banjo, and guitar all about the same time. Having given up teaching to run a dairy farm of thirty cows, Old Man expected his son to help him with the chores.

Woody felt that milking thirty cows by hand gave him strong hands that, in turn, helped with his music-making. As he told Too Slim many times, he got "his rhythmic feel from 'that ol' Surge milker. I used to play my fiddle to that thing. Shu-dit shu-dit shu-dit . . .'" Before he turned ten, however, the family acquired a milking machine. Reared by a father who crafted handsome utilitarian objects and furniture and kept farm machinery working, Woody learned and valued other practical skills that he gladly acquired and later put to good use; he enjoyed applying such knowledge to carpentry and working with automobile motors.[8]

Occasionally, Woody played fiddle while his dad played banjo, in a fashion imitative of the act that Paul Warren and Earl Scruggs did in their shows to suggest the beginnings of string-band music in the rural South. According to Don Cusic, Woody made his musical debut at the age of four at the Murfreesboro Cattle Barn, singing "Home on the Range," and he was rewarded with "a hamburger, Milky Way, and RC Cola." Although his family displayed all of the trappings of down-home rural culture, including dipping snuff, they seemed to be relatively prosperous. Knowing that Woody was a gifted student, they did everything in their power to see that he had the best education possible. Both he and Billy Maxwell attended the all-boys' prep school, Battleground Academy, in Franklin, on the site of the great Civil War engagement. While Billy boarded there, Woody was a day student who, Billy thought, rode each day to the campus with one of the teachers who lived near the Chrismans. Over the years, this child prodigy became an all-purpose music maker, singer, and songwriter. His principal instrument, however, was the fiddle, on which he became proficient at everything from hoedowns to jazz.[9]

Woody had no formal musical training, but he received invaluable instruction from the fiddlers he heard at fiddle contests in the musically rich region of south-central Tennessee and on the Grand Ole Opry. He performed during school plays in middle school, participated in fiddle contests himself—even winning the New England fiddling championship while at MIT in graduate school—and claimed that, while he was a young teenager, he knew and could play the "old-timey tunes" in the "old-timey" way. Never much of a bluegrass fan, he nevertheless considered musicians such as Paul Warren, Howdy Forrester, Tommy Jackson, and Buddy Spicher his mentors. Nearer to home, he became acquainted with two of the veterans of the Opry, the brothers Sam and Kirk McGee, guitarist and fiddler respectively, who lived not too far away on their farms in Williamson County. They both recognized Woody's "real interest," and as they became "really good friends," Woody related that he "played gigs with those guys by the time [he] was fourteen or fifteen." The McGees had been on the Opry since 1926 and had often accompanied the irrepressible Uncle Dave Macon on his tours. They often took Woody along on Saturday nights to the Ryman Auditorium when they played on the Opry. There he heard and loved all the old-time styles even though, at the time, he may not have realized that these excursions linked him to the very oldest traditions of commercial country music.[10]

While traditional fiddling was in his blood, Woody seems also to have always been receptive to modern styles of music. One particularly influential recording that helped to shape his approach to the fiddle was a gift from his mother: Felix Slatkin's *Hoedown! The Fantastic Fiddles of Felix Slatkin*, with Gordon Terry (Liberty, 1962). Slatkin was the conductor of the Hollywood Bowl Orchestra, and purportedly Frank Sinatra's favorite conductor during his Capitol years, while Terry was an esteemed country fiddler and a master of styles ranging from bluegrass to western swing. The twelve recordings on the album consisted of such classic fiddle pieces as "Devil's Dream," "Turkey in the Straw," and "Fisher's Hornpipe," as well as more "modern" country numbers such as "Maiden's Prayer," "Faded Love," and "Orange Blossom Special," all presumably selected by Terry. Throughout his career, Woody constantly experimented with tone and technique and freely embraced any motif that the worlds of jazz, blues, and rock had to offer.[11]

Woody was not simply a master musician; he was also a brilliant mathematician. He enrolled at Vanderbilt University in 1967 and majored in physics. While he had left Williamson County to begin his undergraduate career in Nashville, he did not completely leave the country behind; his parents brought that rustic tradition with them when they moved to Nashville to be near him. Old Man found a small piece of property on Little Hamilton Road and built a cottage for Mama Kat and himself. In 1969, while still an undergraduate, Woody and Cynthia Candeleria married. Before he graduated from Vanderbilt, they were the proud parents of a son, Paul David.[12]

Although he had more family around him than most undergraduates—along with the responsibilities and obligations these relationships incurred—Woody also wanted to play music. He had met a classmate, a wealthy sorority member and guitarist named Marshall Chapman, and found that they both liked old-time music. Marshall was more than his match in her unconventionality and music addiction. A striking blond, six feet tall, she easily attracted admirers who were blown away by her looks, intelligence, and glamour. She grew up the debutante daughter of one of the four families of mill owners in Spartanburg, South Carolina. The first indication that she was not likely to follow the social aspirations of her wealthy family came when she fell in love at the age of seven with Elvis Presley. This was the beginning of her lifelong love for the biracial and working-class music of the South. She chose to enroll at Vanderbilt in 1967 for the same reason that motivated Doug Green: it was in Nashville. Although she did graduate in 1971, she spent most of her waking hours making music. Marshall doesn't recall how they met, but she told us, "Woody got my attention at Vanderbilt, and he was dipping snuff in flannel shirts and jeans instead of being preppy. I had a Martin guitar, and he had a Stella." They started making music together, especially at parties, including one held by her sorority. One memorable evening, Allen Ginsberg was at a party at an old house near the university, and "Woody and I were playing. He was playing old fiddle tunes. I think Mr. Chrisman was on the floor like the Buddha with his peg leg and long hair, which he never washed." Marshall had not written any songs until she met Woody, who encouraged her. Woody, in turn, had written no songs until after he and Cynthia divorced and Marshall moved in with him. Musically, they seemed decidedly meant for each other. In her memoir, *Goodbye, Little Rock and Roller (2003)*, Marshall refers to Woody by the initials CW. She created an indelible image of the two of them and their impromptu music-making:

> Sometimes on a weekend night, I'd call CW from some fraternity party—usually after my date had passed out—and we'd hitchhike, with our instruments, down West End Avenue to lower Broadway and the backdoor of the Ryman. CW had grown up knowing a lot of the Opry regulars, so we often ended up in Roy Acuff's dressing room, where CW and Mr. Acuff would swap out on old-time fiddle tunes while Charlie Collins and I played along.

Roy Acuff, a one-time fiddler, had forsaken that instrument to become one of the leading singers of country music. When Woody was only sixteen years old, Roy gave him a fiddle with his autograph scribbled on the back. Many years later, Woody was honored to give the fiddle, during an Opry birthday celebration, to Ketch Secor, one of the promising young entertainers of country music, and a member of Old Crow Medicine Show.

While Woody may have been an outstanding mathematics and physics student, he was getting Ds in English. His sympathetic adviser recommended that he go to the music school at Peabody, at the time, a separate, but linked, college, and take violin instead of the next level of English. Woody was thrilled to pull As instead of Ds, even though he felt that he didn't actually learn to play classical violin. Because of his interest in fusion—and his excellent grades in his major—after graduation, he headed straight to MIT, where he worked on a doctorate in nuclear engineering. In Boston, as in other towns, Woody discovered, "If you play acoustic music, you go out and meet all the acoustic pickers" you can find. Local music stores, like Old Joe Clark's in Cambridge, served as community centers for such musicians. Woody met Sandy Sheenan, who ran the store in an old house, where musicians both picked and lived. Woody hoped that his wife and child would remain in Nashville while he was at MIT so that he, too, "could have a place to stay and play." That dream did not pan out. Cynthia, however, did move to join him, and they had their second child, Joseph. Since Woody's stipend for graduate school did not cover his living expenses, he also served as a research assistant at MIT, building plasma machines and learning a great deal about plasma physics.[13]

Woody's passion for music, though, was never disguised during his heady intellectual enterprises. He had temporarily abandoned the fiddle in order to devote his musical energy to playing classical guitar and using his intellectual energy to pass his doctoral qualifying exams. When he became depressed that he had not yet identified a topic for his dissertation, he once again turned to the fiddle. Somewhere between the scrimping to live on Woody's limited salary, being far from family support in Tennessee and, very likely, his spending too many hours away from her and their children, Cynthia left him in early 1975 to go back to Nashville and seek a divorce, taking the children with her. Understandably, Woody's depression deepened, and he called Marshall, with whom he had "kinda lost touch" since leaving Nashville. As she wrote in her memoir, "as we talked, I could tell CW was upset . . . I can't remember what all was said, but by the end of the conversation, it was somehow decided that I would go to Boston."[14]

Marshall moved in with Woody the spring of 1975. In addition to typing his dissertation ("Inertial, Viscous, and Finite-Beta Effects in a Resistive,

Woody Paul presenting Roy Acuff's fiddle to Ketch Secor at the Opry. Photograph by Chris Hollio, image courtesy Grand Ole Opry Archives.

Time Dependent Tokamak Discharge"), she and Woody played on the sidewalks in Harvard Square near the Harvard Co-op on weekend nights. As she described, "We had us a good little repertoire going. I'd back him on my old Martin guitar while he fiddled 'Devil's Dream' and 'Sally Goodin,' then he'd back me while I sang 'Your Cheatin' Heart' and 'I'm So Lonesome I Could Cry.' We were a big hit on the street." With the extra money they made, they moved to a nicer apartment in Cambridge, closer to campus. In fact, Marshall said that she told Woody that, despite the hard work he'd devoted to his graduate education, he would be happier as a musician than as a scientist. They were getting along well, inspiring each other musically. Marshall already had songs recorded, and Woody began writing his own. Two of his songs, "The Cowboy Song" and "Blue Bonnet Lady," results of his initial songwriting efforts, later became successful Riders' standards. But his relationship with Marshall became problematic because of his unpredictable drink-induced mood swings. Finally, on Christmas Eve of that year, when Woody got drunk, Marshall became so frightened of his violent outbursts that she left as fast as she could, eventually making her way back to Nashville. Once reestablished and writing songs and performing at the

Exit/In, she became part of Nashville's nascent Outlaw movement, the rebel and rule-breaking contingent of musicians that included Waylon Jennings, Willie Nelson, and Billy Joe Shaver. Stylistically, she fashioned a fusion of country and rock music and, nevertheless, continued to maintain her warm relationship with Woody's mother, whom Marshall described as being "as close to a saint as any person I've ever known. She loved me, and I loved her." Once, Marshall got the flu while living alone in Nashville, and Woody's parents came to her apartment, got her out of bed, and brought her to their home where Mama Kat nursed her back to health. Later, when Marshall decided to put in a vegetable garden, Mama Kat patiently guided her and shared her recipes, including one for canning tomatoes.[15]

Woody obtained his PhD in nuclear engineering in 1976 and knew that he had options in his field awaiting him. While in graduate school, he had worked for the Atomic Energy Commission in Oak Ridge, Tennessee, during the summers of 1973 and 1974, and knew that he did not want to return there or work for the government. Upon graduation from MIT, he was also offered a research position and a teaching assistantship at Columbia University, and though he had earlier contemplated such a career move, it no longer appealed to him. Woody had come to disagree with the way physics, which still fascinated him, was being explored and taught academically. Many years later, when being interviewed for the MIT alumni magazine, he told Jay London, "I knew I'd make more money playing rock and roll . . . But I've never stopped studying thermodynamics. I'm fascinated with entropy—how it's present in every reaction on the planet, yet no one can truly describe it." And Woody had learned a great deal as a graduate student. London commented, "While physics and fiddling may seem poles apart as professions, success in both fields hinges on both passion and practice." Woody agreed, adding, "You need a strong work ethic to be successful . . . That's what MIT is all about. The people there love what they do—they get so excited solving a problem." As music had done with Doug and Fred, it had taken possession of Woody, and all he really wanted to do was play fiddle with a band. While being a nuclear physicist was a far cry from being a cowboy fiddler, his doctorate served as a major reason why the Riders have become known as the most educated band in country music.[16]

After Woody returned to Nashville, Fred recalls, "Woodrow and I met in the audition line for Opryland pit bands. I'd heard about him before, and my friend Charmaine Lanham had told me, 'You should meet Woody

Chrisman. You have a lot in common.' For my audition I played bass and sang 'Dark Hollow,' which underwhelmed the casting crew. I packed up and left and went back to my serial unemployment. Woody auditioned after me, also didn't get the gig, except he flew out to LA a couple days later and got the gig with Loggins and Messina." Kenny Loggins and Jim Messina were popular rock musicians. Woody went on the road with them from March until October 1976 as guitarist and fiddler. When playing with Loggins and Messina, he became fascinated with jazz, especially with the music of Stéphane Grappelli. That summer, Woody also married a Vanderbilt alumna and friend of Marshall, Liza Ramage, with whom he fell in love shortly after Marshall departed from Boston. They had two children together: Rebecca and Jacob. After leaving Loggins and Messina, Woody signed on as a fiddler with the dynamic old-time singer, Wilma Lee Cooper, whose musician husband Stoney had died. Woody admired Wilma Lee's musicianship, but he found his true calling with Riders In The Sky.[17]

The Riders played publicly only once in June and not at all in July, but the gigs picked up again in August, the first real turning point in their then-still-brief career. When the Riders went looking for suitable venues, they found that none of the Nashville clubs catered to cowboy acts. Even the venerable Grand Ole Opry had no cowboy singers on its roster, except for Marty Robbins who only occasionally dipped in to the western song bag. Nashville, however, as a thriving center for live music, had alternative venues that catered to a youthful population that was ready to go out just about every night. And these were the places where the Riders first gained a loyal following. Between December 16, 1977, when they played at the Old Time Pickin' Parlor, and August 17, 1978, when they made their first out-of-state foray to the Kentucky State Fair in Louisville, the Riders performed almost exclusively at such hip, youth bars as Mississippi Whiskers, Exit/In, Springwater, and Wind in the Willows. Similar clubs—including Cat's Cradle in Chapel Hill, North Carolina, the Cellar Door in Washington, DC, the Birchmere Restaurant in Alexandria, Virginia, and Poor David's Pub in Dallas, Texas—have ever since been essential stops throughout the nation for the Riders. Some of these clubs, like the Old Time Pickin' Parlor, of course, featured bluegrass and other forms of roots music, but for the most part, they attracted audiences that had not been turned on to the music of the singing cowboys, but were instead looking for an evening of superb musicianship and good risqué fun. And the Riders were more than ready to present them this heady mix.

Both Tommy and Woody joined Fred and Doug in time for the first out-of-state—"on the road tour." They spent ten consecutive days at the Kentucky State Fair in Louisville, from August 17 to August 27, 1978. They played two sets daily, at 10:00 a.m. and 4:00 p.m. in what Tommy referred to as "The Hall of the Giant Vegetables," surrounded by Future Farmers of America displays. During the intervals between shows they jammed in their hotel rooms or took in other exhibits at the fair. Their shows were interspersed with other acts, including a contingent of trained monkeys. While they earned $2,500 for their appearances, they did not get paid until the end of their ten-day engagement.[18]

This quirky series of shows nevertheless marked their first extensive venture outside of Nashville and presented them with their largest and most diverse audience to date. Witnessing the number of children and older folks in attendance, they quickly realized that they needed to modify their comedy to make it appropriate for all age groups. They also realized that their show actually appealed to a wide audience, which had tremendous marketing potential for their future. Since the Riders had no dates the previous month, they had plenty of time to work up playing as a foursome. Woody brought to the group a droll sense of humor, an ability to sing a tenor harmony, and a dazzling fiddle style. He, unfortunately, also contributed his "Where's Woody?" erratic behavior. Don Cusic and Dan Beck were still managing the band and also drove to Louisville with the boys. Don met Woody there for the first time. The Riders' first appearance was being videotaped for a local TV station, so they were being given directions about the details concerning that performance. As Don wrote, "During this whole time, Douglas, Fred, and Tommy Goldsmith were listening closely so they'd know what to do. Woody was sitting on the floor in the middle of this group. When the guys had finished giving instructions, and we all started to move off, Woody looked up and said, 'What's going on?'" Ultimately, Doug judged the fair a great success because "we got a good enough response," and the fair set the band up with an agent, Triangle Talent, which booked the band for the state fair for another three years and for corporate events in Kentucky. That trip also gave Doug the "go for it" signal that he'd been waiting to receive; he knew he was ready to be a full-time Rider, even though he stayed at the Country Music Foundation several more months.[19]

Just before the Kentucky State Fair, the Riders played two August shows, one at the Old Time Pickin' Parlor and the other at Wind in the

Willows, located behind the Exit/In in what had been an old mansion, built in 1906 by Mr. and Mrs. Alex J. Porter. In 1971, Michael Murphy built a bar there, named it for his favorite childhood story, and began featuring the music of jazz and pop musicians. Returning to Nashville after the state fair, the Riders wasted no time getting back in the promotional/entertainment saddle again. On Tuesday, August 29, they were once again on the Ralph Emery Show on early morning television, and that night, they played for the second time at Wind in the Willows. That was the beginning of a Tuesday night run for the Riders, as the club became virtually their performing "headquarters" for the next year, and the setting for their full-fledged evolution as America's cowboy band. Tuesdays are a traditionally slow night for bars but, as word-of-mouth reviews quickly spread the news of the zaniness that went on there, audience size expanded dramatically. The Riders began their performance by "playing off the props." They entered carrying saddles, saying, as Slim told us, "This looks like a good place to camp. Then I'd light the campfire which was a little pile of sticks covering a light bulb," followed by "a lot of jokes about burning cow chips, phrases like 'Beats the meadow muffins out of me,'" and riffing on cowboy stereotypes.[20]

Tommy said that Wind in the Willows "was pretty packed every time we played, informal enough that the Riders could really work on their shtick." At that weekly gig, Fred explained, the band developed the basic structure of their act—inspired by the Sons of the Pioneers *Lucky U Ranch* and the *Gene Autry Melody Ranch* radio shows—that moved from the stage of an intimate club catering to college and young adult regulars to stages all across the United States and in Europe and Asia, as well as on television and radio programs that appealed to audiences of all ages. Almost all audiences, that is. In late October, the Riders backed up some Opry acts in middle and high school auditoriums, first in Northlake, Illinois, and then, on successive nights, in the small New York towns of Haverstraw, Tarrytown, and Salamanca. Since the Riders were not actually a country back-up band, they did not entirely succeed—artistically or financially. Don Cusic and Dan Beck figured that the Riders' show was so magical and so different from the typical Nashville club act that playing in the Big Apple might be their "Big Break." They had arranged for the Riders to play at the popular Lone Star Cafe in Greenwich Village, but only if the band played for free, since they were "unknown and unseen." They opened for a blues act on Halloween, but the hip audience in New York City didn't "get" the Riders act the way hip audiences in Nashville did. While they were playing, Fred said, "Some guy walks in, looks at us, and says... What's this cowboy shit?" Doug told us that initial response held: upstate New York and New England responded well to the Riders, not so the big city folks.[21]

While the entire trip was a bust on many levels, the time spent on the road actually led to the creation of something essential to the band's future. The Riders always listened to radio shows while on road trips. *Mystery Theater*, hosted by E. G. Marshall and heard on CBS, was a particularly important inspiration. Listening to the show, Tommy said, "I thought we could come up with something for this band that would be a skit." And he wrote the first one, "The Cowboy Who Hated Christmas," based largely on Charles Dickens's *A Christmas Carol*. Doug, then known as the Big Fella, was the principal character. According to Tommy, this sketch "was wildly greeted," and he averred further that "The Riders' humor was very accessible, funny to just regular people. *Mad Magazine* was certainly important, as well as Brother Dave Gardner, *Al White Motors*, and some kind of hipster shows as well." "The Cowboy Who Hated Christmas" was the beginning of what Tommy called Riders Radio Theater, a comedic routine that soon had Fred writing weekly versions. He based each week's content on current events along with the one-liners and stories that were sprinkled among the songs they sang and tunes they played. Too Slim joyously recounted, "I was into the performance art aspect of it." And, as he recalled, they were having so much fun with their shows that it was "like kids in a sandbox." The amazing thing about the Riders is that performing stayed that way for the rest of their careers! At the Tuesday night shows, they also began introducing the performing personae that have since defined them. "Ranger Doug" debuted there. As Fred told us, "In my earliest scripts I called him 'Big Fella,' which he hated. He came in one night and said something like, 'From now on I'm Ranger Doug, Idol of American Youth,'" a title well suited to his dignified and manly bearing. Doug got his idea from a poster that advertised Vaughn Monroe and the movie *Toughest Man in Arizona*, with the wording, "Idol of Millions." Fred explained that this "over-the-top grandiosity seemed hilarious to us... much like 'America's Favorite Cowboys,' which I loved, although at the time we weren't even Davidson County's favorite cowboys." Fred called himself "Too Slim," inspired by Too Tall Jones, a former professional football player, who had a commercial on a Black radio station, WVOL in Nashville. Woody Paul was already Woody Paul, but he also became "The King of the Cowboy Fiddlers," while Tommy became Tumbleweed Tommy.[22]

In 2023, as Fred reminisced about the "fearlessness" of their comedic skits in their early shows, he said, "We felt like Wile E. Coyote, when he'd dash off a cliff and, as long as he didn't look down, he was all right. When he looked down, of course, he dropped like a rock. We articulated that very thought amongst ourselves from very near the beginning. Woody came up with the delightful image of our career resembling 'a cast-iron, steam-powered biplane,' which, against all odds, manages to stay airborne. We embodied that idea: 'Just act like it's going to work and it will.'"[23]

According to their unfolding bunkhouse mythology, the Riders resided at the XXX Ranch. Tommy added, "Woody, Fred, and I were all smoking a lot of pot in those days, which probably flavored the hipster humor part of the band in contradistinction to the 'Idol of American Youth.'" Part of their appeal lay—and continues to lie—in the tension between the music, which the Riders fervently intended to be respected and done right, and the humor where anything goes. "I was conscious of coming up with something new every week to keep the regulars coming back," Fred said, and he took over writing the scripts, drawn from three different models: *Saturday Night Live, Hee Haw, and Melody Ranch*. While he told us that "double entendres were everywhere," the Riders refrained from profanity—"unless warranted. In the dialogue, the XXX home ranch was at the corner of Fifth and Commerce in downtown Nashville, a notorious peep show locale. Later, when people started bringing their kids to Riders' performances, it became awkward. Then the XXX morphed into Harmony Ranch." Slim took on another task when writing for their performances at Wind in the Willows and other club dates. He created "wacky commercials," such as "'Deadwood Darlene's Udder Butter on a Rope,' a division of 'Deadwood Darlene's Prairie Lubricants, the Official Lubricants of (your waitress, your local sports team, whoever was in the news)'; 'Frederick's of Deadwood,' featuring the alluring 'Peek-a-Boo Bucking Cinch.' A big favorite was 'Deadwood Darlene's Natural Rope Wax, with Organic Stiffeners,'" complete with the following dialogue:

TOO SLIM: Say Woody, how's your ropin'?

WOODY: Not very good, Too Slim. Everything I get my rope around just slips right on through. I think I'll just burn it in the campfire.

TOO SLIM: Hold on there, Woody. What brand of Rope Wax are you using?

WOODY: I just grab whatever's on top of the pile. You know all Rope Waxes is the same. [He always said "is."]

TOO SLIM: Ha ha ha! There's your problem, Woody Paul. All Rope Waxes are not the same. Here, try some of my new Deadwood Darlene's Natural Rope wax, with Organic Stiffeners.

WOODY: Hmmm... Organic Stiffeners...

RANGER DOUG, IN HIS ANNOUNCER'S VOICE: Two weeks later.

TOO SLIM: Say Woody, how's your roping?

WOODY: Yeehaw, Slim! I'm nailing everything I can drop my loop around, and I owe it all to Deadwood Darlene's Natural Rope Wax! Those Organic Stiffeners sure make a difference. Hey Slim, wanna try some team roping?

TOO SLIM: Ha ha ha! No thanks, Woody.

RANGER DOUG: That's Deadwood Darlene's Natural Rope Wax, with Organic Stiffeners, the official Rope Wax of... your waitress. And now back to Riders In The Sky.

The Riders had successfully created a structure that suited them perfectly and, significantly, translated well into television and radio performances.[24]

One Tuesday evening at Wind in the Willows, Slim was talking to a "friend's girlfriend" who mentioned a job at the downtown library, telling him that he would be perfect for it, and that he should immediately go for an interview because they were looking for someone who could entertain children. He took her advice and got hired. That position involved Slim's superpower: entertaining. He became Cowboy Too Slim, whose duties included shelving books and working with the "brilliant" puppeteer, Tom Tichenor, and crafting the "primitive" soundtracks for his shows, major productions that were presented to large audiences at paid performances on Friday evenings. Tom trained Too Slim, Tina Walker, and a second children's librarian to man the marionettes for these shows, which Tina described as being quite elaborate. She and Slim also created an act called "Too Slim and

Pickles." To engage their young audiences in reading, Tina and Slim would choose a book they liked and write scripts together, which they then "sang and acted out the books" for the children. Not surprisingly, she found Slim a "charismatic performer," excellent at encouraging audience participation. Tina had been a gospel and back-up singer in Nashville before becoming a librarian, and the two got along famously. In addition to doing a morning show in the children's reading room, they performed this half-hour act, sometimes two shows a day, for classes of children bused to the library from schools all over the city. Working so closely together, Tina and Slim became good friends, and she and her husband also enjoyed watching the Riders perform at Wind in The Willows. Slim said that the library experience was "really good training for me. It helped with my sense of professionalism. I was the show for ten minutes before the puppets began. That kind of structure was really helpful." The job also proved more enjoyable and stable than working in dangerous situations for Manpower, Inc., and the experience of writing scripts from his library days made him more adept at creating material for the Riders.[25]

A Riders' performance was—and remains—not a concert, but a show: pure escapist entertainment. With their western props in prominent display, and the campfire properly "lit," the Riders would stroll on to the stage, and Ranger Doug would typically greet the listeners with, "Mighty fine. And a great big howdy to all you buckaroos and buckarettes." Then a song like "Texas Plains" or "When Payday Rolls Around" would kick off the evening. After that, it was all contrived but controlled mayhem, mixed with western music. On some evenings, the Riders invited other entertainers to join them. A longtime fan since the Wind in the Willow days, Dr. Tom John recalled one occasion when Jill Klein appeared to sing with them wearing clear plastic jeans. "When she belted out the first lines of 'I Want to be a Cowboy's Sweetheart,' her jeans completely fogged up, and everyone cracked up. Fred had to lay his bass down temporarily." Other evenings, the band projected clips from the classic Grade-B western movies on the walls of the club, and then built their own skit or a series of songs around the theme of what had been shown. More often, though, they presented their own outlandish skit.[26]

While their audiences were growing at Wind in the Willows, and their appearances around Nashville increasing, they certainly were not yet making a living as a band. But they were definitely on their way, which Doug had realized after the Kentucky State Fair. As Bill Ivey told us, he was aware, by the late fall of 1978, that Riders In The Sky was beginning to take too much of Doug's time, and that he needed to make a decision about what to do. He should either spend more time with his work at the CMHOF or work on building his band. Bill had seen the Riders perform, appreciated that they were offering something fresh and different, and knew that Doug could not continue to devote himself to a full-time position at the CMF. In asking him to resign, Bill had anticipated the choice Doug would make. In Doug's letter of resignation, dated November 6, 1978, he wrote, "It has been a continual pleasure to be associated with a first-rate staff, an exciting and growing organization, and encouraging Board of Trustees, I nevertheless find the call of my particular Muse too strong. The time has come to hop on my pinto and devote all my energies to the success of Riders In The Sky." An article in *The Tennessean* quoted Bill as saying, "Doug has been an important part of the Foundation's activities for nearly five years and his presence on the staff will be missed.... All of us have been aware of his growing interest in a performing career... and we wish him well in his efforts." Bill also admired the fact that, after leaving the CMF, Doug and the Riders "went out and systematically built a network of live audiences all over the country. They are the shining examples of how to build a career without country music radio hits."[27]

On December 9, 1978, just about a month after Doug left the Country Music Foundation, the Riders made their first appearance on the Grand Ole Opry, followed by another early morning visit to Ralph Emery's show. They were definitely gaining local notoriety. Even as their act was coming together, though, the winter of 1978/79 was a rough one economically for the members of Riders In The Sky. Fred kept his library job, but playing until the wee hours of the morning, then being alert and energetic enough to keep young children engaged just a few hours later was not easy. Woody was working on Volkswagen motors when he wasn't performing, and Doug was chopping trees—for nothing—that had to be thinned in the Montgomery Bell State Park, then hauling, and selling firewood from the back of his pickup truck when he wasn't writing. Since "things had not quite taken off yet" for the band, Doug, ever the record keeper, noted that in 1979 alone, he had 128 pieces published, including articles, liner notes, record and book reviews, news snippets, and book chapters. "These pieces were not scholarship," he pointed out, "just journalism with a historical bent." While his wife, Cindy, had a job as a receptionist, every dollar coming in helped. Tommy was the only one who didn't have another job, but then he was also the only one without a family to support.[28]

The amount of money the Riders earned at Wind in the Willows may have been negligible, but their Tuesday night shows provided them with sufficient interest to yield hefty returns. Davis Ford, a well-respected environmental engineer from Austin, was visiting his sister, a professor at Vanderbilt, when they took in a Riders performance at Wind in the Willows. He was so delighted with the show that he told them he'd try to get them some gigs in Austin, then in the midst of becoming a vibrant and antiestablishment music center. In late February, 1979, they played at an Austin club called General Sam's one night, and then the three following nights at another, 1874 Steamboat Springs. Ford also arranged for them to play for a private party. Serendipitously, Terry Lickona, host of *Austin City Limits* airing on PBS, saw them at one of those performances and booked them for a future appearance, an event that would garner the attention of a national audience. As Don Cusic wrote, "The door that opened in Austin would be a big, wide double door." Townsend Miller, who had a popular country music column in the *Austin American Statesman*, knew both Tommy and Doug, and wrote that he "was excited to know" the Riders were playing at General Sam's, although he had not yet seen them perform. After seeing their act, his review the following November waxed ecstatically: "I don't know what more to say about the Riders except that they are wonderful . . . with their faithful revival of campfire vocal harmonies and relaxing instrumentals."[29]

David Symington, an aspiring songwriter from Washington, DC, began working at Wind in the Willows shortly after the Riders began playing there. He sometimes sold tickets at the door—the show was 50 cents, with beer and popcorn—or tended the bar and became a real fan of the band, telling us that he saw a big difference in the Riders after they returned from their first trip to Texas: "I remember when they went to Texas. When that happened, they got busy, started playing more, really 'hit the sky.' I came in one day when they were warming up, and Doug said [to his fellow band members], 'What did you do for Riders In The Sky today?' They were driven to make it. Every step they took for the next forty years, they took it as a business." When asked about the effect David Symington had noticed about that first trip to Austin, one of the Riders replied in conversation that they recognized, "Oh, we're a road band!" They'd expanded their orbit, exactly what they'd hoped to accomplish. Fred recalled that during the winter of

1978/79 when they were all struggling financially, Doug bought them each a copy of the book by Kenny Rogers and Len Epand, *Making It with Music: Kenny Rogers' Guide to the Music Business*: "how to do the publishing, what to look for in a manager, etc. From the beginning, Doug was thinking of us as a real thing, a career, and we had to approach it in a business kind of way. He had the vision. I had the idea that what we had was commercial, that people would pay to see us." From Doug's perspective, the Riders needed to treat the fun they were having onstage like a business, because that was the only way that they could make a living doing what they loved to do.[30]

Sometime after they returned from that initial trip to Texas, Tumbleweed Tommy decided that he wanted more. After one of their Tuesday night gigs, he realized that would be his last performance with the band. He told Don Cusic that he drove around in an ice storm, going to each of the other Riders' homes to tell them that he was quitting. As much as he loved working with Ranger Doug, Woody, and Too Slim, he needed to make more money to support himself. After playing one weekend with a rock band, he was offered a job on a tour backed by their record label; he decided to take it. And while he realized that "the Riders were so good and so enthusiastic and there was such a great reaction from the crowds," he knew they "were going somewhere—but it wasn't where I wanted to go." Tommy had other things that he wanted to do with his life. After he left the Riders, he built an illustrious career as a journalist and music historian, specializing mostly in bluegrass-oriented studies, and although he had remained with the Riders even less than a year, he made crucial contributions to the band, as a musician, harmony singer, and as a writer of scripts.[31]

The Riders had worked out their initial show as a band of four, and for several months, David Symington told us, they seemed to him to be out of sync when they performed at Wind in the Willows, even though their growing audience may not have been aware of it. The Riders auditioned other lead guitar players, but none seemed to fit the bill. They finally realized that Woody's excellent fiddle playing added more than enough musical color to their performances. The three already contained all the humor, harmony, musicianship, and complete commitment to their adventurous enterprise that they needed to make Riders In The Sky succeed. All of them understood that working together as a team made that happen, that Doug, Slim, and Woody knew they had something unique in their approach to a traditional style. "The commitment to what we were doing overrode the difficulties," as Doug put it. Although they had begun as something akin to a revival band, the Riders had, in fact, created a complete and original show that spliced humor into the revered sounds of the past, while seamlessly integrating their own songs into the delectable mix. While still performing in and around Nashville more often than in other locations in 1979, the Riders also played at festivals and other venues in Kentucky, at a family reunion in North Carolina, and at gigs in Birmingham, in and around Houston, and as far away as the Heart of America Rodeo in Branson, Missouri, and Eastern New Mexico University in Portales.[32]

Before the Riders played their last gig at Wind in the Willows in early October, a couple of Tuesday night "regulars" approached Doug during a break. Dr. Michael Lichtenstein, who had done his internship and was then a resident at Vanderbilt University Hospital, and his fiancée, Mary Flanagan, who worked for a youth services agency, asked if the band would be interested in playing at their upcoming wedding reception. Ranger Doug agreed that they would play for $300, including the performance of the couple's favorite song, "Our Love Is Here to Stay," even though it was not in any way a part of the Riders' repertoire. Doug laughed when he recalled how hard it was to master the unfamiliar chord changes. On October 21, the marriage took place in the nondenominational chapel at Vanderbilt, with the reception held in the Hall of the Divinity School on campus. The newlyweds, their guests, and the band all had a wonderful time. It was the Riders' first wedding reception performance, but it would not be their last.[33]

Along with their gigs at Wind in the Willows, and afterward, they played intermittently at Old Time Pickin' Parlor, a few times at Exit/In, and several times at the Springwater Club and Lounge, which claimed to be the oldest continuous bar serving alcohol in Tennessee. It had supposedly hosted events for Al Capone and Jimmy Hoffa, but by the late 1970s, it was essentially a dive bar. Fred recalled that his signature rabbit dancing ("and the subsequent remarks about his living with rabbits and learning 'The Rabbit Way'") first debuted one night at the Springwater. The idea originated one evening as he and Peggy watched a local television show where the reporter interviewed a "hillbilly codger" who was doing a rabbit dance on his front porch. When Fred laughed at the performance, she told him, "I bet you can't do that." Spurred by the challenge, he immediately began creating his own version of the dance on their living room floor. Too Slim introduced the act in the midst of a Riders' routine they were performing at the time. While

Woody was playing "a fiddle tune at a reasonable tempo, Ranger Doug would tell him to play it faster. And faster. And finally, he—the Ranger—would draw the .45 pistol he wore and shoot blanks at Woody's feet and say, 'I said dance, Woody, dance!'" as "Woody shifted into high gear." While Doug was shooting at Woody's feet that fateful night at the Springwater—unanticipated by the two of them—Fred said, "When Woody picked up the tempo, I put down my bass and hollered into the mic, 'I was born to Rabbit Dance,' and went to it on that disgusting tiny stage. I'll never forget the look on Woodrow's face. A pure expression of 'What the hell are you doing?'" And a new Riders tradition was thus born.[34]

Even this early in their career, the Riders were already gaining national publicity. The late-night talk show host, Larry King, visited Nashville during Fan Fair and did a series of radio shows for the Mutual Broadcasting Network, speaking to guests in the country music industry. On June 9, 1979, the final night of the series, the Riders appeared. They were big fans of Larry King, Slim recalled, to whom they listened while "driving through the night on to our next show," but neither he nor Doug remembered how they got booked on his Nashville show. The Riders had performed on Fan Fair earlier, and they arrived around midnight at the Hyatt Regency downtown. "There was probably alcohol in play. We found Larry sitting at an 8-foot table in a corner of the lobby... just sitting by himself at a table with a couple mics on it and some cords leading to God knows where. The lobby was empty... Maybe an engineer. We'd never seen a picture of Larry and we couldn't believe it was really him until we heard that amazing radio voice."[35]

Larry undoubtedly had no idea what to expect when the three young Riders walked in with their instruments, but it's clear that he expected a straight interview. He was certainly flummoxed when they began supplying humorous responses to all his questions. When he asked where they're from "out west, Doug replied, "western Detroit," and Slim reported, "western Grand Rapids," while Woody declared that he was from the "plains" of Triune, south of Nashville. The Riders performed several songs, greatly impressing the host, and also interrupted with quite a few enthusiastic coyote whelps. At one point, Larry announced that he was going to give everyone Doug's phone number, for he felt certain that this most entertaining group could be booked in "western New York City," "western Queens," and other places in the Riders' favorite, "western time zone," telling his coast-to-coast audience that the band would also be available for "western

Bar Mitzvahs." Then he gave Doug's phone number. Even though he probably expected no responses, the Riders would have welcomed generating any gigs anywhere. Larry complimented the Riders on their talent, "savior faire," the "ambiance" they create, and their "laid back style," to which Woody Paul responded that the band has "a lot of time on the old XXX Ranch, down on their 200-acre spread on lower Broadway" where they can sit around the bunkhouse and develop their talents, and that he had no idea what Larry was talking about. The Riders were at their charming, funny, clever, spontaneous best, and when Larry caught on, he really got into their shtick. Slim "vividly" remembered Larry's comment at the end: "These guys are ready for Carson!" And Slim added that Larry "used our triple harmony coyote howls in his promos for years afterward."[36]

That fall, the Riders decided that it was time to do an album, but as Slim said to Don Cusic, "Nobody in Nashville would touch it." They thought about approaching Rounder Records, an independent label, founded in 1970 as a vehicle for the preservation of old-time music by three Harvard students—Ken Irwin, Marian Leighton Levy, and Bill Nowlin—all of whom were passionate about roots music and those contemporary musicians performing in that vein. Rounder, though, had quickly moved into bluegrass, and eventually gained stature with its recordings of people like JD Crowe and Alison Krauss. By the time Riders joined the label, it had already become famous for its recordings of traditional and bluegrass musicians. Slim said that Rounder seemed like a natural choice, since the label was known for "left-field music like we were doing."

Ken Irwin knew Doug from the bluegrass scene and as a country music historian, when Ken was doing record company research at the Country Music Hall of Fame. He said, "When we talked then, it was more country and bluegrass," and Doug wasn't yet into cowboy music, but when Ken learned that Doug had gone in that direction, he felt it wasn't "all that surprising, since Doug didn't really have a bluegrass voice." As a historian, Doug had written liner notes for Rounder albums, another inroad that he had with the label. Ken and his then-girlfriend, the remarkable singer Hazel Dickens, had come to Nashville, staying at their friend (and another Rounder artist) Anne Romaine's, who was out of town. They were planning to see the Riders play at one of the local clubs, but a snowstorm that night forced the show's cancellation. As Ken told us, "We weren't going to be around so long, and Doug suggested that they come over and play for us, so they came over and set up. They had the little campfire, the cactus... the major elements of what they'd be doing for years to come. They had the basics for their show already in place. They outnumbered us, and we were only six feet away from them, instead of the back of the room where I usually like to sit." As he'd said to Don Cusic,

> They played for us just like we were an audience. That was the very first time that had happened—a showcase just for me. I thought it was very, very cool. It was certainly different from anything we had seen before—it was a real show! Remember, I'd been used to hearing bluegrassers who just stood there and looked at their instruments while they played. It was quite a departure. We laughed a lot. I remember wondering where we'd set it. But my usual instinct was that, if I liked it, then others would, too. So, we agreed to do an album.[37]

According to Too Slim, "Ken Irwin said, 'That's your first album. Just do that,'" and Slim remembers "being tremendously excited, first to be doing an actual album, and also to be on Rounder, which was to me the coolest label around." Ken told us, "We hadn't defined Rounder very clearly back then.... We liked the real traditional, but we also liked people who were taking traditional music and giving it their own spin... I don't think we thought we were taking a risk when we signed the Riders. Having seen their show and having spent lots of time at record tables at festivals, we thought they'd generate sales." Which they did! Over forty-five years later, Ken looked back and made this assessment:

> Having three people as the original Riders was part of the success of their longevity. Rounder is similar in having three, and not four [cofounders]. The Riders were a perfect fit for us. We were all just out of being students and teachers and graduate students. We were always learning, and that's why we loved liner notes. Doug had a sense of humor. We had all gone through pretty much the same upbringing. We liked their music, where they were coming from, their approach, teaching without being didactic.[38]

The Riders approached their first recording date with a vocal and instrumental sound that, though always evolving, closely approximated that of the

Sons of the Pioneers. Their three-part vocal harmony usually consisted of a voice singing the melody of the song, with the other two men taking parts above and below. In the beginning, this usually meant Slim being the leader, and Doug singing a baritone part below, and Woody singing above with his tenor that sometimes ascended into a falsetto (depending on the key of the song). The Riders, however, sometimes altered this approach with each of the men occasionally singing the melody.

Over time, Doug was destined to be the primary vocal leader, with the others finding harmonies around him. With his mellifluous voice Ranger Doug often took the lead on songs like "Back in the Saddle Again" or "Cattle Call," and spiced them up with his acrobatic but melodious yodels. Doug had been yodeling long before the Riders came into existence. He became a student of yodeling and added his knowledge of Swiss and German practitioners to the sounds learned from American country recordings. He listened to all of the yodelers and found much to love in the music of people like Roy Rogers and Wilf Carter (Montana Slim). His chief inspiration, though, came from Elton Britt (James Britt Baker), whose records he first heard in 1968. A bluegrass friend named Lance Leroy told Doug about Britt's album, *Yodel Songs*, which contained such numbers as "Cannon Ball Yodel," "Maybe I'll Cry Over You," and "Chime Bells." Listening to the album, Doug later claimed, was a "eureka moment." Britt was an Arkansas-born musician who entered professional music in 1930 in California as a member of the Beverly Hillbillies but gained stardom in country music during the 1940s and 1950s. He became famous for recording one of the giant hits of World War II, "There's a Star-Spangled Banner Waving Somewhere," but is most valued historically for the dexterity and sky-high vocalization of his yodels. Doug thrilled to the duet performances of Britt and Rosalie Allen (another one of his favorites) on songs like "The Yodel Blues," and to the Britt classic, "Chime Bells." Doug succeeded in learning the subtle but supple intricacies of the Britt style, adding to them the full-bodied richness of his baritone voice, achieving probably the prettiest sound made by any yodeler in American music history. He told reporter Melissa Schorr that yodeling was "not to be undertaken casually," and that if tried at home, "you will lose friends and family. The trick is getting in a truck and rolling up the windows and driving around and practicing."[39]

Instrumentally, the Riders' sound was also an approximation of that featured by the Sons of the Pioneers—as heard in the jazzy fiddle and guitar playing of the Farr Brothers (Hugh and Karl). Although no one used the term during the heyday of the Pioneers, this sound was a facet of western swing, which itself was an expression of jazz. Pioneered in the 1930s and 1940s by such Texas musicians as Milton Brown and Bob Wills, western swing was a thoroughly urban-derived style of music played by rural entertainers—a body of music born in the cities and disseminated by such urban technological forms as radio and recordings. Until Joey Miskulin brought his accordion into the band, Woody Paul's fiddle was the all-encompassing instrumental lever of the Riders' sound. Woody grew up on country hoedowns, but he eagerly embraced all varieties of jazz and pop music and could move easily from an exuberant hoedown to a popular jazz tune like "After You've Gone" or a dreamy waltz like "Lonely Yukon Stars."

Ranger Doug's rhythm guitar playing created the groove for the band's music. Too Slim, a largely self-taught bass player, with a solid improvisational style, "reinforced the rhythmic pulse" that Doug established. By using the notes of his choosing "to color the melody and harmony lines," Slim asserted that he worked to "generate the energy which pushes OK music into really good, and occasionally great, music." Doug had been venturing into the performance of swing even when he was playing bluegrass with Bill Monroe and Jimmy Martin and brandishing his skills as an open-chord guitar player. By the time he organized the Riders in 1977, he had become a full-fledged swing musician, having embraced the closed chord style of Freddie Green, the master rhythm guitarist who played for the Count Basie band for over fifty years. Like his mentor, Doug felt that "less is more," and sought therefore not to compete with or overpower the other instruments, but instead provided them a groove that could be easily felt if not heard. Adopting and working in that style, Doug became revered as one of the greatest rhythm guitarists of all time.[40]

These, then, were the credentials that the Riders took with them into their earliest years of performance. When they made their initial recordings for Rounder in late 1979, they called the resulting LP, appropriately, *Three on the Trail*—the trail they're continuing to ride.

CHAPTER FOUR

THE COWBOY WAY

THE 1980S OPENED WITH THE RELEASE OF *THREE ON THE TRAIL*. During the crucial decade that followed, the Riders metaphorically kept their steeds climbing one peak after another in their ascent of the western mountains. As Bill Ivey had said, the band consciously built their audience through their animated and fresh live performances, without the support of any of Music City's powerhouse producers and publicists. The Riders did it in what they later would term, "The Cowboy Way," one crucial move at a time, focused on making the music they loved and committed to presenting it whenever, wherever, and to whomever as often as they could. According to Too Slim, "What made the band work was that someone always picked up the slack whenever anyone faltered. There was almost a sense of mission in what we were doing, that this music was important to do justice to. During the hard times that we had, the overall sense of what we were doing mattered. It was important that this music be furthered."[1]

As early as their first album, the Riders selected songs that demonstrated their grasp and beautiful delivery of western music and their unique approach to enlarging the tradition to which they were paying tribute. While proudly affirming their indebtedness to the Sons of the Pioneers and to the other singing cowboys who preceded them, the Riders wisely chose to use more of their original songs than those of earlier western artists. Seven of the twelve songs heard in this first album were written by Doug and Woody Paul. Fred also contributed a humorous adaptation of the traditional Mexican love song, "Cielito Lindo." Doug wrote the opening upbeat song, "Three on the Trail," which introduces a band of three cowboys who "vow to stick together," as, in four verses, they ride from break of dawn until nightfall. Before the last verse, Doug interjected the introduction that they used, in one form or another, for the rest of their career: "Well, mighty fine and a big western howdy from Riders In The Sky, brought to you live and direct from the bunkhouse of the old XXX Ranch, bringing you the best in western music for the next thirty minutes, so don't touch that dial." In their final verse, they close with their beautiful signature harmony yodeling. It was a perfect way to announce themselves to their purchasing listeners, giving them a bit of the flavor of seeing the Riders perform in a local club. The second cut, "Ghost Riders in the Sky," the song from which they took their name, was an apt choice, admirably performed by Too Slim. Humor reigns next with Ranger Doug's clever "That's How the Yodel Was Born," a tall tale origin story about a cowboy astride a bucking bronco. As the lyrics graphically spell out, when the bronco "jumped up . . . the cowboy came down/ They met at the old saddle horn . . . And that's how the yodel was born." One can see how it quickly became a favorite. Don Cusic claimed that if any one song defined the Riders, then "That's How the Yodel Was Born" garnered his nomination. Woody plays a jazzy introduction and sings the lead on another classic, Cole Porter and Bob Fletcher's 1930s pop song, "Don't Fence Me In," followed by Doug's mostly solo on his original, "Blue Montana Skies." The Riders continue with a pattern that has endured—intersperseing original compositions by Doug and Woody with silver screen—and earlier—classics. "The Cowboy Song" and "Blue Bonnet Lady," the two songs Woody wrote in Boston, are separated by "When Payday Rolls Around" and "Skyball Paint," both Sons of the Pioneers classics. As Slim told us, "I started with parodies very early. An early example was my take on 'Cielito Lindo.'" He substitutes some clever lines of his own in the Riders' spirited rendition:

> Ricky Ricardo, the late Guy Lombardo
> Cielito Lindo, Don Pardo
> Edie Gormé leased a condo

Cielito Lindo from Elvis Costello
(Spoken) She signed the paper singing...
Ai ai ai yi yi...

The Riders break the pattern with the final two originals: Doug's "Here Comes the Santa Fe," in the venerable tradition of fast-moving train songs. Woody wrote the closer, "So Long, Saddle Pals," something he intended the band to use in the way Roy Rogers had done with "Happy Trails." And Woody's song worked as well for the Riders, as "Happy Trails" had for Roy.[2]

Doug never had a chance to meet Bob Nolan but spoke to him by phone and corresponded with him. He was thrilled when his songwriting mentor agreed to write the liner notes for the forthcoming album. One can palpably sense the emotion in Doug's voice when he told Don Cusic, "That marked a big moment emotionally for me when those guys [the then-still living Sons of the Pioneers], who we almost worshipped for what they'd done, really adopted us and said, 'You guys are carrying it on'... It was a high point for me personally and for the group... another positive factor that kept us going in those early days." Slim recalled, "I was working at the library when Ranger Doug called me with the earthshaking news" about Bob's acceptance. "The Ranger read to me over the phone what our great hero had said about us, how he'd been waiting for many years to hear the next generation pick up on what he and the Pioneers had created, and how we were just going to get better at it, and I just about lost it. Talk about validation! Talk about the one guy who mattered getting spot on what we were doing! I told the Ranger 'Holy xxxx! This is it! This is the Opry! This is our future!' I think it's hard to overstate how much that meant to us, and how it kept us going through some of the tough times ahead."[3]

Ken Irwin had engaged Russ Miller as the producer of the album, although he was primarily producing for Elektra. Slim described him as "a genial, avuncular cat who had a history of working with out-of-mainstream artists and I think in many ways a good fit. We'd worked up the arrangements ourselves and most of them were tried and true in our live shows, and I think Russ was looking to augment our sound but not lose what made us special to begin with. He brought in Eddie Bayers to provide a bit of percussion... I believe, to keep the Ranger and me rhythmically in the pocket." Although Doug had expressed his concern about the drums, keeping the Riders "in the pocket" was a necessity. Initially, the band found difficulty in adjusting to the more exacting demands of the recording studio after the spontaneity of performing live. As Slim emphasized, they were accustomed to "playing off each other in the moment, and the idea of staying strictly in meter like a metronome was not our style." The band, instead, has "always gone where the emotion of the song takes us. Our musical conversation is organic in that way and just feels right." The Riders were not "session players, the type of musicians Nashville is flush with: somebody who can come in, hear a demo, play something appropriate and sometimes brilliant, sign the time card and go home or on to the next session." For the Riders, Too Slim continued, "singing parts in the studio and overdubbing vocals was a bit of a learning curve. We have a nice, fairly effortless blend when we're standing close together and hearing each other without headphones, but singing with an existing track, trying to perfectly match phrasing, feel, tone, and pitch is a whole other world. But we learned, and we did it."[4]

Relieved when the recording was complete, Doug said, "It was done, and it was us," and Slim added that the "album came out and did its job, exposing us to a huge new audience and announcing the arrival of wonderful western songwriters Ranger Doug and Woodrow." Gratifying to the Riders, the widespread reviews of *Three on the Trail* both welcomed and applauded the album. Linda Cain called it a "delight for folks of all ages and of all musical persuasions.... The Riders In The Sky manage to inject this classic [western] music with class and new verve.... Mentor Bob Nolan, who wrote the LP's touching liner notes shortly before his death, must have gone on to the happy hunting ground as a satisfied man, having discovered this trio of revivalists to keep the memory alive and kicking." Stephen F. Davis, who pronounced their live performances "DYNAMITE," felt that the album was "no let down," and cited Nolan's liner notes: "I was going to take each man separately and explore their individual talents and virtues—and they are all loaded with it but when you take that talent and combine it you do not have three individuals, you have a team of formidable potential. And what a joy to listen to!" Michael Bane claimed that the album exceeded being a tribute to the music of the silver screen. Instead, he found it "both contemporary *and* nostalgic, a tribute to the virtuosity of all three Riders.... They are authentic singing cowboys, as if, during Doug's tenure at the Country Music Foundation, he unearthed a secret cache of Sons of the Pioneers material.... Pretension is deadly to good music, and there's not a trace of it on this album. Instead, there's three guys doing something they love to do. Rather than just making records, the Riders In The Sky have given us a gift." Robert K. Oermann, already a fervent local Riders fan and supporter, advised, "buckaroos . . . it's a dandy. Go git it." Looking back on their many recordings, Slim offers a perspective on their overall experience:

> One thing I always think of when I hear our recorded music is that we're the only people on the planet who can make that sound. Everybody else can do those songs, use the same instrumentation and arrangements, and it's a completely different outcome. Somehow, it's our personal expression, and I think that's key to why we're still here forty-five years later. One comment we've heard countless times after shows is "how fresh" we sound, even on songs we've played thousands of times. It's that living in the moment flow that makes it "fresh."[5]

From the earliest days of their performances, the Riders established overall patterns that, despite continual refinement and innovation, endured. Although Ranger Doug has been the most prolific songwriter, Woody and Slim also contribute to the growing archive of their own material. While each of the other band members takes the lead on an individual number, Doug always has solos and yodels; Woody has always played at least one solo instrumental, including an old-time medley; Slim has always led the humor, either with a song (often solo) or with remarks that spark the responses of the others and/or the audience. The Riders' interplay with each other has always been warm and infectious, an invitation for the listeners to embrace the western fantasy they are embodying. Their songs evoke the romance of the region: the mountains and plains, the camaraderie, even the loneliness of a long night camped out with the cattle, but never despair. The Riders' West is definitely the place "where seldom is heard a discouraging word," the perfect wedding of music and humor working seamlessly to facilitate their audiences' escape into *that* West. As Doug has often pointed out, "People want to believe in the clean cowboy image, I think. . . . Why we're out there on the trail on our mission to bring Western Music to new people all the time . . . and isn't that what the good guys do?"[6]

The Riders typically entered the stage, lit the fake campfire, warmed their hands over its "flame" and drank a spot of coffee. Ranger Doug issued the familiar greeting to welcome the buckaroos and buckarettes and introduced the other two members of the trio, with occasionally improvised flourishes: "To my left, and your right, Too Slim, the man of a thousand hats. And to my right, and your left, the king of the cowboy fiddlers, Woody Paul." Then, Woody or Slim introduced Doug as "the idol of American youth, Ranger Doug." They generally launched into a classic cowboy song, often from the repertory of the Sons of the Pioneers, such as "When Payday Rolls Around."

By the time they made *Three on the Trail*, though, they had accumulated a hefty and growing supply of original songs and could open with one of them. Dressed in colorful cowboy regalia, which was greatly augmented after they became able to afford to be patrons of the famous West Coast costume designer, Manuel Cuevas, the Riders presented a picture of western stage-set flamboyance. Each member's outfit revealed an aspect of that musician's stage persona. From the earliest days, Ranger Doug dressed more conservatively and tastefully than the others, distinguishing himself as a dignified, soft-spoken rancher who strived mightily to keep his sidekicks in line. In early photos, he sported a bibbed cowboy shirt, often with a sheriff's badge pinned on the left breast side. Singing cowboy Ken Curtis had seen photos of the Riders and sent Doug two of the shirts he had worn in his early Columbia movies, and later with the Sons of the Pioneers. Ken told Doug, "You guys are soundin' better all the time, y'all put on a terrific show!" What a great thrill for the Ranger, knowing that one of his heroes was paying attention to the band! Woody Paul, often described as a "space cadet" because of his absent-mindedness and goofy antics, often played a clueless role, but his shirts were fringed across the chest and along the arms, the latter swinging and gracefully emphasizing his vigorous fiddle-playing. As the comedian, Too Slim's outfits remain the most outlandish: more decorative, more colorful, more over-the-top than those of the others—as were his wisecracks and pranks.[7]

Woody and Too Slim's improvised back-and-forth trading of quips sometimes dissolved Ranger Doug's composure. While their famous "Cattle Call/Circus Train" sketch of 1988 is the best example of the mayhem brought to the stage by Woody and Slim—and especially Slim—they had earlier frequently interrupted the beauty and/or solemnity of Doug's solos in live shows by Slim carrying on a nonsensical dialogue with Two Jaws, the talking horse skull, or playing a tune by slapping his face, or by Woody and Slim playing "Dueling Faces."

While Ranger Doug played the straight shooter most of the time, he also had opportunities to share his wry, understated humor through the introductions of his partners. All three elicited laughs from their audiences by frequently asserting that though some particular action "would be the easy way, it wouldn't be the Cowboy Way." That defining phrase had originated on April 4, 1980, during a show at the Side Track club in Tuscaloosa, Alabama. Too Slim paid tribute to country singer Red Sovine, who had just died, by saying that although Sovine was not a cowboy, he had done it "the cowboy way." Like any other spontaneous remark that one of the Riders made during a show, if it worked well once and drew a positive response from the audience, the line very likely became a feature incorporated into future performances. The Riders' Fan Club president, Jamie Amos, interviewed Ranger Doug in one of the club's newsletters and asked him the difference between Ranger Doug and Doug Green. Doug responded as follows:

> Well, Ranger Doug, like Gene, Roy, and Tex, goes to sleep in a bedroll on the prairie and wakes up with spotless, perfectly pressed clothes, shiny teeth, and a smooth shave. Doug Green, like all mortals, wakes up bleary-eyed, stubbly, and in dire need of a cup of coffee and a good toothbrushing. To amplify, on a grander scale, Ranger Doug lives "The Cowboy Way"; Doug Green, like the rest of us, aspires to it in his all too human way.[8]

As Carin Joy Condon, a Riders'-dubbed SSP (Super Saddle Pal) in Boise, Idaho, wrote, "There are many bands with excellent musicians. There are some bands with excellent musicians who occasionally say funny things. Then there's Riders In The Sky. From the very beginnings of their career, the Riders had mixed the solemn with the ridiculous, not in one segment of their performance, but throughout each show." These contrasting dynamics have indeed been the key to their popularity. "The Riders weave together musical talent and original humor in a constantly flowing mix of laughter and melody," Carin Joy continued. "Their comedy threads and ripples and bursts and zings throughout the show, as the energy flows and sparks among the . . . men on the stage and the characters they create."

The Riders sang traditional cowboy songs with deep and sincere reverence and followed them with an outlandish spoof of cowboy culture, or with a sketch that was totally irrelevant to anything else previously done on stage during that concert. Ranger Doug, for example, might exhibit his marvelous yodeling on a cowboy classic such as "How the Yodel Was Born" and then

Too Slim playing his face. Riders In The Sky Archives, courtesy New Frontier Management.

Children imitating Too Slim with face-playing. Riders In The Sky Archives, courtesy New Frontier Management.

see it followed by a fiddle instrumental executed by Woody Paul, with one of Too Slim's "varmint dances" breaking in and commanding still greater attention. By the time the Riders performed on their first *Austin City Limits* show in 1980, Too Slim had added an array of other varmint dances to his repertory, including the three-toed sloth dance, and especially for Texans, the armadillo. The armadillo dance featured the little varmint trying to cross a busy highway, warily looking from side to side as the traffic sped by, then, while crossing, Slim flipped over on his back with his legs and arms in the air, demonstrating that the creature had been hit by a passing vehicle that he hadn't spotted. *New York Times* journalist Peter Applebome wrote that the Riders "serve up a vision of the Old West that's as much *Blazing Saddles* as *High Noon*." The Riders had such a great time the first night at Herr Harry's that they wanted to continue to do so. As they say in Cajun Louisiana, "*Laissez les bons temps rouler!*"

Even after nearly half a century, the Riders prefer being on a stage performing for an audience than doing anything else, anywhere else. They simply love to entertain. Carin Joy claims that while the band is having a great time on stage, "the audience gets to go along with them for the hilarious ride." It doesn't matter whether they're doing many of their most-sung songs or cracking some of the same jokes and one-liners, "No two shows are ever the same... that sparking energy is so ephemeral, so much a part of that particular night and place, that you really have to be there, and then you can feel how your face hurts from laughing so much." Woody learned roping, in the style of Will Rogers, adding that to his fiddle-playing, while Ranger Doug yodels softly and strums his guitar and Too Slim narrates the different figures Woody creates with his lasso, such as the flat loop, the vertical loop, the butterfly, the reverse butterfly. As Woody's last rope trick in the sequence begins to fail, Slim announces, "the dead butterfly." When he tangles the rope or makes a mistake, Woody "assures the audience, 'These are real mistakes we're making here... We don't make fake mistakes.'"[9]

Too Slim's comments about a performance at Cat's Cradle in the mid-1980s summed up their delight-producing act of the evening succinctly: "Nice snapshot of how we were onstage in clubs. Loose comedically and tight musically. Some sprightly tempos! Highlights include rope tricks and commentary, Woody and the Ranger's Gene Autry/Tex Ritter impressions, Mercantile pitch of our four Rounder albums." Carin Joy quotes Too Slim as saying, "'I read once that a child laughs 400 times a day and an adult only fifteen times. Laughter is tremendous therapy . . . When people come to our show, they can double or triple their laugh total.' How do they do it? . . . It takes acting, timing, quick wits, and the ability to think on their booted feet . . . and as if all that weren't demanding enough, everything they come up with has to fit in with their theme of western music."[10]

The band has always had a good time together offstage, especially when they were on the road, as Doug wrote some forty-five years and almost 7,800 performances later, "on our endless trail drive." In February 1980, the Riders drove to Chicago to perform at the University of Chicago Folk Festival, their first appearance on a college campus. They traveled in the first of their thirteen "buses"—Ranger Doug's blue van, nicknamed the "Blue Hole of Death." Woody, who honed his technical skills at his father's side, did the first of his many Riders' road vehicle remodeling jobs by removing the front passenger seat and replacing it with a saddle. Whoever rode shotgun, sat in the saddle. Slim told Cusic that as they drove, Woody kept yelling, "'Now we're really Riders In The Sky!' . . . I mean, we were committed . . . We took the cactus and sat in the saddle for hundreds of miles. We were having so much fun!" In an interview with Robert Oermann, Slim vividly described some of the van's other salient features:

> You could tell it belonged to a shot putter because you couldn't roll up the windows unless you were like a huge strong person. Like Ranger Doug could roll up the windows. A normal man could not. And we took out the back seat because we wanted a bed. Ranger Doug had a couch that weighed about 800 pounds. It was made of cast iron all underneath, and we put that in and rode and sat in that in the back and then loaded the equipment around it. It was a short little couch. No air-conditioning.

Yes, the Riders were already amassing their Tales of the Road, amusing themselves in much the same way they amused audiences. In 1980, the Riders had plenty of time to have fun while traveling. After just over two years, the band was hitting the road in earnest. In 1979, they had clocked 102 performances in Tennessee, and thirty-seven in six other states; the following year, they played for 298 audiences, a third of which took place in fifteen different states. Along with regular gigs at several clubs in Nashville, especially J. Austin's and Springwater, the Riders also performed seven times on the

Grand Ole Opry between August and December, and they began getting frequent bookings from several clubs out of state, such as Cat's Cradle in Chapel Hill, North Carolina, and the Quarter Moon in Columbia, South Carolina. The biggest coup of the year, of course, was the national exposure gained from appearing on *Austin City Limits* on November 19—which practically coincided with the band's third anniversary. The program featured two separate shows by the Riders and Bill Monroe and the Blue Grass Boys, also a fortuitous coincidence for Doug, who pronounced it, "a big deal... the first time that put us over." From the time he had stepped onto Bill's bus in the spring of 1967 to be a Blue Grass Boy for a few weeks, he had dreamed of being a traveling musician. Thirteen years later, he had become Ranger Doug, lead singer of the western band he had created, along with his original sidekick, Too Slim.[11]

On June 16, the Riders played with the Houston Pops Symphony Orchestra at the Kennedy Center, a major feat for the young group. Their repertoire for the evening, paying homage to the music from the Lone Star State, featured songs such as "Big Ball's in Cow Town," a western swing classic, and two songs from the Ernest Tubb catalog, "Waltz across Texas" and "There's a Little Bit of Everything in Texas." Strangely enough, considering the association of both Texas and the Riders with cowboys, and that the program notes declared that the band specialized in cowboy songs from the silver screen era, not one of the selected songs mentioned cowboys.

This ephemeral artifact marks the event that brought the Riders into the national spotlight. Collection of Fred LaBour, used by permission.

While playing at the Kennedy Center with the Houston Pops certainly was the Riders' most prestigious association to date and one that prefigured more performances with symphonic orchestras some years later, it may have paled when compared to the band's appearance the following January at both a preinaugural ball and an inaugural ball when Ronald Reagan was sworn in as president. The inaugural event occurred near the end of a tour at Eastern venues—the Paradise Theater in Boston, the Bottom Line (along with Steve Goodman) and the Lone Star Cafe in New York City. The invitation to the preinaugural ball, cohosted by Riders' early fan and benefactor Davis Ford, on January 18, 1981, referred to the entertainment as "A Musical Tribute to California and the Great American West," much closer musically to the Riders' focus. Two evenings later, at the Smithsonian Air and Space Museum, the Riders performed with the Houston Pops Orchestra at the Texas inaugural ball. While the band played the same five songs they'd done with the orchestra at the Kennedy Center, Too Slim recalled that the acoustics at the museum were terrible and the crowd loud. He summed it up: "We did our part. I don't know that people even knew we were there. We stayed at a pretty nice hotel with room service. When Sinatra was singing, Ranger Doug and Woody were throwing food at the TV."[12]

Before they turned in for the night, however, Doug had one of his most treasured experiences. Those who entertained at one ball were free to attend others, and he chose to go to one where Count Basie's orchestra was playing. As he reported, "While politicos dressed to the nines munched hors d'oeuvres and sipped cocktails, and generally ignored the music, I got to watch the guy who became my guitar hero, Freddie Green, chunk rhythm with a great band. Unforgettable. I saw then he was not playing big complex chords, but instead driving that big machine with a pulse. Put me on a whole new journey." Although he and Slim were no fans of Reagan (Woody being apolitical), Doug admitted, "it was really exciting to be there [enjoying the glitz and glamour associated with the inaugural] . . . but to me it was no endorsement of Reagan but a celebration of the presidency itself and a great career boost for us. As it turned out, it was not really that much of a career boost, but it was an adventure in a glittery world I would never have seen had it not been for this amazing career." The Riders drew some jeers and catcalls from a few of their younger fans the following week when they played at Cat's Cradle. Doug announced to his hecklers that the band did not endorse the new president, that it was just "another show—and we had to take 'em where we got 'em and move on." Slim expressed a similar sentiment: "I said it was honoring the office and not the man." Slim and Doug were certainly not alone in their circumspect approach to politics. Liberal country musicians generally have had to balance or hide their deep political beliefs to maintain the support of an audience presumed to be preponderantly conservative.[13]

While the Riders experienced some difficulty with their reception at Cat's Cradle in late January, no such problem existed when they returned there just over a month later. In fact, they began a tour in Lexington, Virginia, at Washington and Lee University and North Carolina State University in Raleigh on February 27 and 28, then went on to Chapel Hill before the Riders reached Baltimore to perform at No Fish Today. No Fish Today was a popular venue in a rough part of town that attracted some of the biggest acts in blues and rock music, such as Stevie Ray Vaughan and the Fabulous Thunderbirds. It was not the kind of place where one expected to find a cowboy band extolling the open spaces of the West, nor was it the place where Too Slim LaBour might expect to encounter true love—a pearl in the oyster of Baltimore nightlife—the person who would change his life.[14]

Roberta "Bert" Samet came to the show that night, March 4, 1981, with a girlfriend, both dressed like cowgirls. Bert had learned about the Riders from a boyfriend who had heard and taped them on a bluegrass show on WAMU, the National Public Radio station in Washington, DC, and had seen them at the Cellar Door in Georgetown. The Riders arrived two hours late in Baltimore, hassled and hungry. Fred recalled that "Bert asked what she could do to help. She got the guys soup, and it took off from there. She loved the theatrical aspect of what we were doing, and she had such great theatrical and design sense. She started coming and visiting me on the road, and the relationship just took off from there." Evidently her take-charge thoughtfulness and spunk proved even more deliciously welcome than the warmth of that soup—the first course of what became a true partnership on every level.[15]

Bert was born February 9, 1958, and grew up in Baltimore. She was only four when her father, Harold, died from complications of diabetes at age forty, leaving her and her older sister, Sandy, and their stay-at-home mother, Inez, without enough financial resources to live on their own. Consequently, the three moved in with Inez's great-aunt and uncle, who were like grandparents to the girls. When Sandy (four years older) turned thirteen, mother and daughters got an apartment of their own because Inez was then working full time as a medical secretary, and Sandy was old enough to help with Bert. Although raised within a Jewish social context, Bert never received any formal religious education beyond the celebration of major Jewish holidays. Yet, Fred maintained, she "absorbed Jewish humor, sarcasm, compassion, and social justice to her core."[16]

Bert was always involved in some artistic enterprise, and that aspect of her personality grew sub rosa, despite the lack of money that governed most of the circumstances of her youth. Marrying at eighteen, predictably, turned out to be a big mistake, so Bert got a divorce, and became a licensed aesthetician. While working at a local makeup store, she met someone shopping for supplies for the Baltimore Opera and felt that such work might be interesting, so she volunteered to help with the production. Intrigued and engaged by the experience, she apprenticed and traveled with Charles Elsen's New York opera wig and hair team, where she learned "wigs, makeup, stage craft, road survival, and dealing with the occasional diva." Having "learned to paint faces, make wigs . . . she began training volunteers. *On Your Toes* was revived on Broadway and she did that show for two years, doing makeup and hair." Those experiences proved invaluable when Bert became involved with Too Slim and the Riders and began making Slim's shirts. When Slim got divorced in 1986, Bert moved to Nashville, and she started doing makeup and hair for the Tennessee Rep. If Slim had an idea for a prop, she helped him carry that project out. Then she moved in with Slim in about 1987, traveling on the road as an invaluable part of the band. According to Jamie Amos, founder of the Riders' fan club, "Bert held the Riders together, and she could do anything that the band needed." She and Too Slim were partners in every sense of the word, and knowing that the band was essential to the man she loved, she became indispensable to the Riders as well. And Too Slim told us, "Ranger Doug famously said, 'When I really need something done, I call Bert, because I know it will get done.'"[17]

One of the many outstanding assets that Bert, literally, brought to the table was designing new products for the Mercantile, communicating with the fans, and selling merchandise. Too Slim explained that as partners, from the beginning of their band, each Rider handled his own domain of responsibilities. At their early shows, Doug kept a book where fans wrote down their names and addresses, which became the band's first mailing list from which he annually mailed Christmas cards. And because Doug was "sort of the ace schmoozer," he handled interviews and promotional material. Woody retrofitted the interior of every road vehicle to accommodate the Riders' needs and then kept it running, necessarily being very creative in doing so as inexpensively as possible. Initially, he also maintained the books. Since Too Slim had been a natural entrepreneur even as a child, he handled all the merchandise, having taken the name "mercantile" from the TV sitcom of the 1950s, *Ozzie and Harriet*. He also took charge of the mail order aspects of the business. During the almost fifty years that the Riders have been on the road, the Mercantile has been well-stocked, and all items come with Too Slim's lifetime guarantee, "Everything unconditionally guaranteed for as long as I live. After that, you're on your own." The following souvenirs are included in the partial list he provided:

- albums in all formats through the years—vinyl, 8-tracks, cassettes, compact discs, DVDs
- lunch boxes
- t-shirts "in every color of the palette, every design known to man"
- hoodies
- sweatshirts
- tour jackets in denim and satin
- bandannas
- masks—thank you, COVID
- kids' cowboy hats
- kids' vintage guitars
- ball caps
- watches
- bumper stickers
- fly swatters, including instructions: "1. Locate fly. 2. Grip handle. 3. Swat"
- "Beanie" ponies
- refrigerator magnets
- "Every Day the Cowboy Way" calendars
- posters
- snow globes
- Christmas ornaments
- Woody Paul trick ropes; keychains
- lanyards

- badges
- bolo ties
- hat pins
- photos
- guitar picks
- washable tattoos
- stickers

Too Slim quickly learned that the point of all Mercantile sales was not about selling a t-shirt or an album; "the point is to make a fan. That was the point forty-five years ago, and it's the point today."[18]

Too Slim introduced the Mercantile at the very beginning of the Riders' career. When the band was playing at Wind in the Willows, "a good friend and huge fan," Carl Meier, approached him one night, asking, "'Have you ever thought about a t-shirt?' 'Um, I can't afford it,'" Slim responded. Carl offered to "bankroll a t-shirt," allowing Slim to reimburse him from the sales, then "keep any profit," since all Carl really wanted was the t-shirt.

The Riders displaying their assortment of merchandise for Too Slim's Mercantile, with the cac-ties designed by Roberta prominently featured. Riders In The Sky Archives, courtesy New Frontier Management.

After discussing the proposal with Ranger Doug, he "enlisted" a graphic designer from the Country Music Hall of Fame, who provided the first design: "three cowboys riding through the clouds." Carl had the t-shirts printed and was reimbursed when they sold well at Wind in the Willows. Thus, the Mercantile—and "another income stream"—was born. As Slim liked to say, t-shirts could be considered "a humane alternative to branding," and they remained a solid staple at the Mercantile. "We found a printable merchandise goddess named Teena Scoggins who had a business on Music Row," Too Slim continued. Like Carl Meier, Teena heard the Riders at a Nashville club, chatted with Too Slim after the gig, and told him that she "had all the contacts and capability to make whatever we could dream up and that it'd be fun and profitable. It sounded right to me, and in my memory, we shook hands. Teena was our principal supplier for the next forty years, until she retired."[19]

Teena and Bert got along famously, and as Bert slowly took over the Mercantile, she and Teena designed and created all manner of Riders gear. Teena described Bert as "a shining light. She was a gentle soul; she was creative, a wig maker, willing to try things . . . and inspired Slim to try things, too." Teena and Bert became very close friends. Teena loved the Riders' music, and their western themes, and Slim made merchandising easy. "I brought ideas as well as Slim bringing them to her, such as canteens that said, "Always Drink Upstream from the Herd." Baby bibs had ABCs with western themes, watches with the Riders logos, bandannas. Bert also had a hand in the Mercantile's "crown jewel—the Cac-Tie," which had its own origin story, dating all the way back to Windy Bill's cactus-shaped wooden bowtie, held in place by an elastic neck band. When he left the band, he bequeathed it to Too Slim, who wore it on stage. Bert had the idea of creating a similar fabric model with a Velcro neckband, then improved the original by extending it into a real necktie. The longer necktie received its signature name from John Hartford who saw Too Slim wearing it on a set of the Riders' *Tumbleweed Theater* and "ad libbed the immortal words: 'Too Slim is wearing a Cac-Tie.'" John graciously allowed Slim to keep that name, and the ties continue to be sold at the Mercantile. The Riders also initiated mail order early on under Slim's purview, passing out order forms at shows that Slim filled when returning from a tour. When "dealing with the Mercantile on the day-to-day level got to be too much for me," he added, "luckily for me and Riders, Bert was there to help every step of the way."[20]

The Riders were now spending over three-quarters of their performances outside of Nashville. *Austin City Limits* had provided them the national exposure needed to put an end to their leanest years, and they were playing in more states, on more college campuses, in a wider variety of venues than ever. Several other firsts came in 1981. They made their initial foray into California in May, playing in San Francisco and Los Angeles, the state in which they eventually racked up their most performances (with Texas as a close second), and on the same tour, they performed three dates at Caesar's in North Lake Tahoe (their first casino resort). In July, they played at the Winnipeg Folk Festival, their first stage appearance outside of the United States. While Woody felt that the financial compensation for folk festivals like this one wasn't sufficiently lucrative to justify their time, Doug disagreed, telling Don Cusic, "Things like that can get a buzz going.... There's a lot of communication between people in this circuit, and they communicate with each other." Slim agreed with Doug: "We were so new and different, and we were the hit of the festival. A lot of folks from Minneapolis came over—and that got us into the Minnesota State Fair and the Minneapolis market, which was really good for us." When they appeared at the Minnesota State Fair the following year, a Rochester, Minnesota, journalist quipped, "I dare you NOT to like this band... It's like Garrison Keillor all rolled into three. That's the best description that comes to mind of these three college-educated performers. Subtle, laid-back humor and polished three-part harmony that blends like smooth pipe tobacco make this group a must to see if you're at the state fair."[21]

In November 1981, they were back in California, this time in Santa Monica, playing at McCabe's, a music store, which had become a popular venue for roots-oriented performers, such as Jackson Browne and Linda Ronstadt. Mike Mahaney, a guitar player who worked as a janitor at McCabe's and hosted an American roots music program on KCRW, the NPR station in Santa Monica, had been playing cuts from *Three on the Trail* on his early Sunday morning show. He invited the Riders to come down to the station for an interview, but he was completely taken aback when they walked in with their instruments, dressed in their pre–Manuel Cuevas cowboy best, ready to play live. As Mike related, "The three stepped up to the mic, tore the roof off the studio, and the phone lines burned up that morning. They played and cut up. It was as if we all knew each other from another life. It was absolutely wonderful." That morning began a long and fruitful relationship between Mike and the band. They stayed with him and his wife the next time they landed in Los Angeles, and he noted that Roberta was there with Fred, already designing Riders merchandise and costumes. Mike commented that he found her a special woman. After he and his wife divorced, he often traveled on the road with the band when they were on the West Coast, working the Mercantile, serving as a driver, or acting as a general "gofer."[22]

The following January, the Riders returned to the Los Angeles area after playing in both San Jose and Coronado. They made their debut at the Palomino Club in North Hollywood, the best-known venue for country music in the entire LA area for nearly fifty years, from 1949 until 1995. Two brothers, Tommy and Billy Thomas, bought the club from country bandleader Hank Penny in 1952, and when asked to what they attributed their success, Tommy responded, "Real simple. We had all the acts that nobody wanted. No one wanted Marty Robbins, Barbara Mandrell, Kenny Rogers, Willie Nelson, Patsy Cline, Jim Reeves, and on and on. So, we had it made. For years and years, we had all these entertainers to ourselves. It was like a private goldmine." The Riders knew that they'd arrived![23]

Even more significant than their appearance in this hallowed venue may have been their meeting the fabled designer for country music greats, Manuel Cuevas, whose shop was down the street from the Palomino. Born Manuel Arturo Jose Cuevas Martinez Sr., in Coalcomán, Michoacan, Mexico, in 1933, he had learned his trade working as a designer for Nudie Cohn, the famous Ukrainian-born tailor whose gaudy, bespangled "nudie suits" had outfitted hundreds of rock and country stars since the 1950s. Fred told us that Viola Gray was Nudie's embroiderer and Manuel, his great tailor and artist. Manuel married one of Nudie's daughters, but when that didn't work out, he moved several blocks down the street and set up his own shop. Working in Los Angeles after 1975, and in Nashville after 1988, Manuel designed costumes for Elvis Presley, Johnny Cash, Gram Parsons, Dolly Parton, Dwight Yoakam, Marty Stuart, and other giants of country music. Manuel told us, "The Riders are not only my clients, they are great lovers of what country music is all about, and their performances are so terrific. I saw the show [at the Palomino] and was overtaken by the show. When I got to meet them personally, it was a great thing."[24]

Ranger Doug was probably the first to get custom pants and a custom shirt. Fred obtained his first Manuel shirt during his initial visit to Manuel's store, paying $75 for a shirt with no embroidery, "right off the rack." When Fred ordered his first custom shirt ($600 or $700), he didn't have the money at the time, and Manuel told him to pay when he could. Manuel said that he enjoyed dressing up the Riders like cowboys "in a way that was unique. It was fun to get on the cutting table and start giving them a look. They were so happy with what I was making for them." Because Roy Rogers was a childhood hero to both Manuel and Woody, Manuel wanted to make "a new Roy Rogers" for Woody. The PhD physicist wanted to have Maxwell's equations embroidered on one of his shirts. He told us, "James Clark Maxwell in the eighteenth century created equations to create simplified terms to explain electromagnetic fields.... Mathematical representation of the relationships between magnetic and electrical fields, how they relate to each other in a dynamic way. How to state that relationship in a simplified way. The shirt tips my hat to my interest in physics."[25]

Manuel was happy to oblige him, and explained, "The others are ranchers, and I wanted to give them each an individual look. They need to be my stars so that I can dress them as they should be. I am trying to make them all original." Slim relayed, "Ranger Doug wanted roses; I wanted something funny on each shirt. I would pick out a couple of colors, and he had all this fabric." Bert had already been making Fred's shirts, with embroidery and "sparkly stuff." But she knew that Manuel was "the real deal," and when she got there, his shop was "like a playground for her." Manuel was never cheap, and the prices for his costumes increased dramatically over the years. But luckily for the Riders, he loved them and their music and, in order to outfit them to meet their performing needs within their tight budgets, Manuel always told them, "Pay when you get some money." By 1983, Bert was also consulting with Manuel, choosing fabric and suggesting suitable designs. "She and Manuel made basic decisions," Fred said, "and then Manuel would do what he did. Once, Bert went to pick up this beautiful shirt, and Manuel gave us the bill, which was twice what they'd [typically] paid, and he said, 'Roberta, you know about Enron. That's why I have to charge you more.'" Of course, the colossal collapse of the Houston-based energy giant in 2001 had no effect on Manuel's rising prices. He did not acknowledge that the real reason was more likely the steeply rising prestige of his brand.[26]

Meeting Manuel early in 1982 was providential, since the Riders found that they were to be inducted as members of the Grand Ole Opry on June 19. Now they would be seen sporting their fancier, custom-made duds. They had played on the Opry over two dozen times when they were finally asked to join. While they had always been well-accepted by the Opry's staff and cast, and most significantly, the audience, Hal Durham, the Opry manager at the time, had reservations about offering the band membership because of Woody's reputation: erratic behavior and serious issues with alcohol. According to Don Cusic, Doug had to reassure Durham that Woody now had things under control: "The hard-drinking days were over by then. . . . It was something we'd all been worried about." Doug and Slim recognized Woody's strengths and were therefore willing to put up with his shortcomings—his lack of awareness of time constraints, his snuff-dipping, his drinking and mood swings, and they had worked with him to handle those issues. Doug used the Finnish term, *sisu*, loosely translated to mean that stubbornness to keep the band going through financially trying times, dealing with wives, ex-wives, children—and Woody.[27]

But Woody, like Slim and Doug, loved the Opry. When he was still a boy, he had gone there with the McGee brothers, and being a member meant a great deal to him, even though he was still about a year shy of what he described as "the talk." He told us, "When I used to drink and smoke pot, Doug and Slim had a good talk with me, and I got tired of being sick and tired. I just went to AA at the suggestion and advice of Bill Wiley, who was a good friend of the Sons of the Pioneers. Wiley suggested that I might want to go to AA to stop drinking and smoking." Even before that "talk," Woody well understood that on the Opry, he would have to bring his behavior under control. Woody remembers that he quit drinking on Doug's birthday in 1982, deciding that "walking out on the stage is so much fun; it's a high." Ranger Doug elaborated that it fell to Slim to keep Woody "in check," that is, to be on time for their engagements and to avoid nonconforming behavior. Slim also has taken the responsibility of reminding the other band members when to show up and what to wear since the Riders always perform in colors that differ from each other.[28]

The Riders had been on a ten-day tour immediately preceding their Opry induction. Beginning in Lawrence, Kansas, at Off the Wall Hall, they then performed the next three days at the Smokey Hill River Festival in Salinas before driving to Oklahoma City to play at a Shepler's western store. They went from there to the Dallas area where they appeared first at a Hyatt Hotel, then on June 18 at another Shepler's in Arlington. This brought them in touch with Jerry West and his wife, Diane, fans living in nearby Duncanville, who had become good friends. The Wests agreed to work the Mercantile that evening when the band played at Billy Bob's, a giant dance hall in Ft. Worth. While the Wests were happy to take on this responsibility, Jerry insists that they didn't sell a thing all night. After that performance, the Riders followed the Wests back to their home. They then asked Jerry to accompany them to San Angelo (about four hours to the southwest) where they were playing the next day at an outdoor arena on an old frontier calvary post, Fort Concho, now a national historic site. The Riders were cutting it close by scheduling a date in San Angelo on the same day as their induction into the Grand Ole Opry. If Jerry drove with them in the bus—by this time, one of the many recreational vehicles that served as the band's transportation—they could then fly back to Nashville immediately after their performance. Jerry would drive the bus back to his home, and one of the Riders would fly out to drive it back to Nashville after their Opry performance. Jerry agreed to help. Of course, it was very late when they left the Dallas area, and they encountered tornado-force winds that nearly blew them off the highway. They arrived in San Angelo exhausted and drove out to see where they would be playing, only to find that a tornado had destroyed the outdoor site—the stage had completely blown away. The Fort Concho Days staff assured them that the concert would take place inside an old large building with high wooden rafters where a makeshift stage had been set up.

Jerry was sitting behind the Mercantile table selling t-shirts while the Riders performed for what he estimated to be about two hundred people. The band had reached the point in the act where Ranger Doug would pull out his blank-filled .44 revolver and shoot at Woody's feet while he played and danced faster and faster. When Doug fired his gun, the vibration that it set off in the old building caused dirt, grit, grime, and bat guano to fall on top of them. The Riders spontaneously began singing "I'm Dreaming of a White Christmas" as the dust covered them. About that time, Jerry noticed three motorcycle policemen, presumably with the state highway patrol, who told him that they had arrived to escort the van to the airport. As soon as the Riders wrapped up their set, they followed the siren-wailing highway patrolmen to the airport. While the Riders enjoyed the escort, Jerry felt panicky driving through stoplights and stop signs in order to get them to the plane on time. The three packed into the small Cessna prop plane with only their instruments. Jerry had no idea where he was in relation to San Angelo itself or the highway back to the Dallas area, but he somehow found his way. A few days later, Woody, Liza, and one of their babies flew back for the bus. What an adventure—for Jerry as much as for the Riders!²⁹

Fortunately, providentially, the Riders made it back to Nashville in time to be inducted as members of the Opry. Doug recalled that as members of that historic institution, we were "really there, a real act, really prestigious. One reason they [Opry management] felt good about hiring us: we were entertaining, different, and we didn't compete with anyone else. Ernest Tubb loved what we did, and he introduced us as members. We did 'That's How the Yodel Was Born' and 'The Rabbit Dance.' What's not to love?" Robert K. Oermann, writing in the *Tennessean* later that year, called the Riders "the ideal Opry act" for revitalizing "one of country music's most appealing genres, western music. Thus, they look to the past which is so much a part of the Opry's appeal. The group is something fresh and new, too, so it is as modern as a jet-speed trip on an Opryland ride."³⁰

From the beginning, the Opry old timers appreciated the Riders, especially since their western act added another level of entertainment to the show's offerings. As they warmed up in their dressing room, Billy Walker, George Hamilton IV, Little Jimmie Dickens, and Jim Ed Brown, for example, would come in and sing with them. Fred and Doug understood that those welcoming them were "the very people on whose shoulders we were standing." All three of the Riders were thrilled to have been on the Opry "with all the old timers," such as Roy Acuff, Grandpa Jones, Charlie Collins, and Bashful Brother Oswald. "Connie Smith would come up to us again and again to tell us how much we added to the show." Over forty years after the thrill of being inducted as members, Doug said to Slim during one of our interviews, "When they [the Opry announcers] say, 'Here are the Riders . . . Stars of the Grand Ole Opry,' so much magic still happens. The Opry has waxed and waned, but now it's waxing. Bill Anderson said, 'We used to get country music fans, but now we got tourists.'" Virgil Dickinson, whose Wisconsin Opry began operating in Lake Delton in 1979, was backstage one night at the Grand Ole Opry when the Riders were performing during their first years as members. Although he hadn't yet met any Riders, Virgil found himself standing next to Too Slim—decked out in his chaps and cowboy regalia—in the men's restroom. Virgil asked if the Riders would consider playing at the Wisconsin Opry, and Slim responded with that famous Ray Benson line, "If you got the dough, we got the show." The Riders played in Lake Delton

The Riders standing with longtime Opry announcer and general manager Hal Durham and Ernest Tubb the night the band was inducted. Photograph by Les Leverett, image courtesy Grand Ole Opry Archives.

almost annually between 1990 and 2013, demonstrating that one of the perks of being on the Grand Ole Opry was increasing their appearances around the country.[31]

The following spring of 1983, the Riders achieved another welcome distinction when the original Country Music Hall of Fame, then located near Music Row, invited the Riders to join their Walkway of Stars in the glass atrium entrance on Demonbreun Street. Their fellow celebrants that year were the Bailes Brothers, R. C. Bannon, Alcyone Bate Beasley, Reba McEntire, Billy Jo Spears, B. J. Thomas, and Carson J. Robison. Fred told us that he recalled that induction "pretty clearly, mostly because of how emotional Woodrow was," explaining that "he had gotten into AA earlier that year and was cleaning up his act."

> We were asked to share a few words with the assembled, which I recall was a pretty big crowd, a lot of Music Row plus all the Hall

The Cowboy Way   117

folks and our families. Woody choked up and could hardly get through it, thanking the Ranger and ME for sticking with him and saying he wouldn't be where he was without us, and he was so grateful to call us his partners. Pretty moving, especially considering all the s*** we'd gone through with him.[32]

Between these two august occasions of becoming officially recognized by the Nashville country music community, the Riders' reputation and bookings were billowing beyond the Lower 48. As Doug assured us, from their earliest days, the Riders intended to be a touring band. Now they were achieving their dream. During the summer of 1982, they played at the Winnipeg Folk Festival again and were back there in December performing at the Playhouse Theater. They also performed in Alaska for the first time that summer, playing several nights in Anchorage at Mr. Whitekeys Fly By Night, where Too Slim added a new element to his varmint dances. The club was next to a lake, and Slim had strategically placed a big rubber fish in the water prior to the band's performance. At a designated moment during the show, giant curtains opened. In Slim's telling, Mr. Whitekeys "turned on the headlights of the car, and I jumped in the lake and when I got back on stage, it turned into a conga dance. It was like an indigenous people's celebration of the harvest." Who had the best time—shivering Slim or the audience? Very likely, it was a perfect balance. After their splendid time in Anchorage, they traveled on to the Alaska State Fair in Palmer. By the following summer, they had added Calgary, Vancouver, and Edmonton to their Canadian venues as well as returning for yet another Winnipeg Folk Festival.[33]

Not all festival performances, however, could be counted as positive. In fact, the enormous US Festival in 1983 certainly scored as the band's worst experience of their illustrious career. The Riders were scheduled to play on June 4, a Saturday afternoon at the tail end of the second (and final) US Festival, in what is now Glenn Ellen Regional Park near Devore, in San Bernardino County, California. No infrastructure existed at the site until Steve Wozniak, cofounder of Apple, conceived of the initial 1982 festival, where he had a huge amphitheater built. The 1983 Memorial Day weekend's lineup was thematically designated by day: New Wave on Saturday, May 28; Heavy Metal on Sunday; and Rock on Memorial Day. Sunday garnered the largest crowds, but perhaps as many as 750,000 people showed up that weekend, with traffic jams as noteworthy. The following Saturday, June 4, was devoted to Country, which had a smaller crowd, but was the largest outdoor concert the Riders had ever played at that point, with several of the biggest country stars to follow them: Emmylou Harris, Hank Williams Jr., Waylon Jennings, and Willie Nelson to close out the evening. Writing about it nearly forty years later, Peter Larsen described it as "a big opportunity that turned into a nightmare of the kind you can laugh about once you've survived it." The nightmare began when their flight from Houston to San Bernardino was canceled, and, as Doug told Larsen, when they realized the next flight was already full, "we ended up paying other passengers, offering them cash money to take a later flight, so we could make it out there." Although they were supposed to go on at one, by the time they reached San Bernardino, they were already so late that they had missed their time slot, and the festival promoters had a helicopter waiting to hustle them to the concert site. Mike Mahaney and his wife, waiting at the airport, rode on the helicopter with the band. In their wisdom, the promoters gave the Riders a new time slot, inexplicably between Waylon and Willie—at ten thirty that night—with about 50,000 people in attendance.[34]

Mike told us, "First Emmylou played, then Hank Jr. ignited the crowd and went a long time. Now it's getting late. Waylon stirs the crowd up, and now it's getting dark. It's now the Riders' turn: three guys on the stage with their acoustic instruments." Doug reported, "While our fans might have enjoyed us at one in the afternoon, the 3,000 or 4,000 Waylon and Willie drunk fans up front sure didn't enjoy it." And, as Mike said, the Riders' sound was "thinner" after all the larger electrified bands. Of course, "the sound was thinner." They opened with "Back in the Saddle," and by the third or fourth number, the beer cans and other "missiles" came flying toward the stage. "The crowd kept shouting, 'We want Willie.' It was one of the most hostile audiences. The Riders understood how badly positioned they were at that festival with a drunken, rowdy, volatile crowed. The other performers were very supportive. Manuel Cuevas was sitting with us [and] Tommy Thomas, owner of the Palomino. They all understood what had happened. Too Slim recalled, "When the beer cooler came across the footlights it was like, oh my god, it's probably time to wrap this thing up," admitting on stage that it was something like performing between "Elvis and Jesus." The promoters whisked them offstage to protect them, apologized profusely, and paid them well. The band understood why they hadn't gone over as they usually did with crowds, and it certainly made for a terrific story long after the shock of the evening had worn off.[35]

While the unruly audience shouted, "We want Willie," as they threw things at the Riders at the US Festival, the band's own fan base was rapidly growing, due in no small part to their visibility on *Tumbleweed Theater*, their show on the then-new Nashville Network (TNN). TNN was the first country-oriented TV channel, and it offered Opry and other country music stars a national showcase for their music. Appearing on their own ninety-minute weekly television show was a huge breakthrough for the Riders, and *Tumbleweed Theater* ran from 1983 to 1988, although it featured the band with fresh songs and skits during the first three seasons and reruns the fourth. The show presented public domain B-western films from the 1930s and 1940s, with Ranger Doug, Woody Paul, and Too Slim providing movie commentary, and songs and sketches in between portions of the films. How did they manage to get such a toothsome spot on TNN?

Woody's then-brother-in-law and close friend, Ned Ramage, worked in video and screen production and, with Randy Hale, formed Celebration Productions, making music videos. In 1982, they produced a show of the Riders' music, which they shared with their friend, Steve Arwood, who was also involved in video production. Although Steve didn't know the Riders before he saw the video, he was won over when he heard them sing "Back in the Saddle Again," and he pitched the pilot to Elmer Alley, the program director at TNN. While the show itself didn't impress Alley, he thought that the Riders would be perfect hosts for a proposed western movie segment, *Tumbleweed Theater*. Ned and Randy were involved in producing the three seasons (twenty-six shows per season) of *Tumbleweed Theater* in which the Riders were engaged. As Fred wrote, "Shooting wise, we cranked out a whole season in three weeks." The Riders had to change outfits three times during the taping to create the illusion that the show was shot weekly. Since Nashville lacked good video production studios, during the first year, the show was produced on Channel Four, which hosted Ralph Emery's morning show and the local news. For the second season the production moved to the stage of the Opry House, and by the third year, moved again to the TNN studios. The ninety-minute *Tumbleweed Theater* premiered on Saturday evening, March 12, 1983, during the first week of TNN's broadcasts, and each new episode appeared on Saturday evenings and was rebroadcast early the following morning.[36]

The Riders of course—mostly Slim and Doug—wanted to write the sketches that they had been presenting. Along with his role as a video producer, Steve Arwood was also a writer, who assumed the false persona of someone who had previously been an announcer on a Mexican border station. Not only did he become Tex Bix Bender, the announcer on *Tumbleweed Theater*, he took the lead with the Riders in crafting the skits. He said, "We got the movies with time code in, and we'd watch the movies, then come up with bits, and they'd write the scripts, and I would tweak them a bit." Too Slim was more specific about the process:

> We'd meet late mornings at the offices of Celebration Productions on Music Row, where Bix had his own office and there was a small conference/hospitality room. We'd screen the movie we were going to show—on 16 mm, all Public Domain, because TNN was too cheap to book anything better—and wisecrack our way through it, with Bix taking notes and whoever was there, mostly Bix and me and Ranger Doug, improvising. Ranger Doug invariably fell asleep after lunch. We'd turn the volume down a bit and let him rest. Bix and I would meet later and improvise some more until we had enough bits. We laughed a lot, sometimes actually rolling on the floor. He'd bang out a script at home, Bert would gather costumes and props, and we were ready to shoot.[37]

Besides playing themselves, the Riders also enjoyed creating other characters to people *Tumbleweed Theater*. Two Jaws existed prior to the show.

> Two Jaws was an early creation. We brought a horse skull along as a stage prop from the earliest days, and I believe it was one night at Cat's Cradle in Chapel Hill where I happened to pick up the skull, articulated the lower jaw, and started talking. Probably the earliest bit was his commentary on Woody's rope tricks. We did that bit on our first *Austin City Limits*, and it proved memorable to a lot of people. His persona, Fourth or Fifth Smartest Horse in the Movies in countless B westerns and failed stand-up comic after he died, developed over time. My puppetry work at the library no doubt influenced how I moved him, and his voice and demeanor owe a lot to my early influence, Froggie the Gremlin, especially the "ah ah aaahhh."[38]

Woody displays his roping prowess. Riders In The Sky Archives, courtesy New Frontier Management.

The other characters, like L. Philo "Larry" Mammoth (Slim), a fast-talking conman, were inspired by late-night television commercials, and Doug adapted his role of Sgt. Dudley of the Royal Canadian Mounties from *Rocky and Bullwinkle*. High Sheriff Drywall (Woody), Slim related, "came out of Woody's Stonewall Jackson/hillbilly/country star impression which he regaled us with on many a mile up and down the road." Ranger Doug dreamed up Slocum (Slim), as the "archetypal villain," taking his name from a line in an old western he liked to quote: "Slocum, get off of my land!" while "his henchman Charlie (Doug)," Slim said, "is a reference to the great B western heavy Charles King, who often glowered in the background as the nefarious plot unfolded." The Riders clearly enjoyed riffing on their childhood fantasies. The rest of the menagerie came to life as Bix and Too Slim wrote. Each episode followed a prescribed formula, opening with Woody and Ranger Doug riding their steeds toward the XXX Ranch bunkhouse, and Too Slim following in Doug's Studebaker pickup truck. One of the Riders then welcomed viewers and introduced the name of the episode's featured film. Next, the band performed two songs on the front porch of the bunkhouse. A "commercial" by Too Slim in the guise of Larry Mammoth followed. Typically, back in the bunkhouse, Ranger Doug as Sgt. Dudley or Too Slim as Side Meat the Sidekick gave a short history of the film or of the actors involved, followed immediately by the movie. During the ninety-minute program, the Riders sang and—mostly as the alter egos they had developed—interjected skits, including additional Mammoth-offered fake advertisements.[39]

Side Meat quickly emerged as the most enduring of all the characters. He came into being almost immediately, because as Too Slim stated simply, "We needed a cook." To create him, Slim started paying attention to, and doing research on, all the movie cowboy sidekicks, such as Gabby Hayes, Smiley Burnette, Pat Buttram, "and the rest of the sidekick pantheon." Inspired by these delightful comic characters, Slim wrote a song, "Sidekick Heaven," as a tribute to them. Gabby Hayes, though, was dearest to his heart. He had seen Gabby's TV show in the early 1950s, "brought to you by Puffed Wheat—it's shot from guns." Slim explained the inspiration:

> Early on I thought of him as Sidemeat, all one word, but Ranger Doug thought Meat was his last name, so Side Meat it was, and is. I got the name when I heard a story that one of Woody's rural

neighbors, concerned with the fast lane lifestyle Woody was living, opined that Woody's complexion looked like "a piece of side meat." I'd never heard of "side meat," but I loved those words together, and I was inspired by the *Rawhide* TV show sidekick, Wishbone. Thus, Side Meat was born. His voice is my homage to Gabby, Walter [Brennan], and all the rest of the stars in Sidekick Heaven. Mr. Meat is my favorite character I've ever done, because I don't have to think of what to say. He just says it effortlessly, and it's always right and always funny and if he can't think of anything, he can revert to "Myah whew," or a variety of old codger noises which never fail to amuse.

As always, resourceful and creative Bert "understood Side Meat completely," pulling together his costume and crafting his beard "one hair at a time." Slim said that they joked about his "gradually turning into Side Meat" as he aged, but that was all right with Bert, since she "loved the old coot." When their daughter Alice "was a little bitty girl, however, she hated Side Meat because 'when he comes out my Daddy disappears,'" which Slim regarded "as a compliment." Side Meat moved seamlessly from *Tumbleweed Theater* to *Riders Radio Theater*, and in the twenty-first century, regained his sidekick status on *Ranger Doug's Classic Cowboy Corral*, broadcast weekly on Sirius XM radio.[40]

After the first three seasons of *Tumbleweed Theater*, TNN informed the Riders that the station planned to do reruns for another season. After that, Slim wrote, "We got the axe when TNN went with another cowboy movie show featuring reminiscences of Gene Autry, Tex Ritter, and Roy Rogers." Less expensive production certainly motivated TNN, but that was not the only reason for letting the band go. In 1985, the Riders had hired David Skepner as their manager. TNN had changed directors of programming from Elmer Alley to Paul Corbin, and Corbin did not like Skepner, so the band was expendable. "Still," as Slim summed up the less-than-perfect experience, "the show ran four years, with the last year of reruns, and put us in front of a lot of people."[41]

After Don Cusic and Dan Beck's venture into managing the Riders not long after they'd organized, the band pursued various methods to enhance their bookings until the mid-1980s when they met David Skepner. For example, appearances at several Fair Buyers Conventions permitted them to showcase their act hoping to obtain bookings at county and state fairs. Then

Side Meat with his Fair Roberta, who designed the old codger's costume. Photograph by Sue Rosoff, used by permission.

in 1980 Bill Fegan (of Bill Fegan and Associates, in Dallas) heard them at the Arkansas State Fair, where they played September 26 through October 5, and approached the Riders about getting them gigs on college campuses, for $1,500 a night. Fegan was a veteran actor, producer, and booking agent who spent most of his active show business life in New Mexico. Based in Dallas in the 1980s, he promoted a wide assortment of actors and musicians, including Jimmy Driftwood, the Chinese Golden Dragon Acrobats, and opera singers. He had extensive contacts with the National Association for Campus Activities (NACA) and Community Concerts, Inc. Fegan arranged for the Riders to appear on a showcase in Texas for NACA, and, as Slim recalled, "We killed that night, and Fegan booked us all over the place." Gloria Gene Moore, who worked for Bill Fegan in Dallas at that time, said that she arranged for many of those bookings. Slim told us that these were "not big paydays, but plenty of 'em, and we played colleges all over the Midwest, Texas, up into the Dakotas. Those dates kept us on the road profitably for a couple years, and we filled in around them in clubs, theaters, birthday parties, yes, birthday parties." One night the Riders played a show at Sul Ross

The Cowboy Way 125

University in the West Texas community of Alpine. After the show, a fan asked the band if they weren't busy the following night, would they appear at a baby shower at his house in nearby Marfa. Slim added, "We said for $300 we'll be there." And they were—for all eighteen folks in attendance.[42]

During these same years, the Riders had also received some managerial assistance from the Record Bar, whose East Coast representative, Lou Viola, proved especially helpful. The record chain's Nashville store was part of a network of establishments located throughout the southeastern United States. Founded in Durham, North Carolina, in 1960, Record Bar grew to at least 180 stores. On August 20, 1980, the Riders played at the chain's convention in Hilton Head, South Carolina. But finding an active and high-powered manager was a difficult enterprise for a fledgling band of musicians who had not yet fully proven their commercial viability. Doug recalls negotiations with one manager, who had worked in that capacity with a popular country rock band and wanted 25 percent of *everything* that they did—songwriting, publishing, Opry dates, merchandise, and any outside work performed in any musical venture. This was an offer that they easily rejected.[43]

At one point in 1981, it seemed that the Riders might be able to obtain the managerial assistance of Bill McEuen, the Los Angeles promoter who had managed the Nitty Gritty Dirt Band and the superstar comedian Steve Martin. McEuen had seen them on *Austin City Limits* and flew the Riders to LA at his own expense. With visions of possible movie contracts and other glittering commercial emoluments whirling around in their heads, the Riders met with McEuen for dinner at his condo. The promising collaboration floundered, however, when Woody got drunk (this was before the "big talk") and created a "kind of debacle." McEuen immediately had second thoughts about the project, the next day informing them that he'd decided that he didn't want to manage anyone. He told them that they needed an agent and put the Riders in touch with the Agency for the Performing Arts (APA), a talent agency with offices in Los Angeles, Nashville, and other cities. APA told the Riders how very much they would do for them financially. Through the APA's Danny Robinson on the West Coast, the agency managed the Riders for a short period of time, including "high-profile gigs": one on Steve Martin's TV show, singing "That's How the Yodel Was Born," and another at the disastrous US Festival.[44]

Ned Ramage was the one who connected the Riders with David Skepner, first through his brother-in-law, Woody. David, as Ned said, "was a neighbor of a business associate and was in the market for another act. He had worked with Loretta Lynn and made her a household word." Well-known Nashville music journalist Stacy Harris wrote that David grew up in Los Angeles, grandson of a Jewish immigrant scrap dealer. He began his career with Decca Records and knew his way around the West Coast music industry before relocating to Nashville. Slim told us, "Skepner was a complicated cat. Some people loved him, some loathed him, some were bemused, and some couldn't stand to be in the same room. With all that said, he did an enormous amount of good for us, in terms of TV and legitimizing us in Nashville. He loved us, in his way." A special plus for Slim was Skepner's recognition of Bert's talents, immediately adding her "to the crew for every TV show, photo shoot, commercial taping, and radio show. I heard him once on the phone telling somebody that 'Slim's girlfriend will handle all of that.' And after a marvelous pause he said, 'I know, but she's not that kind of girlfriend. She's a pro, and she'll do a great job.'"

Doug averred and said that David was "very effective but had a horrible personality." Having managed Loretta Lynn, he had a lot of contacts. George Vecsey, an author, journalist, and friend of Skepner's, described him as Loretta Lynn's "gatekeeper—a big dude, probably 6-foot-3 with matching persona and a big iron on his hip, as the song goes. I don't believe he was ever in the service but he was a big military buff, who wore olive jackets and blue caps with Navy insignias and belonged to a pilots' association." Doug noted that Skepner "tried to intimidate with his size, but he believed in us and got us on some major labels: MCA and Columbia. He just happened to take advances on commissions, which the Riders' bookkeeper discovered. Loretta Lynn had warned us that he would do a lot of good for the group, but 'watch the money.'" Although they acknowledged that Skepner had worked hard on their behalf, and had won wide exposure for them, the Riders fired him in 1997 because of those fiscal improprieties.[45]

Skepner was pitching another artist to Buddy Lee Attractions, a prominent Nashville country and rock booking agency, when he mentioned that he had just signed Riders In The Sky. Coincidentally, Paul Lohr, a relatively new agent for Buddy Lee, was walking by the office and overheard the conversation, inspiring him to say, "I could book the living shit out of that band." As a journalism and art major at the University of Missouri, Paul had worked at the Record Bar in Columbia. When Buddy Lee signed the Riders, Paul became their agent, arguing that the band offered "more than music," that "Riders In The Sky is C and W: comedy and western. Riders chose a genre of music that most people love, but they don't know that they love it." He understood that performing arts centers would be the perfect—and most lucrative—venues, with "sit-down, attentive audiences." He began booking them in 1986 and never stopped. After the Riders fired David Skepner, Paul took over the band's management as well, and has been with them ever since.[46]

As significant as an agent and manager were to the band's career, the Riders did not lessen their efforts to build a fan base in other ways. Jamie Amos from San Angelo, Texas, was one such fan. She was a student at the University of Texas in Austin when she first heard the Riders in 1983 and began going to their performances when they appeared nearby, working at the Mercantile for some of their shows. It wasn't long before she began a Riders fan club while she was in Austin and got tips on how to manage the club from the Johnson Sisters (Loudilla, Kay, and Loretta) who ran the International Fan Club organization. The fan club gathered about six hundred members before the Riders hired David Skepner. At the urging of Ned Ramage, who became her husband, Jamie moved to Nashville in 1985 when the Riders were doing *Tumbleweed Theater*. She sent out the Riders' tour itineraries, ran the Riders' first booth at Fan Fair at the Tennessee Fair Grounds, and put out a quarterly newsletter, the *Riders' Roundup*, begun in 1984. The newsletter included short articles about the band, portraits of fans, and features on *Tumbleweed Theater*. In "Howdy Buckaroos & Buckarettes," her introduction to the second issue (October 1984), she welcomed new fan club members in England, Scotland, Ireland, and Canada and announced the Riders' first live album (*Riders In The Sky Live*, 1984) and "a children's album now in the works [*Saddle Pals*, 1985]." When the Riders produced *Saddle Pals*, Slim told Cusic that the band did not want to market to children "exclusively," but realized that the recording served as "another trail to go down." For this LP, Doug wrote "Down the Lullaby Trail," and the album was voted Children's Album of the Year by the National Association of Independent Record Distributors. Rounder had already produced *Prairie Serenade* (1982) and *Weeds & Water* (1983), which meant, at this point, that the Riders were creating new albums annually. In the *Riders' Roundup*, Jamie let fans know that the Riders' outreach to children went beyond their performances for family and youthful audiences. The band had "adopted" the Bellshire Elementary School as part of "Project Pencil," a Nashville program

Woody and son, Casey, performing together on a Nashville Network Christmas program. Courtesy Nashville Network.

encouraging city businesses and organizations to become actively involved in a local school to help with fundraising and other community-oriented programs. The Bellshire students, Jamie wrote, were indeed "thrilled" and had even changed their name to the "Bellshire Buckaroos" and their motto to "Let's do it 'The Cowboy Way.'" The Riders helped the students write a new school song and "were looking forward to an upcoming songwriting seminar to be conducted by Too Slim for all aspiring 3rd and 4th grade songwriters."[47]

Since 1980, the Riders had been doing benefits for Hospital Hospitality House, a place for out-of-town families to stay while visiting hospitalized family members, and then became involved with Project Pencil. Both community-oriented projects demonstrated the band's commitment to improving the quality of life in their hometown. When the Riders became a touring organization, they initially made a name for themselves in Tennessee and its neighboring states. But they soon conquered the West. Bob Nolan's warm and enthusiastic liner notes for their first Rounder LP provided the welcome evidence of the support that would come from their musical mentors in the western genre. Several years later, on June 13, 1989, when the Riders made their fifth appearance on *Hee Haw*—the incredibly popular

Performing with Roy Rogers on *Hee Haw*. Photograph by Don Putnam, used by permission.

country comedy series that first appeared on CBS—they were thrilled to be featured with Roy Rogers. In another appearance with him at the Opry, Doug and Fred enjoyed hearing Roy say, "It was just like singing with the Sons of the Pioneers," and they recalled, "He got twenty years younger before our eyes." Seconds before the camera rolled on the set of *Hee Haw*, Doug reported, Roy "turned to us and quietly said, 'I wonder what Gene is doing this afternoon.'" During these years, the band learned that such western veterans as Ken Curtis, Wesley and Marilyn Tuttle, Jimmy Wakely, Ray Whitley, and Gene Autry himself also expressed their satisfaction for the music that the Riders were playing. As a band that focused on revitalizing the western genre, Ranger Doug, Too Slim, and Woody Paul added their own original compositions to the repertory of traditional and made-for-the-movies songs and soon found that their biggest following lay in the western United States. With their enticing combination of three-part harmonies, exciting instrumentals, and outrageous humor, the Riders not only won over audiences at their performances, but their unlikely success inspired a renewed interest in western music, storytelling, humor, and an upswing in the formation of other western bands.[48]

CHAPTER FIVE

THE WINNING OF THE WEST

THE RIDERS PLAYED IN EVERY REGION OF THE CONTINENTAL United States, plus Alaska, where high schools tended to be the primary sites of performance. The West, fittingly, was the scene of most of their shows. At the end of the 1980s, and throughout the two decades that followed, they did not simply confirm their legitimacy as bona fide western entertainers, they were in the vanguard of a resurgence of cowboy music throughout the West. And by the early 1990s, the Riders were plying the range on the Pacific coast. Their fortunes lay in both the romantic mountain West and the mythical Hollywood West.

The acceptance of the Riders in the western community came, in part, through their association with Hal Cannon. A prolific author, songwriter, poet, student of the West, and the founding director of the Western Folklife Center, in Elko, Nevada, Hal achieved a national reputation as the producer of the NPR series *What's in a Song*. Between performing at the Utah State Fair in mid-September 1984 and gigs in Edmonton and Calgary on the twenty-ninth, the Riders met Hal, whom they called "a kindred spirit," in Sun Valley, Idaho, on September 26. Hal recalled that the Riders did a concert for him there, adding, "We turned the bowling alley experience into a

Celebrity Bowling Contest. We each played like we were celebrity country music stars, each of us with a different persona, although those personalities could change within that context. That took place while I was trying to organize the Cowboy Poetry Gathering." Hal believes that he and Doug hit it off immediately because they both loved performing, studying, chronicling, and collecting. They easily shared personal stories about their lives beyond music. In the mid-1980s, through Hal, the Utah Arts Council set up a tour combining the talents of his Deseret String Band and Riders In The Sky. Hal conceived the tour as a combination of the Deseret's working cowboy and the Riders' Hollywood cowboy songs. The success of that tour cemented their relationship.[1]

In 1985, Hal and several other folklorists and poets, under the auspices of the Western Folklife Center, created the Cowboy Poetry Gathering, which met in the Center's hometown. Cannon argued that he was continuing an old tradition that dated back to the beginning of the trail drives, when cowboys made up songs in the bunkhouses or as they did their chores. A few of them, like Curley Fletcher, D. J. O'Malley, and Nathan Howard Thorp, had achieved a degree of fame with their offerings printed or published, while many unnamed or forgotten writers contributed songs that chronicled life in the West. Songs were peddled at rodeos and other public gatherings or were occasionally printed in livestock journals or local newspapers. In this way, songs like "Strawberry Roan," "When the Work's All Done This Fall," and "Little Joe the Wrangler" entered public currency. Cannon, though, insists that cowboys had never stopped making poetry, and that he was determined to make this talent known while encouraging modern generations to try their hand at versifying. Even Larry Mahan, a bull- and bronco-riding rodeo champion of the mid-1960s and early 1970s, recorded a Warner country album in 1976, *King of the Rodeo*. Although he admitted in an interview that he "couldn't sing a lick," and that the album was a "flop," he had a great time regardless.[2]

The initial Cowboy Poetry Gathering featured only poets, but Hal invited the Riders to come the following year, and they remained mainstays in Elko, Nevada, for many years. Doug recalled that for their first appearance, "We went there by train from Reno, and it was really fun. Being there got us some national attention, but mostly, we were proud to be part of it, meeting and performing with folks like Waddie Mitchell, Baxter Black, and Sons of the San Joaquin." Fred insists that playing at Elko introduced them to a community they didn't know they were part of, and that poets like Baxter Black and Wallace D. "Wally" McRae—the creator and narrator of the popular poem, "Reincarnation"—were instrumental in making them feel comfortable in the western setting. Fred, in fact, was inspired to increase his own array of poems. Doug noted that "the Cowboy Poetry Gathering grew very quickly. Most of the acts don't try humor, and those that do, shouldn't," which made the Riders a standout from the beginning. The Gathering became a week-long celebration of cowboy poetry, art, and music, which has continued to grow and thrive. The first Gathering in 1985 had attracted about 1,000 people; by 1990 it had "maxed out," with all the local hotel rooms filled, infusing about $2.9 million into the Elko economy. For its tenth annual meeting in 1994, the Gathering welcomed over 9,000 fans. Five or six stages presented programs simultaneously, while jam sessions went on constantly. Guest stars included Gary McMahan, Ian Tyson, Don Edwards, and the Riders. But the most significant Riders' trip to the annual Gathering, especially for Too Slim, occurred in early 1991.

With many of their friends around them, Too Slim married his "fair Roberta" on January 30 at Brenda's Wedding Chapel. Near Elko's Stockman Hotel, the chapel advertised weddings for $129, with a video, $139. Baxter Black read a poem, and Joey Miskulin played the theme from 20th Century Fox as a wedding march. The wedding was attended by about 150 guests, people whom they knew through their involvement in the western music industry. After the ceremony, Slim and Bert went to a lunch counter in the Red Lion Casino and ordered the Challenger Burger for their "wedding feast." They had decided to marry when they were ready to start a family, and soon after the wedding, Bert and Too Slim announced that a new baby was on the way. As Slim said, "The two smartest decisions I've made in my life were 1. Marrying Roberta, and 2. Partnering with Ranger Doug."[3]

The West had always had its local assortment of cowboy singers, such as those who performed for tourists at barbecues, rodeos, and other celebrations. Cy Scarborough, for example, had become locally famous as a comedian, storyteller, and ballad singer since June 2, 1969, when he cofounded the Bar D Chuckwagon in Durango, Colorado. Scarborough said that he modeled the Bar D Suppers, which were popular tourist attractions, on the traditional chuckwagons that followed the herds and provided food for the hungry cowboys.[4]

A few singers had sought professional careers as cowboy entertainers before the Riders came along. Gary McMahan and Chris LeDoux, for example, had tried to gain a foothold with such music in Nashville in the early 1970s, but had won little success in Music City. LeDoux, born in Mississippi, but a longtime resident of Wyoming, had been a champion rodeo rider before he turned toward the performance of western-style ballads. He built a large repertoire of all kinds of country and cowboy songs. His up-tempo numbers, such as "Hooked on an Eight Second Ride," with their rock and roll flavor, strongly influenced the style of superstar Garth Brooks. Unfortunately, LeDoux only lived to be fifty-six, when he succumbed to a rare form of cancer in 2005.[5]

McMahan was a Greeley, Colorado, cowboy who had been singing cowboy songs most of his life. After serving in the navy, he went to Nashville in 1971 to become a cowboy songwriter. While there, he met Doug, and got to know Ian Tyson. Both Gary and Ian soon realized, however, that being in Nashville was a "death knell" since no one was interested in "buying cowboy music." Ian returned to Canada where he succeeded initially as a country singer, but Gary did not really attain prominence until he became associated with the Cowboy Poetry Gathering and Western Music Association. As he told us, he went to the first Gathering and found that Chris LeDoux was singing his songs. Gary felt that he had "*no* career before he found his audience at the Gathering." There, Baxter Black enlisted his aid at various nonmusical gigs, which all paid "ten times better than music did," and Baxter was as good as his word, booking Gary when Baxter was unable to perform. Gary quickly discovered that the Gathering had folks rediscovering cowboy music as well as poetry and knew he had found his niche, becoming highly respected for his songwriting and yodeling. His "The Old Double Diamond" is considered one of the greatest modern cowboy songs. Although the real heyday of this Western Renaissance came during the last fifteen years of the twentieth century, Gary maintains that "it's still going on. The Riders inspired a lot of bands. It gave audiences [who enjoyed acoustic music] something besides bluegrass."[6]

Some of the most active members of the cowboy fraternity, like Ian Tyson and Michael Martin Murphey, came to the western idiom after lengthy careers in other forms of music. A native of Alberta, Canada, Tyson had won recognition during the folk revival as part of the team of Ian and Sylvia (Sylvia Fricker, his then-wife), and then as a country singer, before he converted to the full-time performance of cowboy music. With stellar compositions like "Four Strong Winds," "Someday Soon," and "Summer Wages,"

Tyson could lay claim to being one of western music's greatest songwriters. The unquestioned superstar of western music, Michael Martin Murphey, after a lengthy career as a country rock and country pop singer, committed himself to the exclusive performance of cowboy music in the late 1980s. In 1987 he established WestFest, a festival designed to celebrate the culture of the American West, and his 1991 album, *Cowboy Songs*, went "gold" and has been only one of his many recordings to document the music of the cowboy and the West. The record label Warner Western became the home of Murphey and other cowboy singers and poets such as Don Edwards, the Sons of the San Joaquin, Red Steagall, Waddie Mitchell, and, of course, Doug Green. Superstar Emmylou Harris even made an album of cowboy songs for the label in 1994.[7]

The resurgence of western music *in* the West owes a great debt to the indefatigable work and ambition of Bill Wiley. Doug said that he was "one of the great characters in our career." Bill had been an ardent friend and champion of the Sons of the Pioneers, and during his more prosperous days had outfitted them with uniforms. He also became a great fan of the Riders, seeing them as the successors of the Pioneers. Bill was a flamboyant personality who invested in property in downtown Colorado Springs, on the site of a played-out gold processing plant, in the vain hopes that the remnants of gold there would bring him great wealth if the price of gold ever went up. Fred remembers that gold was trading at about $400 an ounce at the time, but it needed to rise to $800 for Wiley "to reopen the tailings pile in Colorado Springs and regain his former wealth and status." Doug affirmed that Bill was always "struggling to stay afloat waiting for his property to become valuable." He tried to live the good life, though, driving an old red Mercedes automobile—evidence of his past glory. When Fred borrowed the car to pick Bert up at the Denver airport, she described it as a "pimp mobile." Bill may have been eccentric, but he was also an enthusiastic champion of western music. In August 1988, largely through his efforts, a group of western performers and fans met in Las Vegas, Nevada, to organize an association and present a festival. This led to the incorporation in 1989 of the Western Music Association (WMA) as an Arizona nonprofit corporation. After his death, the WMA established its most prestigious prize, the Bill Wiley Award, honoring his memory. The WMA met annually, expanded to twelve states with regional chapters, becoming in 2018, the International Western Music Association (IWMA). The slogan on the organization's website declares that "The WMA represents what is good and wholesome in our society." Since its inception the WMA has presented many awards for western singing and yodeling. The Riders have enjoyed the concerts given by the professional entertainers but were also thrilled to take part in the jam sessions that occurred in hotel rooms and other available spaces, and they were named Entertainer of the Year by the International Western Music Association successively from 2001 through 2005, then again in 2007 and 2010. In 1993, the Riders were named to the WMA Hall of Fame; Joey Miskulin received the Instrumentalist of the Year award in 2002 and 2006 and was named to the Hall of Fame in 2014; and on November 22, 2022, at the annual meeting in Albuquerque, Ranger Doug was happily surprised that he was elected to the Hall of Fame. He joined Roy Rogers as the only other singer with two listings: Rogers had been honored singly, and as a member of the Sons of the Pioneers. Joey also had two listings, one with Riders In The Sky, and as a producer.[8]

Ranger Doug made his own individual contribution to the singing cowboy tradition in 1997 when he recorded an album called *Songs of the Sage*. Produced by Joey Miskulin, and released on the Warner Western label, the recording was Doug's first solo enterprise since 1972, when he recorded a couple of albums in the gospel and bluegrass vein. Doug recalled that the album "came out of the blue" when the Warner Western folks came to him with an offer to record. The Riders were under contract to Rounder at the time, but he said that "they graciously allowed me to do it, with the stipulation that we could not use the Riders In The Sky name or distinctive sound." *Songs of the Sage* revealed a thoroughly romantic Ranger Doug—exhibiting a lovely lyrical majesty and fluidity of phrase somewhat similar to that of late nineteenth-century songwriter William "Shakespeare" Hays. Except for the sad ballad "Jesse," written with Madeline Stone, about an old and broken cowboy, the rest of the compositions are all his own paeans to the West. Doug remains "really proud of the album," especially "Hurry Sunrise," "Amber Eyes," and "Singing in the Saddle." His daughter, Sally, sings harmony with him on "Riding on the Rio," and his sonorous voice and silken yodeling are at their performance best on every cut. The album garnered universal praise, and for us, Doug's "Night Riding Song," complete with melodic yodeling, is one of the most beautifully haunting of the modern cowboy songs.[9]

While examples of earlier performers can be found, it nevertheless seems certain that the real awakening of western music came in the midst of the Riders' popularity and high visibility. Karen Gogolick and Rick Roltgen, a husband and wife singing team from Wisconsin, were among the many performers who found their way into western music through the influence of the Riders. They were part-time folk singers, dabbling with many genres, before they heard the Riders. Rick's day job was directing credit for the State Employers' Credit Union, and Karen created jewelry at her store, Middle Earth Goldsmiths, and also hosted a folk music show on the Madison community radio station, WORT. In the 1980s, she and Rick stumbled on the first album of Riders In The Sky while in the station's library. Impressed with what she heard, she then began listening to the Sons of the Pioneers and soon became a convert to all things western. Seeing the Riders on their *Austin City Limits* debut was "like a light bulb's going off." She and Rick became KG & The Ranger, performing their first official show in 1989, and by 2000 had decided to go full time. Rick learned rope tricks after asking Woody what kind of rope he was using. While Karen patterned her yodeling after that of Patsy Montana, the harmony yodeling that she and Rick developed came directly from the Riders. KG & The Ranger have since become active participants in the western arena, with over 100 concerts a year and winners of three awards in the WMA's harmony yodeling category. Ranger Doug wrote a glowing review of his disciples, printed on their website: "KG and The Ranger are among the best-known proponents of the western style, and it's easy to hear why: they sing with charm and style; they yodel spectacularly; choose great material with unerring taste and write fine new songs as well. Their growing and continuing success is well deserved."[10]

Looking back, the Riders could not help but marvel at the distance, literally, they had traveled since that first appearance at Herr Harry's. Too Slim had been absolutely right when he predicted that people would pay for what they did. By 1907, they had taken their music around the world and had presented it to a wealth of roots-conscious fans through their appearances on television shows like *Austin City Limits*, *Hee Haw*, and their stint on *Tumbleweed Theater*. Their success can be attributed to many factors, not the least of which was their incessant hard work, measured in miles traveled, vans driven to death, and venues played. They loved the road and were ready to play *anywhere* at a minute's notice: at elementary schools, chuckwagons, rodeos, colleges, county and state fairs, folk festivals and clubs, the Cowboy Poetry Gathering, casinos, dive bars, symphonies, and the Grand Ole Opry.

Yes, hard work played an immense role in their success, but one must not forget that they were also splendid musicians and quick-witted humorists.

Although Ranger Doug, Too Slim, and Woody Paul had demonstrated repeatedly that three musically talented cowpokes were enough to captivate an audience, they nevertheless longed for greater instrumental diversity and an opportunity to relieve some of the pressure on Woody, their only soloist. In 1988 they found the man who eventually became the fourth Rider, the wondrously talented Joey Miskulin, who soon adopted the moniker of the CowPolka King. With his super-charged accordion prowess, phenomenal musical acumen, storehouse of songs, and the joy of trading solos with Woody, Joey began a tenure with the band that has lasted another thirty-five-plus years.

Joseph Michael "Joey" Miskulin was born in Chicago on January 6, 1949, the son of a Croatian American father, Joseph John Miskulin, and a Slovenian American mother, Mary Ann Baskovic Miskulin. After his parents' divorce when he was still a young boy, Joey and his mother lived with her parents, Frank and Mary Baskovic, in the suburb of Oak Lawn, now known as Hickory Hills. His Slovenian-born grandfather and he were "very, very close," and his grandfather's brother was an accordion player. The Croatian side of his family played string instruments. Joey never doubted that he would make music his whole life, so, as he told us, "I kept my ears open." Joey's first accordion, though, had been the twelve-bass instrument brought back from Italy by his father after his service in World War II. Joey recalled that when he was about four and a half years old, he had picked up the accordion while staying with his father and had begun "picking out the rudiments of some very simple songs." His father, impressed with Joey's display of musical precociousness, asked if he'd like music lessons, which he began at five. His early training led to the joke around his grandparents' home, that he could read music before he could read English. In retrospect, Joey believes that his taking up the accordion provided a bridge that linked him to both his dad and the musical heritage of his beloved grandfather.[11]

By the time he was twelve years old, Joey was playing professionally in Chicago polka bands, first for Ronnie Lee and then for Roman Possedi, "Mr. Chicago in Cleveland-style polka music," for whom he made his first recording at the age of thirteen. Joey's real ascent to fame came when he was hired, still at age thirteen, by Cleveland's own Frank Yankovic to be part of his touring band. Yankovic, another musician of Slovenian ancestry, was

Joey already determining his prodigious musical future. Collection of Joey Miskulin, used by permission.

the most famous polka band leader in America, and the person who, arguably, had made "Just Because" the "national anthem" of polka music. Joey made $35 a day in 1962 playing for Yankovic, more than his parents earned together. His schedule had become so intense that he later claimed to have missed 234 days of high school. Playing with older and more experienced musicians pushed Joey to begin his own self-tutoring program, telling Don Cusic, "When I was on the bus, I disciplined myself to study music theory and counterpoint.... Once I started getting in the groove it started making sense, and I could apply everything." A motivated lifetime learner, his musicality immediately began expanding. Except for a Far Eastern tour made with the Hawaii International Review when he was nineteen, Joey remained with Yankovic for thirty-six years, a period of intense on-the-job education as a "road scholar" that saw him become not only a musician of great fame but also a producer of four Grammy-nominated albums, including a

Joey and Frank Yankovic. Photograph by John Kausek Studio, Cleveland, Ohio, courtesy Collection of Joey Miskulin.

winner in 1986 with Frank Yankovic's *Seventy Years of Hits*, the first Grammy awarded to a Polka record.[12]

Joey married his first wife, Joanne, in 1970 but, quite understandably, she did not want him to continue to be a touring musician. "I tried for a very short time to lead a normal life.... It was ridiculous. So, it was the wife's ultimatum—music or me—so what can I say?" He chose to return to being a full-time musician, leaving Joanne to raise their son. When he was eighteen in 1967, the already road-weary musician had relocated to Cleveland, the center of Slovenian-style polka music in the United States. There he began working in clubs and, by 1978, Joey had become the owner of Miskulin's Lounge, which he ran with his second wife, Patti. Patti Hlebak Miskulin, a Cleveland native, considers herself a very independent woman, and she had her own career as a respiratory therapist at that time. After working second shift, she'd head straight for the club, where she'd bartend and help with whatever needed doing, and she and Joey would head home together after 2:00 a.m. when the club closed. At the Lounge, he did everything from

The Winning of the West 141

entertaining to bartending and keeping the books while also hosting a popular local television show called *Polka Time USA*. As a musical polymath and a student of all kinds of music, he admired accordion players like Art Van Damme and Dick Contino but said, "Very early on, I stopped listening to accordion players, and started listening to clarinet players," such as Benny Goodman and Artie Shaw, musicians from whom he learned phrasing and articulation. By the time he moved to Nashville, he had already played on over 150 albums.[13]

Cowboy Jack Clement lured Joey to Music City in 1986, after he had flown Joey back and forth for sessions as both a musician and producer. As Joey told Peter Cooper, "Clement was ... well, what wasn't he? ... a songwriter, a producer, a publisher, a filmmaker, a raconteur, a tipsy philosopher and, mostly and always a ringleader. ... He knew most everybody, worked with most everybody, laughed with most everybody." Flying frequently between Cleveland and Nashville, Joey and his wife Patti decided that a move to the country music capital would be more feasible for his work. Patti agreed to remain in Cleveland while Joey moved into a house in Nashville on the street immediately behind Jack Clement's studio. Clement liked to brag, "I've got my personal accordion player living in my back yard. Greatest in the world. Take him with me wherever I go." When Patti and Joey were living there, their three children had the run of both yards, were climbing the trees, and Cowboy Jack called them the "yardvarks."[14]

In the meantime, a mutual friend of Joey and the Riders, Jay Broderson, had begun sending tapes of their music to each other. Joey was already fond of cowboy music, having been a childhood fan of Chicago's kiddie TV cowboy favorite, Bob Atcher, whose *Meadow Gold Ranch* show was scheduled opposite Joey's other hero, Frank Yankovic. Joey remembers toggling back and forth between the two stations during commercials so that he could catch some of each program. One night after moving to Nashville, Joey responded to a request made by his friend Vic Willis, former accordion player for the Willis Brothers, that he and Cowboy Jack play at a Make-a-Wish benefit for the city's children with critical medical conditions. There he met Too Slim who had come to the affair to play with Dickey Lee. Their extended conversation may have provoked the telephone call that Joey received sometime thereafter from Woody Paul, asking him to play on March 7, 1988, when the band began recording their forthcoming MCA album, *Riders Radio Theater*. After his album appearance, Joey began playing regularly on tapings for the

Riders' National Public Radio show, which also got underway in 1988. Joey was not yet a fourth Rider—that would not come until 1993—but he had begun a fruitful and loving relationship that has proved enduring.[15]

Riders Radio Theater, the Riders' eleventh album and their second for MCA, was more than a collection of songs. It was also a compendium of the onstage humor that the group had been presenting since their days at Wind in the Willows. The album and the radio shows that followed were vehicles through which they became almost a household word in American popular culture, offering an indispensable means of widespread exposure. The phrase itself, along with an early script, "The Cowboy Who Hated Christmas," came from Tumbleweed Tommy Goldsmith, and was introduced in 1979 by the Riders at Wind in the Willows. The Riders mixed in short scripts at the club, and elsewhere for a few months, but soon abandoned the practice for their live shows because it hampered their efforts to achieve a spontaneous and freewheeling form of entertainment.

The LP harkened back to those early stage shows, containing many of the elements, including a short skit and some fake commercials. Who could resist a Sagebrush Sports Report that said, "Folks, the deer and the antelope play later today, and we'll have all the scores?" The album also included their classic performance of "Cattle Call," the version where Ranger Doug's beautiful rendition of the song is "destroyed" by the "animal calls" and ad libs of Too Slim and Woody. It is probably the funniest skit they ever performed on stage. The Riders had been doing "Cattle Call"—written in 1934 by cowboy singer Tex Owens—since at least 1981, when they performed it on *Austin City Limits*. But at that time Ranger Doug merely sang the song in progressively higher registers as a response to the challenges of his band mates.

The 1988 rendition was much different from the Riders' earlier version. As Carin Joy Condon wrote, "This [later version] is almost impossible to convey in writing, it is so manic and so crowd-arousing. It depends on Slim's rambunctious antics, Woody's unbelievable ability to do animal impersonations up to and including crickets (do you know anyone who can make convincing cricket noises?), Joey's musical accordion vignettes enhancing the plot, and Ranger Doug's acting ability." On the recording, Doug began with a simple strumming of his guitar and an evocative, sentimental, soft-spoken preface that portrayed the song as a picture of a lonely cowboy tending the herd in a West that is now part of history. Then he sings, complete with a beautiful lonesome yodel, "The cattle are prowlin', the coyotes are howlin', out where the dogies bawl..." But in the midst of this idyllic portrayal, Too Slim injects the cry of a sick calf that had strayed from its mother. Over the next few minutes, as Doug stands dumbfounded, Too Slim adds other animals with their sounds to the overall portrait of the West, while Woody supplies appropriate sound effects: a cow, a horse, a night bird, a cricket, a dog, a cat, a jackass, a duck, a pig and, finally, a circus train wreck, with its wide assortment of exotic animals running wild. The full five-minute, fifty-six seconds' rendition of "Cattle Call" is a real tour de force, giving listeners an excellent example of the fun that the Riders have playing with each other.[16]

Riders Radio Theater as an album led immediately to *Riders Radio Theater* as a real radio series. Bruce Nemerov, an old friend of Doug's, banjo player in his bluegrass band, and later a distinguished folklorist, originally came up with the idea of the Riders doing their own radio show, especially since they already had characters developed on *Tumbleweed Theater* that could transition beautifully to radio, and particularly a radio show with a live audience. From their experiences with *Tumbleweed Theater*, Steve Arwood and Randy Hale agreed. Bruce willingly funded a demo show, in which he tried to interest American Public Radio, distributors of *Prairie Home Companion*, but was turned down. They delivered the demo to Nashville's public radio station, WPLN, but it somehow never saw the light of day until Ranger Doug mentioned it to a staff announcer at the station. That encounter finally awakened the station's interest. As Steve told us, Brenda Loftis and Judy Liff were working there at the time as producers and were looking for a show that they could originate in Nashville and syndicate nationally. They took it to the NPR convention and got a deal where WPLN produced fifty-two shows that year.[17]

Discussing the forthcoming program in the *Tennessean*, Tommy Goldsmith wrote that "metro officials" were touting *Riders Radio Theater* as the first NPR series to originate in Nashville. Steve described that it took a few shows for the Riders to deliver their best. "We taped the shows two at a time at the Johnson Theater in front of a live audience.... When we started, the sound guys had to help us learn what we could/could not do. We didn't have any real sound effects." That's when they got Zeno (Bruce) in, and then Joey came on board. Bruce had been collecting sound effects for TV shows and thought that there would be "lots of places for them that just make things more fun" during the radio show. Bruce became Big Zeno Clinker.[18]

When the Riders and Steve sat down to talk about creating scripts for the show, the process sorted itself out as it had for *Tumbleweed Theater*. Slim already had one script, "Dialing for Dogies," but as Steve pointed out to Cusic, "Woody would show up, then have to go somewhere, and Ranger Doug would be there but usually fell asleep. Most of the time he'd add some key sparks at the end when he awakened, and Woody would add some good ideas when he came back. But this became Slim's baby—he really took ownership." David Skepner had told Tommy Goldsmith, "The comedy is the bricks of the whole thing, and the music is the mortar." The first taping of the radio series came on April 25, 1988, at the Johnson Theater in the Center for Performing Arts in Nashville and continued there through December 6 that year. Presented on Nashville's public radio station WPLN, the programming consisted of four series of shows, thirteen segments in each—"Meltdown on the Mesa," "Mysteries of the Lost Ozone," "Singing Six Guns," and "Curse of the Lost Goldscri." Each show began with a succession of coyote calls done in harmony, followed by a gunshot, and then the mellifluous voice of Bix Bender—described as "the voice that sold a million baby chicks on border radio"—introducing the performers. Music, of course, figured prominently in each show, with the Riders harmonizing beautifully on traditional cowboy songs like "When Payday Rolls Around" and "When the Bloom Is on the Sage," or on songs written by the boys themselves, such as "Bluebonnet Lady" or "That's How the Yodel Was Born." Ranger Doug always displayed his trademark yodeling, and Woody Paul exhibited his fiddling skills on hoedowns and jazz tunes.

The Riders continued to exploit aspects of popular culture, especially in their comedic routines and songs, as they did in their riffing on the Beach Boys' 1963 superhit, "Surfin' USA." And it wasn't just older cowboy singing acts that the Riders emulated in their choice of materials. Cowboy singer, songwriter, and Riders' friend Johnny Western (born Johnny Westerlund in Two Harbors, Minnesota), who'd known Doug through his work at the Country Music Hall of Fame, told us that when he first met the Ranger in 1986 in Wichita, they "hit it off immediately" because they both had Gene Autry as their hero. Johnny counted himself lucky to have toured with Gene during the last year that the famous cowboy singer and actor performed. Johnny had also toured with other greats such as Johnny Cash. Johnny Western wrote the immensely popular "The Ballad of Paladin" for the long-running TV series (1957–63) *Have Gun Will Travel* (still in reruns). The ubiquity of the song sparked Too Slim's ever-receptive creativity. Nonsensical but clever wordplay was a constant feature of the Riders, with their palindrome skits probably being the most well-loved. Based on the television gunfighter, Paladin, the fictional Palindrome spoke in language that, when repeated backward, said the same thing. For example, when the bartender asks, "What will you have?" Palindrome answers "Lager, sir, is regal." Or the Bartender: "You want some fruit in it?" Palindrome: "No lemon. No melon." Their "Ballad of Palindrome" introduces their Palindrome skit that can be heard on their album, *A Great Big Western Howdy*, released on Rounder in 1998. Joey Miskulin, who arrived at about the tenth episode, brought a strong measure of musical gravity and soon became a presence in virtually every facet of their programming. As Steve said, when Joey came on board, "his music really heightened the show." Joey told us, "When I played with the band on *Riders Radio Theater*, things instantly jelled," and they'd played "like we had grown up together."[19]

As the titles suggest, the shows contained preposterous plots, including a touch of science fiction, that were a bit reminiscent of the 1935 movie serial, *Phantom Empire*, which had introduced a young Gene Autry to Hollywood. The series featured a continuing cast of characters, all played by the Riders, that dated in some cases as far back as *Tumbleweed Theater*: the villains A. Swinburne Slocum and his dim-witted sidekick Charlie; the fly-by-night salesman and entrepreneur L. Philo "Larry" Mammoth; the slightly goofy and self-important country and western singer High Sheriff Drywall; the morally upright but stuffy Royal Canadian Mountie Sergeant Dudley; the cantankerous but lovable cook and sidekick Side Meat; and the talking horse's skull, Too Jaws, which had been a part of the Riders' sketches as far back as 1981. Doug loved doing five different roles in an hour. While all of these characters appeared in virtually every Riders' Theater episode, Side Meat—spouting gibberish in a classic Gabby Hayes fashion—was arguably the central figure of the show's roster.[20]

Broadcast on the Armed Forces Network and the Australian Forces Network, the show received syndication on at least 150 American public radio stations. Despite its popularity with listeners, someone in WPLN's management did not like the show. The station refused to renew its contract in 1989. After an eight-month hiatus, Dr. J. C. King and Larry Ashcraft of Cincinnati stepped in and, supported by a local subscription drive, arranged a series on the local public station WVXU. The show resumed at the Emery Theater in Cincinnati on January 22, 1990. The Riders commuted to Cincinnati once a month, along with Joey Miskulin—whose music had become indispensable to the show—and over the course of a couple of days in front of a live and enthusiastic audience, recorded about four shows. Every other week they featured guest stars such as Alison Krauss, Michael Martin Murphey, the Dixie Chicks (now known as the Chicks), John Hartford, and Marty Stuart, who appeared more often than anyone.

The Riders made earnest attempts to ingratiate themselves with the local Cincinnati market, for instance, with players from the Cincinnati Reds baseball team, along with the team's owner, Marge Schott, sometimes asked to take on bit parts. Local journalist Linda Pender covered one of their shows, skeptical at first, then thoroughly appreciating both the performance and the audience's response. She commented, "During intermission, there's a Too Slim look-alike contest. A 3-year-old in chaps and a moustache wins by a mile." In the fall of 1993, Boise resident and Riders' fan Allen McNeely heard *Riders' Radio Theater* on KBSU from Boise State, but the following January, he was disappointed that the station had stopped carrying the program. He went down to KBSU and offered to pay for the show to be kept on, then paid for it for three years, taping each show. The last Riders Radio show in Cincinnati was presented on August 18, 1995. The band members were burned out, trying to come up with original ideas, and Fred said that he was tired of writing the scripts. But even in 2022, when we spoke with Allen, a hair stylist and coffee connoisseur with his own shop, he was continuing to play the taped shows for his customers, who still enjoy them. *Riders' Radio Theater* had a larger future life as well. David Skepner negotiated a contract with TNN that authorized the Riders to do a series of television specials— including a Christmas show—that ran sporadically throughout the 1990s. These shows were very much like those earlier heard on radio and featured big-name guests like Barbara Mandrell and Kathy Mattea.[21]

Joey was having such a good time playing with the Riders on the radio show and enjoying the audience response to the band's interactions with each other and their listeners, that he went on the road with them for about a year and a half, but, as he admitted, he and David Skepner didn't get along. Although Slim, Ranger Doug, and Woody treated Joey as an equal, he got a very cold reception from David. Doug said that David felt like three was an optimal number, and that four people diluted the "look" of the group. "I think he thought that musically, it made it more crowded. It didn't matter to the audience, nor to us." At that point, Joey got a call from Michael Martin Murphey, who wanted him to produce albums for him for Warner Western and to go on the road with him. Joey accepted Michael's offer but continued working with the Riders on the radio shows. Working with Michael Martin Murphey, however, did not provide Joey with the same kind of creative outlet—and fun—that he had experienced with the Riders. Murphey wanted the same set played every night exactly as it had been on the recording, so in late 1992, Joey returned to the Riders. The band let Skepner know that Joey was going to be a partner. End of discussion. Joey explained the magic that playing with the Riders holds for him:

> When the Riders hit the stage, it is still absolute fun. When we're playing, we still feed off each other. We never make fun of the music, but we have fun *with* the music.... The only time we rehearse is when we're cutting a record. The outline of the show remains. When it's my turn, I play anything that I want, just like everyone else does. The truth of the matter is there are no other four guys who do it like we do. Nobody's got the musical chops that we have and that get along together like we do.

As Slim put it, "Joey has become an integral part of the band and has helped us tremendously with his musicality and with his production knowhow... and he knows us intimately, probably far more than he would ever need to or care to. He knows what we can do and is never satisfied with what we do—he always wants to do better and tries to pull out the best performances.... When we thought that three was it, we hadn't met Joey."[22]

While *Riders Radio Theater* commanded much attention from the Riders, it did not monopolize their time. They continued to display their talents in a wide variety of enterprises. In 1992, the Riders had felt sufficiently established, and grateful, to publish a commemorative and highly illustrated account of their career—*Riders In The Sky*—stressing their meteoric rise and noting their delight in having come such a long way in fifteen years. They could not have known, when the book was first compiled, that they were on the verge of their greatest national exposure yet. Hollywood beckoned. While still doing their *Riders Radio Theater* tapings, in 1991, they got the opportunity to do a kiddie television show in California, carried on a major network, CBS. Hosting a kiddie cowboy show proved especially gratifying for Doug, Fred, and Joey, who had spoken often of the formative role played by such shows during their own childhoods. Woody, whose family did not have a television set when he was a child, seems to have gotten his love for cowboy music later, primarily from such television shows as *Rawhide* and *Bonanza*. The Riders were now recording *their own* CBS show at the old Republic Studios, for which Doug, remembering those sessions, wrote, "What a Thrill! . . . it looked like all the Roy Rogers movies!" It was, indeed, where the Sons of the Pioneers had practiced their matchless harmonies. As Doug had told journalist Joe Rhodes, "There's not a day I don't walk along here somewhere . . . without wondering where did Gene or Roy walk? Where did the Sons of the Pioneers practice their harmonies? I get goose bumps every day."[23]

Brooklyn native Alan Sacks, who had made his mark as a television producer with such successful shows as *Welcome Back, Kotter* and *Chico and the Man*—shows with a decided urban bent—was also a fan of cowboy music and culture. Fond of wearing cowboy boots and hats as he went about his business, Alan played a vital role in making the CBS show happen. His affection for the Riders' music was such that he even asked them to sing for his wedding in 1990, and the eccentric "Texas Jewboy," Kinky Friedman, served as his best man. Sacks had seen a brief article on Riders In The Sky in *People's Weekly* on February 27, 1989, and had begun thinking about a possible television series that would feature the group. He persuaded Judy Scott, vice president for children's programming at CBS, to attend a Riders' concert, on May 27, 1990, at McCabe's in Santa Monica, and she was favorably impressed by what she saw and heard. Alan had originally envisioned a plot that would have the Riders moving from a frontier town into Hollywood, where they'd be like fish out of water. But the idea was rejected as being too much like the *Beverly Hillbillies*. Instead, Alan and Judy hatched the idea for a children's television series featuring Riders In The Sky.[24]

The Riders had rentals that summer at the Oakwood Apartments on Barham Boulevard, in the Toluca Lake district of North Hollywood, less than two miles from the Walt Disney Studios. Designed for transient actors, the cluster of 1,151 units specialized in temporary furnished apartments, usually rented for a month or two. A twenty-four-hour security guard was stationed in a kiosk at the entrance. The apartment complex liked to call itself, "a home, not a hotel," and it offered such amenities as a rehearsal hall, a clubhouse, two swimming pools, a tennis court, two fitness centers, and other conveniences. The complex was ideal for someone as health conscious as Doug Green. He and his second wife, Cindy, had divorced in 1985, and in

1989, he married Dianne Rau, who was with him that summer in Hollywood. Five years later, their daughter, Grace Elizabeth, was born. While still doing occasional shows elsewhere, they settled down in their temporary residences and taped shows at Studio City from July 17 to September 14, 1991. The Riders, of course, were thrilled with the opportunity to showcase their art through the powerful medium of CBS. As veteran TV performers, they had no trouble in working effortlessly before the cameras (although, as the show's producers suggested, the band did take some acting and improv lessons while living in Los Angeles).[25]

The prospects for the television series, *Riders In The Sky*, looked extremely promising, which was to be presented on Saturday mornings. Unfortunately—for the band and for the ultimate reception of the series—CBS did not offer Ranger Doug, Too Slim, or Woody the creative independence and control that they had enjoyed on *Riders Radio Theater*. Too Slim and Bix Bender had no hand in writing the shows, nor did Bix in narrating them. The network instead chose George McGrath, who had won success as the principal writer for *Pee-Wee's Playhouse*. Unfortunately, as Doug said, George wanted no input from the Riders and was unwilling to be flexible with his work. "His grasp of the characters wasn't really deep enough, and we were stuck with the script." In its corporate wisdom, the station also brought in a slew of new elements: other actors, puppets (including a talking buffalo), and a group of children, meant to augment or complement the action. McGrath had not paid attention to the genius of the characters the Riders had already created and inhabited, and either replaced them or designated Hollywood actors to play the Riders' parts, except for Ranger Doug, who remained the hero. Other guest stars appeared, and characters came and went. Instead of the fake but funny commercials featured in the Riders' earlier programs, the network interspersed standard ones. The Riders were the stars, yet still sidelined. Understandably, they felt very restrained and immediately saw that what they were experiencing was not the *Cowboy Way*, after all, but *real* show business.[26]

The thirteen episodes of the show ran from September 14 to December 7, 1991. They spent approximately a work week on each: setting up one day, rehearsing the next, and shooting the following couple of days. The shows were somewhat similar—but not similar enough to succeed—to those heard on *Riders Radio Theater*. The Riders' longtime friend Mike Mahaney helped with some of the casting, especially getting kids on, and sat in on some of the episodes and agreed that CBS "totally dropped the ball." He put most of the blame for cancellation on CBS's poor preparation and misunderstanding of the Riders' appeal, feeling that the TV shows were as "stale as yesterday's muffins," because the pre-recording of the Riders' music took the magic out of their performances. He maintains that the shows would have profited from the writing of Too Slim and Texas Bix. Furthermore, when the series aired in the fall, CBS kept changing the time it appeared on Saturday mornings. After the broadcast began, the network didn't think the show was very good, and it wasn't. It didn't really get a full season, since CBS could not recapture Pee Wee's audience. The Riders' music was almost incidental to the action; they sang snippets of an opening and closing theme but did very few complete songs. More often, they engaged in innocent but energetic horseplay and were the centerpiece of a skit that aired in two segments. Because it was only a thirty-minute show (including six minutes of commercials), the action and music were highly compressed. Although Mike Mahaney's reasons are sound, George McGrath was later asked to give his assessment of why the show had not gone on to a second series: "Well, I was proud of the puppets and the actors in the supporting cast. The problem with *Riders In The Sky*, and this may be a weird thing to say, was the Riders In The Sky. They were used to doing a college-touring kind of vaudeville act . . . and they didn't have a sparkle in their eyes. It was hard to get the Riders In The Sky to light up the screen." It's funny that McGrath should mention his pride in the puppets, because that's what he had done to the Riders. With all the pre-recordings and wooden scripts, he had effectively reduced them to puppets. No wonder their eyes and performances lacked sparkle.[27]

A few weeks before the CBS premiere of *Riders In The Sky*, the Riders released *Harmony Ranch*, their second children's album and their first recording for Columbia. Characters from the show adorn the cover of the album. Involvement with CBS clearly elevated the Riders' national profile. And meeting Gene Autry on the CBS set was a decided bonus that the band would never forget. The LaBours had additional reasons to remember those Los Angeles days with special affection—a very pregnant Bert was one of two costume designers, and she received a Daytime Emmy for her work, and their daughter Alice was born in Cedars Sinai Hospital sometime between the eighth and ninth tapings. Alice, in fact, went to her first Riders show when she was three weeks old. While the cancellation of the series was disappointing to the Riders, they nevertheless were very glad to have had the

The Winning of the West

Gene Autry visiting with the Riders on the set of the CBS series *Riders In The Sky*. Photograph by David Skepner.

experience. Ranger Doug told an interviewer, "What struck me most was how professional the crews were; it was not a good old boys' network." And he added, "It was fun to be a Saturday morning cartoon hero." More recently, he told us, "It still boggles my mind. We had a network show on CBS. I never could have dreamed that. I look back on that summer with a lot of fondness and a minor bit of frustration."[28]

Furthermore, the Riders could not have known that within just a few short years, they would be back in Hollywood. And this time the rewards would be unimaginable. In the meantime, they went on with their intensive life as road musicians, with Joey rejoining them, first as a partial, and then as a permanent and full-time partner. In 1994 he became their record producer, with the Columbia release *Cowboys in Love*, a contribution that Joey has continued to make in their subsequent recordings. He returned to the band with the attributes that made the foursome an outstanding ensemble: his storehouse of musical information honed over his already-long career; an expertise with the accordion virtually unmatched by any other musician; and experience as a producer that the Riders eagerly embraced. As Joey explained the partnership: "Everything is split equally. We're four owners of the band. No sidemen. It's *our* band. It's a real amazing thing in the United States today, to have four guys who love each other and love playing together."[29]

The Riders constant slate of tours netted them a comfortable income, but it came at the expense of lengthy separations from family, strained marital relations, and numerous hours driving over often dangerous roads. One of Doug Green's most affecting songs, "I Always Do," included in the *Harmony Ranch* album, was written to his daughter Annie Laurie when she expressed sadness about his lengthy absences. He assured her that he would always return. His several wives could not be so easily reconciled. The Riders' various "busses" (RVs retrofitted by Woody to accommodate the band, and sometimes wives and children on summer tours) driven over thousands of miles, and under uncertain road conditions and often-hazardous weather, similarly could not be easily salvaged, even with Woody Paul's ingenuity and mechanical expertise.

The Riders, in circumstances endemic to touring musicians, suffered at least a couple of serious road crashes but, fortunately, without debilitating physical consequences. Traveling late at night after one performance in order to get to the next often took its toll, however, and while road weariness may not have been a factor, Ranger Doug's vocal performance suffered greatly. On March 30, 1994, in Winston-Salem, North Carolina, he mysteriously lost his voice. An ardent fan named Tom Cole attended one of the Riders' shows at a Las Vegas casino during this period and wrote about it a few years later in his blog. Meeting the group before they performed, Tom said, "I was surprised at how soft-spoken he was. This guy could yodel louder and better than anyone I'd ever heard. I wondered how his off-stage demeanor could be so subdued." He then recalled his shock at hearing Doug restrain his singing while Woody took over the task of yodeling. During their breaks, Doug smiled cordially at his fans but wore a badge that said, "No questions, please, I'm on voice rest." Returning to Nashville, Doug checked in at the Vanderbilt Voice Clinic, but physicians could never conclusively determine the cause, although some speculated that the condition might have been Bell's Palsy, a disorder of the nerve that controls facial movements. For eight or nine months he could sing only with difficulty and could not reach some of the notes that he had earlier mastered—a scary prospect, indeed, for the Riders' lead singer and master yodeler. Doug was limited to one octave for a few months, but at the Minnesota State Fair, he reached one and a half octaves, and his progress was steady and satisfactory after that. By October 7, when the Riders were at the Aladdin Theater in Portland, Oregon, thankfully, his voice returned to normal. Doug's vocal issues did not prevent the Riders from singing but forced them come up with some creative vocal arrangements to offset Doug's loss. Gradually, over a year or so, Doug regained much of his original strength and range.[30]

The Riders continued to record prolifically, with a new album appearing almost every year. They, of course, hoped for significant monetary returns from these albums, and sometimes experimented with methods to enhance their commercial viability, but the albums served primarily as souvenirs for Riders' fans. As Carin Joy Condon insisted, the Riders must be seen to be fully appreciated. But they made albums available to viewers of their stage shows who wanted to take along a remembrance of what they had seen, along with other artifacts from the Mercantile table. In 1995, the Riders returned to the Rounder label, a company that had preserved its mission to record roots-based musicians, but which now had the economic means—thanks to the presence of superstar Alison Krauss on its roster—to market its performers with greater economic efficacy. Both David Skepner and the Riders felt that Rounder now had the "sophisticated distribution machinery" to generate album sales. Joey, of course, produced the Riders' new album, which sported the clever title, *Always Drink Upstream from the Herd*, a bit of advice attributed to Will Rogers that had always been crucial to the health and mental outlook of cowboys on the long drive. The band typically used the phrase when they closed out their concerts, and Too Slim included it in the cleverly written "The Trail Tip Song," which he wrote for the album and often performed thereafter. The other selections revealed the breadth of material that favored their concerts: traditional cowboy pieces like "Take Me Back to My Boots and Saddle" and "Cattle Call" (without the verbal horseplay heard in other versions); Tin Pan Alley pop tunes like "After You've Gone" (an instrumental tour de force for Woody and Joey); a TV theme, "Rawhide"; a Nashville cowboy song, "Running Gun" (written by Jim and Tompall Glaser); and five songs written by Ranger Doug or Too Slim (including "The First Cowboy Song," cowritten by Green and Gary McMahan). In 1996, the National Cowboy & Western Heritage Museum presented its Wrangler Award to the Riders for *Always Drink Upstream from the Herd*—the best traditional western album of the previous year. This outstanding collection's cover shot proved providential, since it depicted Ranger Doug, Woody Paul, and Too Slim standing beside each other looking intently into the distance—presumably west—a pose they continued to assume as "The Cowboy Way" in all their subsequent concerts.[31]

In February 1996, the Riders appeared in a TNN special, "An Evening of Country Greats." As they celebrated the music and life of Gene Autry, the great cowboy hero looked on with approval from the audience. The evening inspired the Riders to produce a tribute album, *Public Cowboy Number One: The Music of Gene Autry*, released on the Rounder label that fall. A childhood hero to all of the band members, Autry did much to create the genre that they now personified, and the recording included twelve of Autry's most significant songs, items like "That Silver Haired Daddy of Mine," "Back in the Saddle Again," "South of the Border," "Riding Down the Canyon," and "Be Honest With Me" (an Academy Award nominee in 1941 for the best movie song, from Autry's *Ridin' on a Rainbow*).

While this was the first album made by the Riders that consisted solely of covers, they did not imitate Autry, but instead gave respectful interpretations of his songs complete with close tasteful harmonies and superb yodeling. In reviewing the album for the *Western Way*, music critic and historian O. J. Sikes wrote that Gene Autry himself loved the CD and played it frequently in his office, commenting that "had the Riders been around in the glory days of the singing Western, he'd have loved to have ridden the musical trail with them." The recording had an additional significance for the band: it saw the first appearance of Brent Truitt as chief audio engineer. He asserts that the Riders have been his best customers—Brent has engineered their subsequent recordings—and great friends. He also claims to be the back-up man to Joey, "who is definitely the boss."[32]

The Riders maintained their extensive array of personal appearances, over 200 shows a year, and in an eclectic variety of venues unmatched by any other entertainers. In 1998, they even appeared in the popular childhood television show, *Barney and Friends*, where Ranger Doug sang "How Does He Yodel?" One of their most satisfying gigs, to which they often returned, was playing benefit shows for Hospital Hospitality House. For nineteen years in a row, the Riders had played at a National Guard Armory in Nashville, raising money for the Hospitality House. On Valentine's Day in 1980, they had raised $1,300; in 1998, a concert and silent auction raised $75,000. They played frequently in Nashville, of course, at the Grand Ole Opry, at the Ernest Tubb

Hillary Clinton posing with the Riders at the annual congressional barbecue at the White House during the Clinton administration. Photograph by Barbara Kinney, courtesy William J. Clinton Presidential Archives.

Record Shop, and at assorted music industry events. Throughout the nation, they played at elementary schools, junior high schools, colleges and universities, including the United States Military Academy. They kept making the rounds of county and state fairs, from Alaska to Texas, and continued to appear in clubs, from the Birchmere in Alexandria, Virginia, to the Palomino in Los Angeles. Folk festivals in places like Kerrville, Texas, and Winnipeg remained on their itinerary, with the Strawberry Festival in California being the locale of some of their most memorable performances. They played at the Reagan inaugural ceremonies, and at annual congressional barbecues during the Clinton and George W. Bush administrations. They even played at zoos, and at the giant Harley motorcycle rally in Sturgis, South Dakota. Ranger Doug said that the Riders approached the rally with some trepidation but were pleased when the motorcycle riders accepted them with good-natured ease. According to Slim, it was a "pretty calm" affair.[33]

Obviously, it was generally a relief, physically, monetarily, and socially, to land a gig that lasted several days and gave the band a bit of down time to relax away from the constant travel. The Knoxville World's Fair, for instance, along with the various state fairs, like that of Minnesota, had provided many advantages, yet casinos offered more lucrative consecutive evenings and more upscale accommodations. These money havens had long been attractive to the likes of entertainers such as Frank Sinatra, Dean Martin, and Elvis Presley, but it was rare for a singing cowboy group to be featured. The Riders performed at establishments like Cactus Pete's in Jackpot, Nevada, and the Red Lion Casino in Elko, Nevada, often on the same trip that took them to the Cowboy Poetry Gathering. Their favorite, though, by far, was John Ascuaga's Nugget Casino in Sparks, Nevada, about three miles outside of Reno, an establishment known for "clean acts" and for being free of the influence of organized crime. John, a colorful entrepreneur with several other enterprises, continually brought in big-name entertainers, but his main attraction was an elephant named Bertha that had been bought from the circus museum in Baraboo, Wisconsin. Bertha was trained to dance and play instruments and was eventually joined by two other elephants named Tina and Angel. Following the elephants, and often a juggler, comedian, or mind reader, the Riders presented an hour of their own entertainment. Beginning in 1982, they appeared frequently at the Nugget, and did so extensively until about 2000, generally earning $50,000 for their two-week stay. Playing at the Nugget meant two weeks off the road, lodging in luxurious and commodious rooms, eating sumptuous food, using the swimming pool, sometimes taking the family along.[34]

Ranger Doug particularly welcomed the time at the casino to read—although he did that everywhere—and to write. He told writer Jon Johnson that "the things that sent it [his writing habit] over the top were the invention of the laptop computer and bookings at casinos that lasted up to two weeks where you really don't have anything to do but go down and do a show between 8 and 10. And boy, that's a lot of free time." He also had his files from interviews at the Country Music Hall of Fame and Museum. Although, Doug admitted, "Songwriting is more fun than academic writing. Writing is the hard part." A deeply spiritual man, he wakes up in the morning and thinks about his writing as he is doing his morning gratitude reflecting, then is ready to get on the computer and write. He considers himself "a fairly fluid writer, hearing his sentences in his head before he writes them." Such perseverance resulted in his 2002 publication, *Singing in the Saddle: The History of the Singing Cowboy* (Country Music Foundation), an overview of the

Hollywood Singing Cowboys, a history missing from previous accounts, as well as a loving tribute to the people and genre that had inspired his career. The publication grew out of a fifty-six-page article that Doug had written in 1978 for the *Journal of Country Music*. Reviewer Travis Stimeling wrote that the book reveals Green's "deeply personal passion for western music," and that "his investment in this topic had opened innumerable pathways for future research into film studies, cultural studies, history, and musicology."[35]

As the twentieth century neared its end, the Riders saw no diminution in their schedule of concerts. They were still doing 200 shows a year. For their twentieth anniversary they planned an intensive schedule of events, including their fourteenth album for Rounder, *A Great Big Western Howdy* and a November 6, 1997, appearance on TNN's *Prime Time Country* where they were featured for the entire hour. Brad Paul, then vice president at Rounder and in charge of the label's promotions and publicity, commented, "Nobody who's ever seen these guys walks away bummed out." Two days later, the Riders performed on the stage of the Grand Ole Opry—their 751st appearance there—where they heard spoken tributes from Garth Brooks, Kathy Mattea, and Reba McEntire and, best of all, letters from Gene Autry, Roy Rogers, and Dale Evans. Doug told a journalist, "Well, that was about the coolest thing that ever happened to us... and we owe it all to sheer orneriness... choosing in 1977 to make a living out of doing cowboy music—in the face of all reason and logic." He informed *Billboard*'s Jim Bessman that, as of July 4, 1998, the Riders had presented 3,781 shows. According to David Skepner, the Riders had achieved success just by being themselves, and Bessman added that the "high family-entertainment value" of the band "is further reflected by the increase in 2,000-seat community bookings," then quoted Skepner:

> We don't use industry formulas; the Riders are a cottage industry unto themselves... it's not uncommon to see three and four generations of a single family at a Riders' show. Little kids come because there's just something friendly about this music... and their parents are happy their kids are into something besides Ninja Turtles and Power Rangers. And grandparents and great-grandparents come because they remember when they were that age and going to the movies Saturday mornings to see Gene, Roy, and Hoppy. Everyone in the family comes for different reasons.[36]

Signing autographs during the Riders' tour in Japan. Photograph by David Skepner.

When he made those observations, David Skepner's days with the Riders were already numbered. In 1997 the Riders obtained convincing evidence that Skepner had been taking checks intended for them and other entertainers and placing them in his own bank account. He had worked tirelessly for the Riders, aggressively won new and commercially viable marketing outlets for them, engineered the public radio affiliation of *Riders Radio Theater* in the 1990s, and had successfully negotiated the band's appearance on several television specials in 1995 and 1996. But David's financial mismanagement went beyond the pale, and the Riders severed their relationship with him. Their agent Paul Lohr now added management to his responsibilities.

Alice LaBour had made her appearance the summer of the Riders' CBS children's show taping, and her little brother, George Harold LaBour, was born near the end of the decade, December 21, 1998. Slim called him "our solstice child: the brightest light on the darkest day of the year." On his way home from the hospital following George's Christmastime arrival, it was snowing, and Slim wrote, "beside myself with joy at having a baby boy . . . I

Paul Lohr joining the Riders on the set of Melody Ranch. Photograph by Michael N. Marks, courtesy New Frontier Management.

couldn't help rolling down the windows and singing at the top of my lungs: 'Hark George Harold angels sing.'" That joyous birth turned out to be a good omen for the entire band, heralding a major breakthrough in their career in the following year.[37]

On September 10, 1999, the Riders sent out an email to fans, announcing that the band had just "wrapped up our 4000th performance in Puyallup, Washington," which averaged "an appearance every other day for twenty-two years." They included a list of trivia-laden statistics—some accurate, others both funny and phony. For example, they'd driven seven vehicles "into the ground," twelve engines "which gave their last full measure," all of which had their windshields cracked. Then they added that they'd

160   CHAPTER FIVE

given 784,000 autographs, and that fans had asked "'Where's Woody?', 36,400 times." The Riders were galloping toward the end of the twentieth century when they encountered some of the most high-profile moments of their career. Hollywood, the scene of their recent disappointment with CBS, this time both beckoned *and* delivered. With an astonishing piece of luck, they appeared in *Toy Story 2*, a Pixar/Disney creation, issued on November 24, 1999, and one of the most successful animated films of all time. Randy Newman, who had written the score for the first *Toy Story* movie, had also composed a song for the sequel's animated cowboy hero, Woody, who had once starred in his own kiddie western show, *Woody's Roundup*. At a conference held before the movie was in production, someone suggested that an "authentic" cowboy singer or singers should be asked to perform the song (rather than Newman), someone with a "real 40s or 50s feel." Many years later, when Ranger Doug was asked how the Riders fortuitously received this commission, he said "we had a mole at Pixar." He was kidding, but they *did* have a fan there. Doug was referring to Ash Brannon, the movie's young codirector, who had long been a fan of their music. Brannon searched for *yodeling* on his computer, and up came the Riders. The other conference attendees, including director John Lasseter and Randy Newman, agreed that the Riders were the perfect choice. When they received the invitation, the Riders jokingly said that they deliberated for about an eighth of a second and agreed. When the movie premiered, Doug, Dianne, and little Grace traveled to Hollywood to be there. The Riders performed at the after-party in one of the little rooms at the venue, but Grace, by that time, had "conked out."[38]

The movie soundtrack, produced by Joey and Frank Wolf, featured the Riders singing their rendition of "Woody's Roundup," which was nominated for the Academy Award as the soundtrack song. That would have been sufficiently exciting in itself, but then Jay Landers, of Disney Records, asked them to create a companion album of songs about the characters, which Joey produced. Landers declared, "I think the Riders sleep in their spurs. They didn't need help from anyone in capturing that western sound." *Woody's Roundup: A Rootin'-Tootin' Collection of Woody's Songs*, was their twentieth album and their third for children. With liner notes by John Lasseter, the album contained thirteen songs: one traditional piece ("Home on the Range"), one country and western number, with altered cowboy lyrics (Johnny Russell's "Act Naturally," popularized by Buck Owens), two songs by Randy Newman (the title cut, which they recut for the record, and "You've Got a Friend in Me"), three each from Ranger Doug and Too Slim, and one from Joey. The Riders have always been, with good reason, exceptionally pleased with this album, and Ranger Doug insists that "Jessie, the Yodeling Cowgirl" is one of his favorite songs of the many that he has written. Doug told us that when Disney records had asked the Riders to write songs about the backstories of the characters in *Toy Story 2* for their accompanying album, he "kept mulling over Jessie." He was on his way to a Sunday morning meeting of the Religious Science gathering when he remembered a suggestion made by John Lasseter that Jessie came from Oklahoma. "So, the first line was easy: 'She was born in Oklahoma in the rolling Osage hills.' The tune, more or less, was just THERE." Once at the service, he grabbed the program and began writing on it . . . "and when I got to rhyming 'caught us' with 'epiglottis goddess' I just laughed out loud, causing a small stir. I didn't care; I knew I had written something wonderful in its own way, whether it was a success or not."[39]

Riders and their families at the premier of *Toy Story 2*. From *left to right*: Grace Green, Ranger Doug, Ann Marie Flores, George LaBour, Too Slim, Alice LaBour, Roberta LaBour, Kaitlyn Chrisman, Woody Paul, Casey Chrisman, Teresa Chrisman, Joey the Cowpolka King, Katie Miskulin. Riders In The Sky Archives, courtesy of New Frontier Touring.

Riders with their Grammy Awards pose the Cowboy Way. Riders In The Sky Archives, courtesy of New Frontier Management.

The Riders' longtime friend, Jerry West, went with the band to a Gene Autry festival in Gene Autry, Oklahoma, on September 25, 1999, and Ft. Worth singer and yodeler Devon Dawson of the Texas Trailhands and Marilyn Tuttle were jamming outside the Riders' bus. Doug thought that Devon would be perfect on the album for Jessie the Yodeling Cowgirl. Jerry knew Devon and her family, and he agreed. Devon told us that Joey called about three weeks later to invite her to be Jessie and asked if she could yodel in E flat and G, where Doug was singing. She said that she saw the movie three times before going to Nashville to record, her first time in a high-powered Music Row environment. "It was one of the most exciting days of my life," she reported, and a "very emotional" experience. The Pixar album proved,

The Winning of the West   163

John Lasseter (between Ranger Doug and Too Slim) roped the Riders into *Toy Story 2*. Songwriter Randy Newman is in the foreground. Riders In The Sky Archives, courtesy of New Frontier Touring.

of course, a tremendous boon to the Riders' career, released on August 29, 2000, in conjunction with the home video release of *Toy Story 2*. According to Doug, the album sold about 300,000 copies, and, at the Grammy awards ceremony on February 21, 2001, it became their first CD to win a Grammy for the Best Children's Album. The Riders were also nominated that year for the Best Country Performance by a Duo or Group with Vocal for "Jessie, the Yodeling Cowgirl." Devon was once again thrilled to be in Nashville, when she appeared on the Grand Ole Opry with the Riders the following March 2, which was their first performance on the show after the award ceremony. The medley of songs from *Woody's Roundup* played frequently at the Disney theme parks, on the Disney website, and even on United Airlines flights. As Joey said, "The Disney thing was huge for us. When we did the promo, we did it at the Silver Dollar Saloon at Disneyworld, with just us and the Disney Folks there."[40]

Best of all, the album's popularity inspired Disney to call on the Riders two years later when another movie, *Monsters, Inc.*, was filmed. There was nothing cowboy about this film; it presented the animated story of a city of monsters, Monstropolis, in which the screams of kids were collected to fuel the city's power company. The fantastic story, however, was used as a subterfuge to promote the message of confronting one's fears through laughter, reputed to be ten times stronger than screams. With Joey producing the album, and arranging much of the featured music, the Riders rose to the challenge presented by the story and recorded another Grammy winner, *Monsters, Inc.: Scream Factory Favorites*. The album included covers of songs heard in the film, such as Randy Newman's "If I Didn't Have You," along with a bevy of songs written or cowritten by the Riders. They, in fact, did a song for every character and exhibited their skill with jazz, pop, and other styles of music far beyond the scope of usual cowboy fare. An animated Pixar short film, *For the Birds*, which preceded *Monsters, Inc.*, also featured music by the Riders. The delightful instrumental tune, "Big High Wire Hop," arranged by Joey, comprised the entire soundtrack, and *For the Birds* won an Oscar in 2002 for the Best Animated Short Film. When the director, Ralph Eggleston, accepted the Grammy, he thanked the Riders "from the stage 'for their wonderful sound work' in the film."[41]

All the Riders agreed that their favorite all-time performance occurred at the Hollywood Bowl on August 11 and 12, 2000, adding luster to an already-successful West Coast foray. Playing with the Bowl's famous orchestra, the Riders performed a few songs from *Toy Story 2*, along with "Lonely Yukon Stars" and a few classics like "Cool Water" and "Tumbling Tumbleweeds." The shows brought no awards, but, musically, they assumed almost spiritual dimensions for the Riders. Mike Mahaney attended the event and recalled the impressive contributions that Joey made. He worked with all the arrangers to make the symphonic charts fit the Riders' style of music, and "really got to shine with the bowl orchestra. Watching Joey onstage at the rehearsal was great, as the orchestra finalized the charts, and the experience brought out his artistry." The design of the amphitheater alone is enough to evoke feelings of wonder. The Riders played there when it was still a series of concentric arches, set off against the backdrop of the Hollywood Hills where the famous Hollywood sign could clearly be seen northeast of the arena. While the Bowl had become famous for its acoustics, it gained equal renown for the quality of the acts—both classical and popular—who performed there, and for the superb musicianship of its orchestra. The Riders had played with symphony orchestras before, but they had only superlatives to describe the music that they heard at the

Bowl. Slim told us, "The concert master hit the downbeat, and it sounded *so* good. The orchestra was having a ball; they dug what the Riders were doing." Doug described the entire experience as "magical." And Slim, recalling the records of Hollywood Bowl performances that his parents had listened to, said that he felt that his late parents "were there emotionally," that he "could look up and say, 'I'll bet my folks are tuned in tonight.'" And Joey, with his "golden ears," could not have asked for a more appropriate setting than the Bowl and its fabulous orchestra. Their peak performance, combined with their two Grammy-award-winning albums—which made them the toast of the younger set—demonstrated that they had come a very long way from the singing cowboys at the XXX Ranch whose slightly raunchy humor had once advertised Udder Butter on a Rope and Deadwood Darlene's Prairie Lubricants. There couldn't have been a more auspicious way to enter the twenty-first century.[42]

CHAPTER SIX

BAND OF BROTHERS

As the riders rode into the twenty-first century, they basked in the glow shimmering from their involvement with Pixar/Disney and from the two Grammys that came in its wake. They truly testified to, as Slim told us, the "power of the Mouse." References to *Toy Story 2*, and to *Monsters, Inc.*, became standard in their promotions for show dates, just as "Woody's Roundup" and "Jessie, the Yodeling Cowgirl" became basic and oft-performed items in their repertory. New songs emerged frequently but, otherwise, the Riders' performing patterns remained very much the same. Slim was quoted as saying, "It's different now ... thanks to the Grammys and Pixar. We've got a confidence in our abilities which translates into a comfort level. We don't feel the need to have to prove ourselves." Their loyal audience members expected, and their newer fans were initiated by, recognizable elements in each show: the campfire, the cactus, armadillos and, more recently, the Woody doll from *Toy Story 2* decorating the stage; Ranger Doug's introductions; the coyote calls; Slim's face playing and, of course, the paeans to the Cowboy Way immediately followed by the iconic pose of the Riders with hands on hips, gazing off into the distance. And Doug continued to give the number of the show they were presenting. The Ranger once said that everything done in this new era was "gravy" (or he could have said "icing on the cake") for they had accomplished just about everything else. The Disney/Pixar relationship generated many, mostly uncountable, spin-offs. The Riders appeared in several short vignettes on television, and in assorted commercials about real products, as opposed to the spoofs that appeared on *Riders Radio Theater* or in their stage shows.[1]

These inveterate road warriors could not—nor did they want to—stay off the road. For at least a decade and a half at the beginning of the twenty-first century and virtually until the onset of COVID in 2020, the Riders followed an almost-incredible itinerary of mostly one-night stands that took them all over the country. Slim recalled that, in terms of income earned, 2007 proved the best touring year they had ever had. The incessant and sometimes punishing schedule, however, took its toll. He wrote that at one point he "feared" for the band's future, noting that "petty annoyances could seem pretty substantial when you're together a couple hundred days a year in an RV." Slim even pondered a meeting to "discuss the unthinkable," that is, cutting back their travel. Although 2008 similarly turned out to be a banner year, the aftermath of that year's Great Recession rendered such a discussion moot as "dates fell out of our calendar in bunches" because the public money for community concerts, festivals, and symphonies dried up almost overnight. After the initial decade of the new century, they enjoyed no more symphony collaborations. Frugal Slim thought he'd "better see about another revenue stream or two. He and Tex Bix Bender collaborated on *The Sidekick Handbook: How to Unleash Your Inner Second Banana and Find True Happiness*, which was published by Gibbs-Smith. Slim also made a solo CD: *Say No More, It's Freddy LaBour*, "a bare bones collection" of his songs and a few "bits," and he did "a few solo dates, including opening for Riders In The Sky, which added a wee bit to my paydays." But Slim never invested much energy into his act, since he always preferred working with the band.[2]

Riders' manager Paul Lohr summarized the financial picture of the band's late twentieth and early twenty-first centuries as follows:

> In the 1990s, the band saw their annual earnings rise from a few hundred thousand a year to around $500,000 a year, quite an accomplishment for a little yodeling cowboy outfit that started out in a bar in Nashville. But when *Toy Story 2* featured their music, well . . . things really took off.

In 1999 they grossed close to $750,000, and the year 2000 saw them earn a whopping $962,000 while playing 132 paid appearances! Annual gross revenue continued to maintain in that $800,000 to $900,000-plus ballpark, but in 2007, their gross earnings topped $1 million for the first time, coming in at $1,038,000. 2008 saw the momentum continue, where they earned a band-record $1,182,000 in touring that year, performing 171 paid shows, NOT counting the Grand Ole Opry... and logging 26 shows in the month of November alone (followed by 24 in September!). That is perhaps the largest annual haul ever for an exclusively Western touring artist. Sure... a fraction of what country artists make but considering the genre... it is unlikely that the Riders' record will ever be surpassed.[3]

By 2010 the Riders' road schedule had returned to "normal," that is, hectic and grueling. Jay Peterson has provided us with a glimpse of the rigors of the band's traveling life. The Riders had met Jay, a musician and commercial artist, at the Winnipeg Folk Festival in 1979. He had worked for *Prairie Home Companion* for several years, where he designed the show's famous Powdermilk Biscuit logo and soon began working for the Riders as an artist, painting their road vehicles and preparing logos for their t-shirts and posters. He also traveled with them on a harrowing road trip, in 2010, through what he called "the square states." He remembers that they drove through Nebraska and South Dakota four times, presenting forty-one shows in forty-six days, and then hurriedly drove the 800 miles or so back to Nashville to play on the Grand Ole Opry. Jay was thrilled that he got to sing a couple of songs with them on the Opry stage. As soon as their Opry gig ended, the Riders had no chance to go home. Instead, they simply returned directly to their "bus" to resume their tour.[4]

Woody's old friend and former schoolmate, Billy Maxwell, could tell similar stories about the Riders' battles with their beloved, but problematic, road. Reconnecting at their twentieth high school reunion, in 1987, Woody had invited Billy, who was then a golf pro at Fall Creek Falls State Park in Spencer, Tennessee, to join them on an upcoming tour. From November 27, 1987, to 2012, especially during the winter season—then full time after he retired until the pandemic—Billy traveled with the Riders. He shared the driving and other duties and, incidentally, kept a journal. The very first trip he took with the Riders almost immediately turned into an adventure. He had flown to join them in Seattle and from there to travel to their next gig in Las Vegas. About 10:00 p.m. after their show, they began the drive in the Riders' then-current bus, a bread truck that ran out of diesel after about a hundred miles. Woody had to thumb a ride, get a can full of diesel, and get a ride back to the bus, which took about an hour, getting them to their destination at two the next morning. And that was just for starters. Not only did Billy help with driving, he told us about the work it took to get the Riders and the Mercantile ready for a show:

> When we got to a gig, we had a lot of props, and I managed where all the materials went, to the stage and to the lobby. I would set up the cactus, the fire, the stuffed armadillos, Woody dolls, Buzz Lightyear. Slim had a canteen. Woody had to have a drink holder on his mic when he was doing his rope tricks. . . . I set up a clock onstage that I laid right behind the fire to make sure he knew what time it was.

Billy's responsibilities, of course, continued after the performance. While the Riders changed from their stage clothes and put away their instruments, Billy reversed the process of setting up: repacking the gear and making it all fit back into the bus, so they could drive on to the next venue on their itinerary and repeat the experience.[5]

In an email, Slim recounted the hazards of the Riders' road travels and summed up the experience by asking, "How is it possible we survived?" For one thing, wheels were sometimes literally driven off vehicles, once on I-81 in Virginia, and another time on I-5 in California, when the wheel bearings wore out and the wheel crunched into the vehicle's housing. Automobile fires, of which there were a few, were much more terrifying. Again, in California, traveling toward Fresno, on I-5, the Riders pulled on to the median to check on an overheated engine. As their skilled fixer-upper, Woody went to work under the hood, and the dry median grass caught fire. They beat it out with blankets and t-shirts. Their good friend Cowboy Ken Jones, owner of the Home Ranch, and Bert, who were traveling with the band, stayed in Fresno a few days while the bus was being repaired. They then drove the bus to Nashville while the Riders were fulfilling some other engagements. This fire, however, was not nearly so scary as the one that leaped out of the engine into the cab of their RV during a harrowing trip through a blizzard one night near Laramie, Wyoming. Slim recalled that "flames started shooting up INTO THE CAB! I mean big flames. Billy [Maxwell] said later he was sure that... we were all going to die." Although the fire was quickly extinguished, the experience made them rethink the wisdom of long and hazardous road journeys, particularly as they grew older in the new century.[6]

Automobile collisions, of course, had always been one of the perils of country road touring. The Riders certainly experienced their share of them. All four of the Riders took turns at the wheel, with each cowboy driving about 250 miles, so the blame for such mishaps could not be placed on any one person. Long taxing hours, dangerous roads, perilous weather conditions, and unsafe vehicles were the real culprits. On one occasion, they drove into a ditch, in the middle of the night, at the junction of I-81 and I-40 in Virginia. Another accident could be blamed on those free-ranging creatures of the mid- and far west, deer. The Wisconsin folk singers Lou and Peter Berryman captured in their lyrics a moment that the Riders and other itinerant entertainers could well understand: "Dem deer, dey're here, den dey're dere, dey're here, dey're dere, dey're everywhere... Just when you think that the coast is clear, there in the road is a whitetail deer." One night in 2018 on I-25 in Wyoming, Joey hit not one but several deer. The airbag on the Riders' rental SUV deployed, breaking Slim's right wrist and several fingers.[7]

One of the Riders' scariest road moments occurred one very early morning during a bad rainstorm on I-30 in Texas, with trucks "blasting by," when Doug steered a bit into the passing lane and was "sideswiped by a semi." Thinking of the disastrous consequences that *could* have occurred, Fred saw this incident as the beginning of the end of night driving and hard traveling. Almost miraculously, though, the Riders only once completely overturned a vehicle. This accident occurred on December 23, 2016, after leaving a Christmas show in Steamboat Springs, Colorado. Ranger Doug, Woody, and Billy Maxwell were traveling alone, because Joey had flown home and the LaBour family had stayed in Steamboat Springs for an extended Christmas vacation. With Woody driving the RV during a snowstorm, the vehicle hit a patch of black ice and flipped over on the median. Doug had been asleep in his bunk and quickly escaped the vehicle through a window, leaving his boots behind. He was fortunate to have broken only a couple of ribs. "That was the end of that RV and the end of that era of Riders travel. Still amazing that those three weren't killed."[8]

The Riders' bus after the accident on December 23, 2016, which ended this mode of tour traveling for the band. Photograph by Billy Maxwell, used by permission.

Woody's mechanical expertise kept their many vehicles running and saved the Riders from additional (although arguably necessary) and expensive repairs. Slim acknowledged that Woody's "bus fixes on the road are quite properly the stuff of legend," and he quoted Ranger Doug as saying that "Woody doesn't fix things, but he gets them to work." More than once, during severely cold or freezing evenings, Woody crawled under the bus with matches and a newspaper and thawed the fuel lines enough to get the vehicle moving. When Slim asked rhetorically, "How is it possible we survived?" he was thinking about those moments, and about the time when the bus's alternator almost fell out of the engine. Woody "worked for a couple hours to get it back together with duct tape and—in his finest achievement—a guitar string he borrowed from the Ranger."[9]

Slim also told us that with "Woody at the wheel, stories are legion." For instance, Woody liked the late-night shift, and more than once, Slim saw him "driving with his knees while eating his supper off of a plate on his lap, simultaneously balancing and reading a book on the steering wheel, and occasionally tearing a piece of a page out of the book and eating it." Woody also had

172   CHAPTER SIX

a notorious penchant for getting lost. Once, as the Riders were returning to Nashville from Kentucky, Woody yelled out to Slim, who was dozing in his bunk: "Hey Slim! Are we supposed to be going through Missouri?" No, they definitely "weren't supposed to be anywhere near Missouri." The other Riders all also endured living (gratefully) through Woody's "movie era," the "several years when he balanced a small TV on the dashboard and played movies all night long, while he was driving." Miraculously, they all survived. More recently, Slim has taken over most of the driving, with Doug doing the balance. Joey and Woody are relegated to the back seat, since those up front no longer trust them behind the wheel.[10]

Being an active road band for so many years (basically from 1979 through the present, excluding most of 2020) exacted a huge toll on both the Riders and their families. Joey's first marriage ended long before he joined the Riders, and his wife, Patti, has always been supportive of his career as a musician. Slim's second wife, Bert, traveled with the band more than any of the other wives (until Alice went to school) and became more completely involved in their performing lives as well. Her sister, Sandy Wilkerson, said that all the Riders depended on Bert because she was "like the team mom, their road manager." It's not the purpose of this biography to analyze what went on in Doug's five previous marriages or in Woody's three, although they both are currently happily married: since 2019 for Woody to Lisa Reed; since 2020 for Doug to Dezarria Donzella "Desi" Smith. But, as Doug's daughter, Sally, said, the Riders "have stayed married to each other all this time." Doug had admitted to her that he "retired" over forty years ago when he started the band. Being gone from home for weeks at a time, repeatedly many times per year, inevitably added stresses to marriages, especially when the children from multiple marriages were growing up. Patti Miskulin recalled that when their three children were very young and Joey had been on the road for three weeks, she told him that she was planning to go to the grocery store. The kids all began begging to go, and just as Joey started to grant them permission to do so, Patti said she turned into the Incredible Hulk, telling him she just wanted to go somewhere *by herself*, and, of course, he understood. Being gone so much was such a burden on Bert, as Slim told us, "With a daughter navigating high school, a ten-year-old son, and us living outside of town . . . meant long car trips to get anywhere. My daughter Lily, who lived with us some of those days, remembered it as being 'pretty much a one-woman show.'"[11]

Absence from home also meant that temptations along the way were hard to resist. Whatever the circumstances, family life was necessarily compromised. For example, in about 2000, when Don Cusic interviewed him, Woody was in his third marriage. After his divorce from his second wife, Liza, Woody married Teresa Goicoechea from Boise, Idaho, in 1989, and they had two children: Casey and Katherine Ellen (Kaitlyn). Although Teresa tried living in Nashville, Woody's repeated and lengthy absences made it too difficult to raise the two youngsters alone, and she moved back to Boise. They tried, unsuccessfully, to preserve their marriage, and were still trying to do so, when Woody told Don, "Wives . . . are awfully unhappy with musicians . . . I think that when you do what we do—spend a lot of time on the road—they're upset because you're not there and they have to raise the kids." He went on to say that many husbands are unavailable, like those in the military or who work long hours and come home exhausted. He completed his thoughts on the subject with the philosophically resigned, "So, you can't win for losing, whether you bring 'em money or you don't—it's always your fault. They're unhappy and you're the reason. I just get tired of that." Although Woody missed being with his young children, he allowed, "It's sure frustrating, but it's just the way it is."[12]

The Riders' children, now adults, shared their perspectives about growing up in families with divorce and with loving fathers who were away so much of their kids' childhood years. Slim's youngest child, George, said, "My dad told my mom when they got married that he would always be married to his work as well. That she joined in surely benefited his work and our family." Alice LaBour Fair told us that Woody's third wife, Teresa, and Bert "really leaned on each other when the guys were gone," while Doug's third wife, Dianne, and Bert were best friends. After Doug and Dianne divorced, he married Ann Marie Flores in 1998. When that marriage ended, he married Carolyn Gann ten years later, but that, too, ended in divorce, and these rather brief marriages did not result in more children. Doug admitted, "I'm a romantic guy, and if I really like someone, I tend to fall in love too soon." His children, Annie and James, concurred, "We consider Dad hopelessly romantic—just like his romantic view of the West: all grand. The band was Dad's lifelong marriage." As they worked day in and day out, year in and year out, Woody, Joey, Doug, and Slim had become much more than a touring band, they had formed a tight band of brothers.[13]

All the siblings, from multiple marriages in each family, had good relationships with one another as they were growing up, no matter what the tensions were between their parents. And Slim and Doug also maintained friendly relations with the mothers of their kids, even after divorce. The Riders' children's best-remembered times, of course, were playing backstage at the Grand Ole Opry, at Opryland, or summers when families often traveled with the Riders to state fairs, amusement parks, and other family-oriented venues. Except for the panic-inducing times their children sometimes wandered off at a venue and were feared lost—Woody's Jake got away from his folks in Indianapolis and Rebecca in Louisville; Joey's Katie temporarily disappeared at a crowded Christmastime Opryland—both parents and kids enjoyed the times spent together on the road or at the Opry. Woody's oldest boys, Paul and Joe, Doug's oldest girls, Liza and Sally, and their stepbrother, Turner, were all peers, with Slim's kids, Frank and Lily, just a bit younger. The next group of Riders' children, Alice LaBour, Annie and James Green, and Rebecca and Jake Chrisman formed the next set; then Grace Green, Casey and Kaitlin Chrisman, and George LaBour. Katie Miskulin spent time with the youngest girls. Annie told us it was like having extra brothers and sisters. Lily recalled the older kids—unsupervised!—running around backstage at the Opry, eating popcorn and drinking punch in the green room, playing, then falling asleep in the dressing room amid the smells of guitar cases, waking up back home; "rolling down interstates while Woody practiced the fiddle for hours and hours." James and Annie conjured up other sensations of the road: "Woody's chewing tobacco, stale coffee, the food and the rides [at amusement parks and fairs]." Woody had outfitted at least two of the vans with a thin mattress in a loft or platform above the driver's seat, which became a nook where all the kids could travel together. Grace Green remembered being in the RV with Woody driving and telling ghost stories to his young listeners. All the kids worked at the Mercantile during summers and school holidays, likely beginning with Liza Jane, who started when she was twelve. Looking back at what he sees as the "mythic quality of traveling around America," George LaBour said that his dad would sleep on the couch so that George could have his bunk when they were on the road. He also recalled Woody trying to fix the RV at every gas station. While Opryland adventures colored the memories of the oldest of the children, the younger ones relished their times at the Tweetsie Railroad Park in Blowing Rock, North Carolina, which became a beloved Rider tradition every summer from 1997 on (except for 2020).[14]

The Riders always looked forward to their own annual visits to Tweetsie Railroad Park where their children could delight in the many forms of available entertainment. Patti and the Miskulin kids, who did not otherwise make road trips, all enjoyed visiting Tweetsie when the Riders were performing. Named for a narrow-gauge mountain railroad that ran from Johnson City to Boone between 1918 and 1940, it became known as "Tweetsie" for its shrill and distinctive whistle "tweets." The amusement park featured a Wild West–themed village, populated by costumed cowboys and cowgirls, and two steam-powered locomotives, one of which—number 12—had been owned briefly by Gene Autry. Visitors can enjoy a twenty-minute train journey through the Smokies on the narrow-gauge line. The park provided western music since at least 1959, when Fred Kirby, a longtime fixture on WBT in Charlotte, became a popular kiddie sensation as a singing sheriff. The Riders made their debut at Tweetsie in 1981, as Doug wrote, "playing six or seven fifteen-minute shows in the saloon, alternating with the dancing girls and a Mark Twain impersonator." After a sixteen-year hiatus, they returned in 1997 as "featured artists," where they played two hour-long shows each day, and which they continue to perform annually.[15]

The Riders were always immediately alert to spontaneously responding with humor to any unforeseen circumstances. A dedicated fan from Cincinnati, Donna Jagodzinski, first saw the Riders when they were doing their *Riders Radio Theater* performances there and recorded every show. She has seen the Riders close to two hundred times, and along with her husband, Ed, has enjoyed seeing them at Tweetsie. Donna suffers from MS, and she and Ed took their old and well-behaved service dog, Bob, with them—a veteran of many Riders' concerts—as well as April, a younger Norwegian elk hound Ed was in the process of training. When Doug started yodeling, April began "yodeling" along with him. When Ed pointed out April to the Riders, Too Slim started egging her on, barking at her, so she started barking back at him. In 2002 the Riders commemorated their experiences at Tweetsie with an album of train songs, *Ridin' on the Tweetsie Railroad*, which was sold at the park. Consisting of a mixture of self-penned and traditional songs—like "Casey Jones," "Rock Island Line," and "I've Been Working on the Railroad"—it was their nineteenth album, and the first produced independently of a record company. Five years later, the Riders celebrated their thirtieth anniversary at the park, and by happenstance, Tweetsie was also commemorating its fiftieth anniversary, as North Carolina's first theme park.

Donna Jagodzinski posing with her dogs and the Riders at Tweetsie Railroad. Collection of Donna and Ed Jagodzinski, courtesy Tweetsie Railroad.

Now that the Riders' own children have children of their own, these young families are partaking of the tradition, as they did in the summer of 2023.[16]

The Riders' twenty-fifth anniversary occurred in 2002, the same year that they recorded *Ridin' on the Tweetsie Railroad*, and it turned out to be a banner year for the group. An issue of *Western Music* magazine honored the Riders, and their anniversary was celebrated at various sites around the country. When the Western Music Association met at Sam's Town in Las Vegas that November, they won, for the second year in a row, Entertainer of the Year, and won the Traditional Western Album of the Year award for *Riders In The Sky Present a Pair of Kings*, a recording that featured their two instrumental aces, Woody Paul and Joey Miskulin. With songs as diverse as "Texas Sand," Johnny Mercer's "I'm an Old Cowhand," "Clarinet Polka," "How High the Moon," and "Never Go to Church on Sunday," the two musicians demonstrated their wide-ranging versatility and ability to play off each other's skills. They also sang on several numbers. Joey won instrumentalist of the year as well. Slim was quoted, rightly, as saying "It means we are still alive and kicking, still bringing good energy and creativity to the hoedown." To top it off, at the Las Vegas convention on November 15—almost exactly

Band of Brothers

twenty-five years after that first night at Herr Harry's—they were roasted at a dinner by a host of friends and celebrities. Texas Bix Bender served as "roastmaster," and "roasters" included Ray Benson, Alan Sacks, Pixar's John Lasseter, and a special surprise roast by Tommy Smothers. One of the "statistics" that Too Slim included in the program is particularly telling, "Hours Onstage, *Our True Home* [italics ours] . . . 6,355." The last of these: "Number of times thanked from the stage of the Academy Awards in front of an audience of 1,000,000,000 . . . 1;" he followed with "Well, that's 25 years. Seems like 250 years on some days, but on others, when the sound is good, the audience is hot, the boys are playing and singing their hearts out, it feels like that first time . . . See you in 25 more . . . on November 11, 2027." And, as we are writing, we're edging ever closer to that date.[17]

Just two days after the roast, the Riders were on a ship in Hawai'i, the advance brochure inviting their fans to accompany them for a seven-day cruise aboard the *Norwegian Star*, to visit the islands of Maui, Kaua'i, O'ahu, Hawai'i, and Fanning. The literature promised touring during the day and listening to "the relaxing sounds of the Riders after sunset as we sail on to our next port." What a way to continue the twenty-fifth anniversary celebration—adding the islands to their itinerary as the fiftieth state in which they had played! This cruise was not the Riders' first; in 1998, they had sailed from Brazil to Uruguay and Argentina. One cruise seemed to beget another. The twenty-first century found the band aboard several other cruises with the Grand Ole Opry to the west coast of Mexico, to the Caribbean, and to Cozumel on country music cruises, and stateside aboard the *American Queen*, on the upper Mississippi River in Wisconsin and Minnesota in mid-September, when fall color is at its most vibrant.[18]

The following year, in 2003, they released *Silver Jubilee*, which consisted of two CDs, with several bonus tracks. The cleverly designed CD cover depicted the four Riders carved into stone on Mount Rushmore. The album consisted of a wide-ranging anthology of their best material, including humor and skits. Reviewer Steven Stone accurately assessed the Riders' magic: "Pulling off a successful musical parody is tough. Keeping the parody going for over twenty-five years is nearly impossible, but Riders In The Sky did just that. I don't care how cool, how *outre*, how bleeding-edge your musical tastes may be, if you don't like Riders In The Sky, you're a square."[19]

The Riders extended their silver anniversary achievements by being inducted into the Walk of Western Stars in 2003, in Oldtown Newhall,

Santa Clarita, California. Enshrined on a bronze plaque implanted in a terrazzo tile, the Riders' names joined a stellar cast of honorees that included Gene Autry, Roy Rogers, Gary Cooper, John Wayne, Tom Mix, and William S. Hart. In the northern valley of Los Angeles County, Santa Clarita had often served as a site where John Ford and other illustrious western directors and producers liked to film, which made it an ideal setting for the Walk of Western Stars. The induction ceremony appropriately occurred in conjunction with the city's acclaimed cowboy festival. Honoring the media legends who had contributed to "America's heritage," the event, in large measure, validated the Riders as an authentic facet of the western myth.[20]

Although his almost fifty years' of experiences playing with the Riders remains Doug's most significant commitment and pleasure, he has not confined his performances to western music. At the Opry in the late 1990s, a group of all-star musicians enjoyed jamming backstage as a respite from the music they played on the Opry or in Nashville's many music sessions. In 1998, they began to call themselves the Time Jumpers. Sometimes Doug sat in with them. The principal founders were veteran performers: fiddler Hubert Dwane "Hoot" Hester and bassist Dennis Crouch, both staff musicians at the Opry (along with their other myriad activities) who began playing western swing with each other in Hester's garage. From there they took their music to dressing room six at the Opry and soon found other musicians eager to play with them. According to one of its longtime members, lead guitarist Andy Riess, the band took its name from a statement made one night by Hoot. After Dennis told him that he had missed a beat, Hoot retorted that he had come from a long line of time jumpers.[21]

In December 2000, Doug, well-known for his abilities as a strong rhythm guitar player, was asked to join. As Kenny Sears, a veteran Time Jumpers fiddler, said, "It really started out as a therapy session. It's just nice to be able to play what you want to play and play it the way you want to play without the constraints of having to try to please whoever you're trying to make a record *for*." Doug echoed this observation: "I don't have to front the band and remember jokes and make up the set list and drive 500 miles. I just get to show up and play with people I respect enormously." The Time Jumpers love traditional country music. Dennis, for example, had an impressive history as a bluegrass bass player, but he and the others strongly enjoyed the western swing of Bob Wills, Spade Cooley, Hank Thompson, and others. In a sense, the Time Jumpers thrived because of a renewed interest in western swing that got underway after 1970 when Merle Haggard recorded a tribute album to Bob Wills, *A Tribute to the Best Damn Fiddle Player in the World*, which Andy Riess called "a landmark record." At about the same time, Ray Benson (born Ray Benson Seifert, in Philadelphia, Pennsylvania) moved his great band, Asleep at the Wheel, away from the roots music they were playing, and began playing western swing exclusively.[22]

The Time Jumpers took their music to Station Inn, a bluegrass-oriented venue in Nashville, on Monday evenings, a traditionally "slow" night for clubs. At first, their audience consisted primarily of other musicians who appreciated their talents or fans who sought alternatives to the standard Nashville fare. But soon, the eleven-person band, with its frontline of three fiddlers, and its great singer, Dawn Sears, was the talk of Nashville and a tourist designation in a city crawling with musicians of all stripes. The group's popularity only grew stronger—even as its music grew a bit more country—when, in 2010, country superstar Vince Gill joined, like Doug, content to put his stage persona aside and just be one of the boys. The crowds strained the confines of the small club, as news of this innovative and creative band spread far and wide.[23]

On June 11, 2012, the band moved to Third and Lindsley, a much larger venue better equipped to accommodate the increasingly large audience. Thronging to hear the best musicians that Nashville had to offer, listeners also included occasional visitors such as Bonnie Raitt, Elvis Costello, Robert Plant, Reba McEntire, Jimmy Buffett, and Norah Jones, who were sometimes invited to take the stage. Doug usually sits unobtrusively at the back of the throng, playing rhythm on his vintage Stromberg guitar—one of only 640 guitars made in Boston by the father and son team, Charles and Elmer Stromberg, between 1906 and 1955. Stromberg guitars, distinguished for their big nineteen-inch width, remain famous for their volume, a quality that made them useful for a jazz band. As a connoisseur and collector of guitars, Doug also values playing his somewhat smaller DeLuxe model Stromberg, especially since Freddie Green had played a Stromberg while providing the rhythmic core of the Count Basie band from 1937 to 1987. Like his jazz mentor, Doug sees the rhythm guitarist as "the ultimate team player" whose role is to provide total support for the soloists and singers. With both the Riders and the Time Jumpers, he employs the Freddie Green style, playing mostly three-note chords, using five or six strings, with three of the strings muted. The chord changes occur each half measure; consequently, Doug's left, or chording, hand is constantly moving. He told Chip Chandler, an Oklahoma PBS producer, "As a rhythm guitarist, I'm all about the feel, all about the pulse.... My job in the band is the beautiful heartbeat, and I love that role." During each Time Jumpers' show, all of which are unscripted, Doug does sing and yodel a few songs with the band. One of his most popular numbers has been "Bloodshot Eyes," from the repertory of the pioneer western swing musician Hank Penny. Doug played on two Grammy-nominated albums with the band, *The Time Jumpers* and *Kid Sister*, both on the Rounder label; the band won the Grammy for Best American Roots Song in 2017 for Vince Gill's, "Kid Sister."[24]

Doug has kept his guitar chops fit by playing with the Time Jumpers as well as the Riders, and while Too Slim exudes the most onstage energy, offstage, both he and Doug exercise at the gym religiously. Doug also employs another form of exercise, reading. When not taking his turn behind the wheel of the bus as the Riders tour, Doug reads. Just as he keeps meticulous statistics of where and when the band has played, he maintained a list of his progress on the 1,001 books that "you must read before you die," an ambitious—and somewhat arbitrary—list that one hundred scholars created and packaged into a book first published in 2006. Knowing how much the former academic liked to read, Too Slim gave him the list, which Doug completed in five years (2014), sometimes with pleasure, sometimes without, but always with his well-known persistence to achieve a goal he set for himself.[25]

Although playing with symphonies was never a Riders goal, they certainly enjoyed doing so, as they had as early as 1981 when they initiated that aspect of their career performing with the Houston Pops Symphony. Although they did not have another opportunity to play in such a setting until 1998 when they played in Florida with the Jacksonville Symphony, they began to be booked increasingly for more performances during the next decade, beginning in 2000 when they played with symphonies in Jacksonville; Williamsport, Pennsylvania; Milwaukee; and St. Louis. These collaborations probably came about because of the notoriety won by their association with Disney and *Toy Story 2*. On July 20 and 21, 2001, they played with the Utah Symphony, featuring a medley of songs from *Toy Story 2*. The Cincinnati Pops and the Pittsburgh Orchestra (with Marvin Hamlisch) had also been scheduled. Doug argued that it should not seem unusual for western songs to be played in symphonic fashion:

If you think about it, every great Western had these beautiful themes that worked perfectly with the symphonic sound [he could have added "The William Tell Overture" that introduced *The Lone Ranger* radio and television shows]. And in fact, many of the songs almost seem to be written to be put to symphony accompaniment. It's actually a beautiful match. You stand up there singing "Tumbling Tumbleweeds," and you feel like you walked out of a John Ford Western in 1948. It's that big, sweeping sound that perfectly accompanies those big, sweeping melodies.[26]

To celebrate the Fourth of July, 2007, the Riders played again at their favorite arena, the Hollywood Bowl. This "Salute to the West" featured the band, along with the Los Angeles Philharmonic, paying tribute to Gene Autry and John Wayne, in honor of the centennial of their births. The performance began with the Philharmonic tribute to Wayne, including a montage of film clips from three of the actor's most-beloved films. The Riders appeared in the second half of the performance, dedicated to Autry, and presented a clip of him singing "Don't Bite the Hand That's Feeding You" from *Bells of Capistrano* rather than the better known and more popular number, "When

The Riders at the Hollywood Bowl with Bowl conductor Edwin Outwater. Riders In The Sky Archives, courtesy New Frontier Touring.

the Swallows Come Back to Capistrano." The event had a slight ideological bent, not simply because of Autry's and Wayne's politics, but also because the song selected from this film was an anti-immigrant number written in 1915.[27]

The Riders, however, neither chose nor endorsed the politics of the song. Only two of the Riders are political—Doug and Slim—both of whom are progressives, and that song and the overall theme did not reflect their own views. In their music they have stayed clear of the machismo and right-wing politics that has too often characterized the world of singing cowboys, feeling instead that their mission is to celebrate the beauty and wholesome community of western culture. On the other hand, few western songs, if any, document the multiracial nature of that culture. The songs the Riders have sung and continue to sing—including the "classics" from the 1930s and 1940s or those the Riders have contributed to the genre—still present the mythic picture shaped by Hollywood's singing cowboy films: that of white-hatted Anglo cowboys. In the decades that followed the Riders' emergence as a cowboy band, a wealth of historical literature appeared to more accurately capture the history of the cowboy and the West—studies that brought women, Native people, and other ethnic groups to the fore while sometimes presenting the seamier side of the region's history. Dom Flemons, founder of the former all-Black string band the Carolina Chocolate Drops, in 2018 produced a well-received album, *Black Cowboys*, that successfully challenged the myth of white exclusivity in the West by presenting a variety of cowboy songs that came from African American tradition. In his recent photography book, *Eight Seconds*, Ivan McClellan documented an all-Black thriving rodeo culture he had discovered in Oklahoma. Doug and Slim are well aware of these new perspectives and cognizant that their music does not reflect the complexities of this historical and social reality. Slim told journalist Steve Hochman, as recently as 2018,

> We are of our time.... And what we foster is a good feeling, an escape in a way... a reinforcement of timeless values of contentment, sincerity, being true to your word and humor. And I think that's why people still come back to our shows. They like the feeling we engender on stage.... But we all recognize that there was part of the West that had to do with genocide, the underbelly of American history. We're aware of that.[28]

The Riders posing with Wilford Brimley at the Opry. Photograph by Chris Hollio, image courtesy Grand Ole Opry Archives.

Since the Riders never let their own political views interfere with playing the music they loved or with whom they loved playing it, they had no hesitance in recording with the veteran character actor, raconteur, and conservative Republican Wilford Brimley, in 2013. *Home on the Range*, a collection of mostly sentimental country and cowboy songs, was a perfect meeting of the minds. Brimley had appeared in numerous movies and television series, such as *The Natural, Cocoon,* and *The Walton Family*. He was also a good singer, with some recording experience. Only a couple of overtly western songs appear on the album made with the Riders—the title cut and "I'd Love to Be in Texas, When They Roundup in the Spring," but it is an affecting album with such classic country songs as "That Silver Haired Daddy of Mine," "Roly Poly," "Won't You Ride in My Little Red Wagon," and "Put Me in Your Pocket." The most contemporary song on the album, and probably Brimley's favorite of the lot, was the 1957 country hit, "Fraulein." The Riders also appeared with Brimley on the Grand Ole Opry and *Larry's Country Diner*, a show hosted by longtime country DJ Larry Black, from Branson, Missouri, on RFD-TV. Recalling Brimley a few days after his death in 2020, Too Slim said that "the stories and jokes between takes are what I remember most. He could spin a ten-minute joke to where you couldn't breathe from laughing so hard, and then sing 'Danny Boy' and break your heart." Two years later, the Riders did a tribute album, *Riders In The Sky Salute Roy Rogers: King of the Cowboys*. Rogers was now deceased, but they had performed with him during his lifetime, including spots on the Grand Ole Opry and *Hee Haw*. The album included several of Rogers's most popular songs, such as "Along the Navajo Trail," "Blue Shadows on the Trail," and "Happy Trails," but also included Slim doing his own composition, "A Tribute to Gabby Hayes,"[29] a longtime sidekick of Rogers.

In the spirit of tributes, Doug and Slim (as Side Meat) in 2006 put together their own weekly radio show, *Ranger Doug's Classic Cowboy Corral* on Sirius XM. Eddie Kilroy (born Alva Dave Moore, and a rodeo cowboy before becoming a Nashville producer) had been hosting a cowboy-themed show on Sirius, but Doug believed that too few classic songs were being played, and that consequently the full range of cowboy music was not being presented. He persuaded the people at Sirius to let him host the show. Doug puts together the shows from what he has in his library: always Roy, Gene, Tex Ritter, and then entertainers like Foy Willing, Andy Parker, Carolina Cotton, or Rosalie Allen. He described the process to us: "I burn a CD, then I give that to Joey, and he processes them. Then Slim and I fly to Cleveland, do three or four shows a day. We did 'Cowboys Salute World War II,' for example ... Weekly, we've got Sidekick Corner, Old Time Disc of the Day, one instrumental." With Joey producing and recording the show, first at his home in Nashville, and later in Kirtland, Ohio (about thirty miles from Cleveland, where he'd eventually moved), the programs run on weekend evenings: Saturday, then repeat on Sunday. A typical recording session in Ohio begins with a trip to the Y by the boys and then a series of tapings that permit the duo to make about twelve or thirteen shows. Ranger Doug plays a few vintage cowboy songs, while Side Meat offers nonsensical commentary. Slim says that "my job is to be the sidekick and to interrupt him all the time." They receive no compensation for the show nor for the expense of getting to and from Cleveland, but they enjoy getting the songs they love on the air for those who appreciate them and for those who are being introduced to these vintage numbers.[30]

Ranger Doug's Classic Cowboy Corral functions as a logical extension of the Riders' oeuvre, but the band also enjoyed the opportunity to play once more with classically trained musicians. Arguably, the Riders most significant classical collaboration came with the Nashville Symphony in February 2009, which, like the 2007 Hollywood Bowl event, took place over three nights—completely sold out—sandwiched between their performances in the Livingston, Texas, high school auditorium and the Grand Ole Opry. Thirteen of the songs, recorded live, appeared on the album *Lassoed Live at the Schermerhorn*. Backed by the lush instrumental sound of the Nashville orchestra, the Riders attained what they believed was a high-water mark in their career. Doug declared that "it was the best we've ever done. It was a rush for all of us." The Western Music Association apparently agreed, because it named the recording as its album of the year in 2010 (one of three awards that the Riders received that year from the WMA). He told journalist Don Rhodes that although they'd played with other symphonies, they had never before recorded one of these collaborative shows, and "It feels wonderful having a huge orchestra behind you; like being on the music soundtrack of an old John Wayne western movie. It's an incredible physical experience that translates so well to western music." Rhodes interviewed Doug before the Riders' appearance with the Augusta Symphony Pops on March 18, and he asked what the Ranger thought when, just weeks earlier, at 6:53 a.m. on February 26, NASA Mission Control played the Riders' recording of "Woody's Roundup" from *Toy Story 2* to awaken crew members on the final mission of the Space Shuttle *Discovery*. "Wasn't that amazing?" Doug replied. "We just loved it. That was just something that came out of the blue. We didn't know it was going to happen and read about it on the Internet like everybody else."[31]

While the Riders' "Woody's Roundup" played aboard the *Discovery*, the Riders themselves played on western dude ranches that recalled the memories of real working ranch roundups. As railroads, and then automobiles, opened the West to tourists, especially from the Northeast and the Midwest, the presence of dude ranches grew, especially in Texas, Colorado, and Wyoming. The mid-twentieth-century spate of cowboy films and singing cowboys contributed to a boom in tourism for tamed reenactments of the mythical West, and Riders In The Sky have done their part to keep the tradition vibrant for the late twentieth and early twenty-first centuries. After meeting Ken Jones, owner of Home Ranch in Clark, Colorado, when the Riders first performed there in 1988, Ken graciously offered the band members the chance to return solely for a week, bringing their families along, singing some each day, and otherwise enjoying the activities that the dude ranch offered. Doug brought two of his children, Annie and James, with him at least one summer and Grace along on another in what became the family vacation for those years, and Liza Jane worked at Home Ranch one summer when she was in college. Slim and Bert and their kids often vacationed at the ranch during the Christmas holidays, with Slim's two sisters joining them. The cover of the Riders' 1992 album, *Merry Christmas from Harmony Ranch*, was photographed at Home Ranch with Doug and Woody atop the ranch's old chuckwagon and Slim standing beside it after they "hauled it out in the snow, even though it was April." Ken also credits the Riders for encouraging him to record his own album, *Ken Jones: Meanwhile . . . Back at the Ranch*. Joey produced the entertaining recording, and Doug and Slim joined him on the vocals, with Slim on the bass.[32]

On one of those trips to the Home Ranch, Doug and Gary McMahan did a side excursion to a festival in Colorado. Doug invited Gary to drive somewhere with him and his two kids. While he and Doug were writing a song ("The First Cowboy Song)" in the front seat, Annie and James played with bows and arrows in the back seat. Every so often, a rubber-tipped arrow whizzed between the two songwriters and hit the windshield. Despite the bizarre circumstances of the song's creation, it appeared on Gary's *Saddle 'Em Up and Go* album and on the Riders' *Always Drink Upstream from the Herd*. Even better, the song won a Wrangler award twice, the only song to achieve that distinction, and Gary and Doug have been "fast friends ever since."[33]

Every year from 1998 through 2019, the Riders entertained at the Bar D Chuckwagon, a cowboy supper club, with music, in Durango, Colorado. The Bar D had been cofounded in 1969 by Cy Scarborough, Big Jim Blanton, and Buck Teeter, all of whom had entertained at the original western chuckwagon, the Flying W Ranch, in Colorado Springs. Cy, a longtime western comedian and singer, maintained a resident band, the Bar D Wranglers, whose primary mission was, in Doug's words, "preserving western music and carrying on the tradition." Doug considered Cy a "genius comedian," whose chuckwagon was one of several inspired by the first of this brand of food-and-entertainment site. Currently, six chuckwagons exist in the West, and most feature a little pioneer village and offer family-friendly entertainment and solid country cooking, traditionally open from Memorial Day weekend through Labor Day. When we spoke with Gary Cook, National Flatpicking Guitar Champion and the Bar D's lead guitarist, he had been playing at the chuckwagon since 1989, where he got to know the Riders very well. Gary and the Bar D Wranglers played with the Riders at the Bar D and on the Grand Old Opry. He and Doug recorded *Springtime in the Rockies*, a CD with both traditional and original songs, the latter the creations of both performers. Gary even filled in for Slim on the road while he recovered from a broken wrist and some fingers, injuries that happened in the bus accident in December 2016, after the Riders had left Eagle, Colorado.[34]

Slim told us that he always enjoyed playing at chuckwagons because it reminded him of his childhood in the 1950s, driving out west for family vacations on dude ranches. "Dinner at chuckwagons felt like an adventure, eating off of tin plates, hearing cowboy music, lots of jokes. It was really fun." Then, as a performer, think of the joy to be giving families the same kind of experience as a member of the Riders! In the summer of 2002 when wildfires were burning all over the mountain West, Slim, Bert, and their children were vacationing at Home Ranch before meeting up with the rest of the Riders at the Bar D. Two days before they left for Durango, Slim learned that the Missionary Ridge fire near Durango had destroyed the Bar D, but found out the following morning that brave Cy Scarborough, his crew, and professional firefighters had fought like mad and finally saved it. When the LaBours arrived, they saw that "stumps were still smoking [and] ash was everywhere right up practically to the stage." The honored guests at the Riders' performance were the firefighters. When Cy thanked each individually by name, Slim reported, "there was not a dry eye in the house."[35]

Musician, broadcasting engineer, writer, DJ, and lover of bluegrass and western music, Nebraska native Orin Friesen had admired Doug's music scholarship long before he booked the Riders in Wichita (early December 1981), in between their scheduled dates in Wellington, Kansas, and York, Nebraska. From 1999 to 2008, Orin led the Prairie Rose Wranglers, the house band for the Prairie Rose Chuckwagon Supper in Benton, Kansas, a venue owned by promoter extraordinaire, Thomas Etheredge. The Riders played at the Prairie Rose several times between 2002 and 2006, but their most memorable experience performing with this and similar organizations, however, occurred far from Wichita. Etheredge had organized what he called the Great American Cowboy Concert held at Carnegie Hall in 2003 and 2004. The Prairie Rose Wranglers played both years, while the Riders were part of the sold-out show the second year. Also appearing with them was their old friend, Johnny Western—composer of "The Ballad of Paladin"—who'd performed annually for several years at the Prairie Rose. Johnny thought that the Carnegie Hall show was great, and he felt that it was "wonderful to see that kind of [positive] reaction in New York City." Slim and Doug, however, remembered the event quite differently. Slim said that Etheredge's boorish, rude behavior, and his bullying of a youth choir that performed that night, obliterated anything positive about the concert, rendering the event a nightmare. But while Etheredge's shady ethics eventually caught up with him and landed him in prison, the Riders' friendship with Johnny and Orin endured. Doug told us that when he was heavily into his research on country music pioneer Carson Robison, Orin drove Doug around southeast Kansas and to the Robison archives at Pittsburg State University, for which the Ranger was immensely appreciative.[36]

Although the Riders' other venues may not share the prestige of Carnegie Hall, they engendered much warmer memories for the band. For example, they appeared at Cain's Ballroom in Tulsa on April 14, 2012, a venerable site that had served as the headquarters for Bob Wills and His Texas Playboys from 1935 to 1942. The ballroom was an appropriate spot, not only for the Riders' brand of western swing but also for the simultaneous induction of Woody Paul into the National Fiddlers Hall of Fame, along with other fiddle greats, Herman Johnson, Keith Coleman, and Kenny Baker. Each of the living inductees (and in Woody's case, the Riders) entertained with a few songs. Woody has often described his unique fiddling style as "traditional," but he has modestly neglected to reveal *how many* traditions he has mastered—from jazz to bluegrass to Cajun to Irish as well as country music and cowboy. Whatever the style, Slim has rightly noted that the King of Cowboy Fiddlers defined a vital aspect of the Riders' sound. Woody further added that playing with the Riders constantly encouraged him to keep experimenting, "looking for something new." Slim told us that legendary jazz player, arranger, and composer David Amram, "used to show up at folk festivals and club gigs and jam with whomever" and seemed particularly interested in Woody's playing. Slim quoted Amram, saying that Woody is "the encyclopedia of correct licks." Not bad for a PhD physicist from Triune, Tennessee.[37]

The Riders' name and music also circulated widely on commercials, promoting such products as Levi's 501 jeans, Taco Bell, Budweiser, Coke, Cheer, and for Opryland (during its twenty-fifth anniversary in 1996). They also made public service announcements for the National Park Service, but, beyond a doubt, their most unique commercial endeavor was the spots made for Yella Fella in 2008, ads promoted by the Alabama lumber company, Great Southern Wood. *The Tales of the Yella Fella* series featured owner Jimmy Rane, dressed in mostly yellow attire, promoting the product of his company, YellaWood—a pressure-treated pine, mainly used in exterior building projects. Rane first hired commercial filmmaker and musician Norton Dill's company in 1986 to produce and film commercials for Great Southern, and he and Rane have done business together since then. Rane had always loved cowboy movies and was "a fanatic about John Wayne." In fact, he insisted that the episodic YellaWood commercials be shot on 35 mm film, the standard film for all motion pictures, even though a lot of commercials were shot using less expensive 16 mm film.[38]

In the Yella Fella short films that recreated the westerns of the 1930s and 1940s, Rane appeared as a cowboy character in the mold of Wayne and similar cowboys, fighting against villains and saving the virtuous. And along the way he showed the value of his product in preserving longtime buildings and structures. The episodes were filmed in Arizona, Utah, and Monument Valley, an iconic western location near the Arizona-Utah border where John Ford had shot many of his films. The Riders were ecstatic to be exactly where the great western movies were filmed. After the series was launched in 2008, the Riders, who came in for season 2, introduced each show with a song (authored by Joey) standing against a backdrop of splendid western topography. Some of the shooting was rigorous and difficult for both actors and crew. Dill said that "there was a lot of moving around shooting in the desert, and the stagecoach scenes when you're far from civilization really get hard. They had to encase the camera in plastic to keep the dust out." Even though the Riders stood in the heat with their instruments and in all their regalia, they did much to lighten the mood of the occasion, at least psychologically, playing cowboy music for Jimmy Rane and the rest of his entourage. Rane was happy being entertained by the most outstanding cowboy group in the country. Dill said that they spent three weeks out West, with the first week for preproduction and the last two for shooting.[39]

The "most outstanding cowboy group in the country" continued to rack up new devoted fans and to keep on keeping on as they celebrated their fortieth anniversary—and show #7,180—at Nashville's City Winery on November 12, 2017. They issued a glossy lavishly illustrated magazine-brochure, *Riders In The Sky: 40 Years the Cowboy Way*, and announced a forthcoming new album, *Forty Years the Cowboy Way*, on their own Riders Radio Records label. The Riders' anniversary tour took them to Durango,

The Riders entertaining the Yella Fella at Monument Valley. Photograph courtesy Jimmy Rane and YellaWood.

Colorado, for a two-night gig at the Bar D, joining the Bar D Wranglers for comedy and music that celebrated the West. In an interview with Katie Chicklinski-Cahill from Durango, the Ranger talked about the key to their longevity: "The real secret is separate hotel rooms. You need your space if you're together 40 years, let me tell you." Much of the Riders' perseverance and pleasure derives from their larger mission of innovation within the tradition of the singing cowboy; as Doug said to Katie, "We are in the business of entertainment, making people laugh and have fun, but we're also in the business of keeping this music alive and presenting it to the next generation so that this wonderful, uniquely American style of music can continue to live."[40]

The Riders' extensive celebratory tour was tragically tempered on Friday, January 26, when Slim lost his beloved Roberta after her seventeen-year bout with cancer. Even as she battled the disease, she was still giving to those around her. Her sister Sandy remarked how Bert taught women at Gilda's Club how to deal with wigs, false eyelashes, and to cope with their cancer. Bert's obituary noted that "she was the quintessential backstage person... who took great joy from standing in the wings seeing something beautiful she made in the spotlight." Slim had told us early on that he and Bert "brought out the best

Ranger Doug: truly, the Idol of American Youth. Photograph by Erick Anderson, courtesy New Frontier Touring.

in each other." The celebration of her life was held at Christ Church Cathedral in Nashville, the spiritual center that had anchored the LaBour family's religious faith. Less than a week later, on February 4, when the Riders played at the Western Folklife Center in Elko, veteran bass player Mark Abbott replaced Slim. The year 2018 had become a solemn memorial of the couple's storied supportive relationship, and soon after his soulmate's death, Slim began writing a series of "Bert Poems," some serious, and some funny, which he sent to his children. His active spiritual life at Christ Church Cathedral and support of his children and his Riders "family" ultimately helped Slim transition back to the life of touring and performing. The joy in making others smile and laugh ultimately provided its own kind of fulfillment to compensate, if not cover, the loss of his life's partner.[41]

On March 27, 2019, America's best-known documentary filmmaker Ken Burns and his longtime narrative writer and collaborator, Dayton Duncan, hosted an evening at Nashville's historic Ryman Auditorium. The recorded event featured some of country music's leading performers highlighted in

Joey the Cowpolka King, doing what he does best. Photograph by Erick Anderson, New Frontier Touring.

The Riders rehearsing for *Country Music: Live at the Ryman*, the concert that introduced the Ken Burns's PBS series, *Country Music*. Photograph by Erika Goldring, image courtesy Grand Ole Opry Archives.

the *Country Music* series and served as a provocative introduction to launch the entire eight episodes that aired the following fall. Riders In The Sky were among those, such as Vince Gill, Kathy Mattea, Marty Stuart, and Rhiannon Giddens, chosen to play that night—quite a coup for the band. Duncan explained, "All of the talented artists who performed at the Ryman also appear in our film, as commentators or as characters or as both.... But on this night, they sang and played the music they love, brought the crowd to tears and to their feet, and in one concert took us all on an unforgettable journey across time, one song at a time." Terry Gross's interviewing of the Ranger on her popular NPR show, *Fresh Air*, was a welcome spin-off from the Ken Burns experience; the appearance gave the Riders additional and welcome publicity.[42]

One of the most significant additions to the Riders' schedule in the twenty-first century was their participation in the giant Bonnaroo Music and Arts Festival—named for a Cajun expression for party or celebration. Held over a four-day period on a 700-acre farm near Manchester, Tennessee, the festival began in 2002 as a tribute to New Orleans–style music, but typically featured multiple stages presenting virtually every type of music heard in the United States. Although shut down during 2020 because of the pandemic, each year the event attracted 60,000 or more. The Riders appeared at the festival in 2018 and 2019 as part of an array of Grand Ole Opry acts. After the 2018 event, Doug was quoted as saying, "We found out the huge audience of mud-caked millennials knew the chorus to 'Ghost Riders,' which they sang along with at top-volume. And they really, really, really liked Too Slim's 'Eminem Rap.'" And the Ranger told a journalist before the 2019 festival, "The response was tremendous last time. We got a lot of great press out of it and as soon as we broke into 'Woody's Roundup' all the kids jumped up. It was just very exciting." He may have been thinking, too, of the vivid contrast between the reception they received at Bonnaroo with the disastrous audience response way back in 1982 at the US Festival in California.[43]

The year 2020 began well, although, as Slim reported, "Joey was MIA ... his back finally had enough of supporting a heavy accordion; his shoulder cried out for mercy; his fingers were a mess; he needed a lot of work done." He was staying at home in Ohio, spending the year getting his body back in shape by undergoing twelve surgeries; he only returned to the Riders in March 2021, although he continued to produce *Classic Cowboy Corral* on Sirius XM for Doug and Slim. Otherwise, "Jeff Taylor rode to the rescue when Joey was out." Jeff was from near Batavia, New York, but grew up west of Rochester. Like Joey, he had been exposed to music since he was a child. His dad had a polka band, and his mom was Polish and loved polkas. "I always thought that the accordion was the weakest instrument, but God made it my calling card. He put Joey, Slim, Woody, and Doug in my life to be a friend to me." Jeff had always loved the music of Roy Rogers, Spade Cooley, western swing, Commander Cody, various styles that prepared him for the Time Jumpers, where he and Doug also got to know each other well. Slim said, "Jeff is still first call when we need a sub, usually on the Opry. He likes calling himself Faux Joe." Jeff also bonded with the band on their very first road trip, sitting up "until three in the morning listening to Slim tell the craziest stories." He'd bought a couple of cheap cowboy shirts for the tour, but the second night out, "Doug held up a Manuel shirt that ... fit me like a glove, and Doug told me to just hang on to it" because he'd never fit into that shirt again. Doug also gave him a white hat, and Jeff wears both when performing with the Riders, an experience he relishes since "whenever I get onstage with them, I feel like I need to buy a ticket... they just bring a form of entertainment from another age and another time."[44]

Even though the Riders had been on the touring trail for over forty years, things were going about as well as possible for an older group, as Paul Lohr indicated. Talking about the years after 2010, he wrote, "Artists' careers ebb and flow, and... they averaged approximately $550,000 a year, until... THE PANDEMIC! The entire music industry in fact had fallen off a cliff. It was almost a miracle that 2020 saw them earn any money... $175,000 gross to be exact." The Riders had performed forty-eight times between January 2 and March 14, but once the pandemic hit, they did not play again until October and only had nine gigs the rest of the year. Slim said that he didn't pick up an instrument for those months, while his son George came home from Northeastern University when the campus closed, and Slim and daughter Alice worked virtually, both at the kitchen table. Slim also wrote poetry and spent time mentoring his grandchildren. Self-described as "notoriously cheap," Slim had a paid-off home, retirement funds, and solid investments, so finances were not a problem—very likely a rarity for a musician.[45]

During the pandemic Doug said that he and Desi "lived on social security, union pensions, Desi's salary, a trickle of royalties, and as a lifeguard at the YMCA." Because he lifted weights and used the elliptical at the neighborhood Y every morning, it didn't seem too much of a stretch to apply for a lifeguard job there when it was posted. He enjoyed being possibly the oldest and probably the country's only yodeling lifeguard. During the summer of 2020, he also became a census worker. And even though the Ranger preferred writing songs rather than books, the months off the road also afforded him time to write his long-anticipated biography of Carson Robison. Born in Oswego, Kansas, Robison was a pioneer performer in country music—a singer, guitarist, whistler, and composer. He was part of a vigorous music scene in New York City that included Vernon Dalhart, Frank Luther, and Adelyne Hood. He was also country music's first professional songwriter—with songs like "Carry Me Back to the Lone Prairie," "Wreck of the Number 9," "Little Green Valley," "Zeb Turney's Gal," "Carry Me Back to the Mountains," and "Life Gets Teejus"—that ran the gamut of country music's substyles; a collaborator with Vernon Dalhart; and the first performer to take country music to Europe. Writing the biography became Doug's academic pandemic project. Acknowledging that writing is "real work," he nevertheless considers himself "a fairly fluid writer, hearing his sentences in his head before he writes them," a facility that helps move the process along more easily.[46]

Doug also had a very happy pandemic experience: he married Desi Smith, on June 20, 2020, on the front porch of his house. They had met initially in 1978, when she was working as a receptionist for *Billboard* in Nashville, and he was seeking publicity for the Riders from the journal. She was in the music business for twenty years, at Elektra and Mercury Records, in addition to *Billboard*, and at Cigna for about the same amount of time. Doug had been captivated by her good looks and personality, or what he calls her "million-dollar smile and a traffic-stopping figure." As an attractive Black woman in the country music field, she found many men disingenuous in their intentions and truly appreciated Doug's graciousness with her. They had what he described as a "torrid but brief romance" in 1988. Then, Desi said, "We didn't see each other for 33 years." After his last divorce, he got on match.com, found her photograph, and rekindled the romance with an email. She told us, "I was raising my grandchildren, foster kids, my neighbors' kids. I hadn't had a date in twenty years" when that email arrived. They had a date to see *The Messiah* at the Tennessee Performing Arts Center and have found happiness ever since. In Doug's words, "She loves me with an unconditional love I have never known and I never knew existed. She accepts the love from my too romantic heart as well . . . We accept each other. Completely . . . I am thankful in my morning meditation EVERY morning."[47]

Woody had married Lisa Reed on August 31, 2019, before the pandemic was in sight. Both marriage and grandchildren nearby served to keep him happy and busy when the music world shut down. Lisa was originally from Franklin, not far from Woody's childhood home of Triune. In 2014, Mama Kat needed help when she became frail, and Woody learned that Lisa Reed was the person to call. Lisa knew nothing about him or the Riders, but because she was staying with his mother while he was on the road for two weeks at a time, she had assumed he was a truck driver. He had never given her a hint of his occupation. She and Woody grew close, and they have been a couple since his mother's death. Lisa is the mother of three daughters and one living son and a grandmother of thirteen, and Woody himself now has seven grandchildren. The Chrismans' home in Donelson is very close to the Opry, and one of Lisa's daughters lives in a duplex next door with her two children, and her son lives on the other side. Woody truly appreciates his role as grandfather to all the children, whom Lisa claims, "are crazy about him. . . . He would love it if we had a big place, and we all lived together." Woody concurs, "I get to stay home and raise kids, which I am really enjoying, since being a road musician was really not good for me." He loved playing the fiddle at home and proved just as adept at fixing things around the house and working on lawnmowers and chainsaws for friends and neighbors as he was at maintaining the Riders' buses. And according to Lisa, Woody also "loves to trap moles."[48]

Slim expressed what the other members of the band undoubtedly felt as the pandemic-restricted venues finally reopened: "When we geared back up for a gig or two at the end of that year [2020], I was really glad to get back to it. There's a sense these days that our road won't last forever, and I cherish every time we get up onstage and create that Riders feel I've loved for forty-five years, ever since that first night at Herr Harry's." Doug told us how hard he found being away from the Opry for nine months and how good it felt to return. Their first date back on December 19, 2020, marked the Riders' 2,024th appearance on that stage. When the Riders returned to active music-making, they were thrilled with the enthusiastic response that they received at the Opry, and from January 2, 2021, thru August 2021 they played there almost exclusively (one big exception came on August 14 and 15 when they played for the Tweetsie Railroad). The Opry had become largely a tourist attraction, rather than a mecca for ardent country music fans. The Riders typically receive standing ovations, which occur very rarely at the Opry. Because of their western charisma, warmth, and receptivity to the audience, they had become star attractions, true ambassadors for the show. The Opry has a policy of offering fans backstage privileges—with fans agreeing to pay an extra $500 for "meet and greets" with certain stars—and the Riders are often called on for these occasions, for which they receive additional pay. Paul Lohr affirmed that sense of the Riders being back in the saddle when he made this prediction: "2021 had spits and spurts of shows to see the earnings creep up to $205,000 that year. But with the pandemic in the rear window, 2022 saw another increase to $325,000, and . . . their 2023 gross [was] over $400,000 . . . With a little bit of luck and determination, the band hopes to return to the days where they can average $500,000 a year again."[49]

The Riders were living up to Paul Lohr's projection when Doug, a strong believer in and practitioner of daily exercise, went in for a routine examination on September 12, 2022. Assuming he was in perfect condition, he was shocked to find out that he flunked the treadmill test, and the doctor told him he needed open heart surgery. With road trips finally reappearing on the Riders' calendar, Doug asked if it could be postponed, and the doctor replied, "not if you want to live." Dates were canceled, and on September 26, Doug underwent the surgery. He wrote, "I was able to (barely) play the Opry with my lightest guitar on October 12 (don't tell my surgeon or cardiologist)." Less than two weeks later, by taking it easy, he considered himself ready "to go back on the road by October 27 for three days in the Midwest," probably sooner than his doctor would have wished, but being in good shape before surgery surely helped that rapid recovery.[50]

And the Riders hit their stride again as they performed at the Franklin Theater for their forty-fifth anniversary, November 10, 2022. The next night—which was the actual anniversary date—they celebrated the event on the Grand Ole Opry. Their playlist included "Ghost Riders," for obvious reasons, along with "There's a Star-Spangled Banner Waving Somewhere" (chosen because it was Veterans Day), a medley of old-time fiddle tunes (including "Liberty" and "Golden Slippers"), and they closed with "Happy Trails," on which the audience was asked to sing along. The guys slipped in a number of familiar quips. Recalling their beginnings, Slim said that he had originally wanted the group to be called the Spice Girls but had been vetoed. Doug noted that Woody had recently been inducted into the Fiddlers Hall of Fame, surprisingly in the "Living Category." Woody gave a few parting words of advice, "Never take a sleeping pill and a laxative at the same time." Ranger Doug remarked, "Look how far we've come since that first night at Herr Harry's," and Too Slim responded, "Yes, about twelve miles." As another tribute to their forty-five years of professional activity, Doug was chosen to give the keynote speech to the IWMA conference in Albuquerque. He gave an overview of his own experiences with the organization and said that western music had a distinct niche in the American musical mosaic. "It is still about the outdoors, free living, fresh air and self-reliance."[51]

As the Riders galloped toward their fiftieth anniversary, their postpandemic schedule had been greatly altered. When they embarked on a lengthy tour of the West in February 2023—just like the old days—they were justifiably thrilled. Speaking of the tour, Doug said, "This has been a very good run, good crowds, strong mercantile, lots of laughs, and we proved we can do 5 nights in a row with travel and not be tattered and torn. It's been since before COVID that we've taken a trip this long." While they still always prioritize road bookings, they fill in more empty weekends with Opry dates. As Paul Lohr confided, the Opry pays union scale, and though this means hundreds, not thousands of dollars, those dates give the band the benefit of publicity on powerful WSM, being at home, performing less time, and with no expenses and other travel-related travails. Being on the Opry regularly will not pay the bills for younger musicians, but for the Riders, those performances make a nice supplement to their income. Pete Fisher, the longtime Opry vice president and general manager, offered only positive comments about the Riders as "perfect Opry members," saying that without their membership, something would be lost, since they provide "so much color" to the more complete experience of country music. As a radio show, the Opry needs to have a great flow, and the Riders have such "tremendous timing"; they perform "in first-class fashion, plus their passion for the music is so evident. I always felt I had an ally in Doug and Riders in the Opry's mission to both respect the legacy and maintain the relevance to the evolution of the Opry's response to the present. The Riders provide the espresso version of western music. Nothing like it."[52]

The Riders had earlier maintained that their recording days were over, but in December 2022, they began recording a new CD. Their postpandemic success at the Opry, with their multiple encores, must have revitalized them. The acquisition of new fans meant a new need for souvenirs. Their reliable engineer, Brent Truitt, worked for them again on the new album. He had been their engineer since 1996, when he engineered their Gene Autry CD. *Throw a Saddle on a Star* (released as their "forty-somethingth") was released in June 2023. Doug wrote that they decided to make a new CD "because there are great old songs out there that can't be forgotten. Because we are still creating new ones. Not because we have to create, but because we can't NOT create." Three of the songs are his: "Golden Lockets," "The Happy Yodeler," and "The Shelter of the Wildwood." Woody composed "Getaway Gallop," an affectingly spirited instrumental; and Fred created a poignant tribute to Roberta, "Waiting for the Echo." Joey contributed an arrangement of the beautiful "Colorado Trail," and Gary McMahan wrote "Ol' Cowpoke." The other six songs included two from the Sons of the Pioneers' repertory, "Cherokee Strip" and "On the Rhythm Range," as well as Carson Robison's "The Little Green Valley," and two classics from the western song bag, "Texas Plains" and "The Wayward Wind." Doug was especially thrilled that the National Cowboy and Western Heritage Museum presented him the 2024 Western Heritage Award for Original Western Composition for "The Shelter of the Wildwood," and he and Desi were in Oklahoma City for the ceremony. Forty-seven years on that winding trail, and the Riders still sound like they're rarin' to go![53]

Almost from the beginning of their storied rise, the Riders evoked a devoted and enduring loyalty among their fans. In some cases, this commitment manifested itself merely in the purchase of items from their Mercantile table—t-shirts, bandannas, cac-ties, CDs and LPs, books, and other mementos of the fancied West—and the wearing of Riders' and other western gear at their concerts, just as Bert did when she first saw the band playing at No Fish Today in Baltimore. These fans, though, pale in contrast to others who became so entranced by the Riders that they not only show up at nearby concerts, they also travel great distances to attend them, and volunteer to work their Mercantile tables and do other chores, sometimes even traveling with them and driving their road vehicles. Fred said of these highly motivated fans, "We've referred to them mostly as Saddle Pals through the years [or, as Carin Joy Condon explained in her case, an "SSP" or "Super Saddle Pal"] with one interesting iteration: when the internet happened, they became Cyberpals." These folks include several already discussed in this book: Nashville music journalist Robert K. Oermann who promoted the Riders early on; Jamie Amos, founder and president of the Riders' first fan club; Jerry West, multirole player in the band's life and inveterate collector of Riders' memorabilia; Allen McNeely, who kept *Riders' Radio Theater* on local Boise radio; photographer Donna Jagodzinski, who traveled to concerts near and far with her husband and service dog; Home Ranch owner Ken Jones and Santa Monica DJ Mike Mahaney who traveled with the Riders; and, of course, the incomparable Billy Maxwell, who proved essential and roadworthy for so many decades.

Other committed Saddle Pals include Jayna Henderson from Parsons, Kansas, who saw the Riders for the first time in 1980 on the stage of the Grand Ole Opry but didn't meet them that night. When she saw them next, Jayna joked with Slim, asking if he remembered her. That conversation served as a bond, and they had someone take a photo of the two of them—a tradition that continued for the next 162 shows (as of June 2023). Jayna, who is a "charter buckaroo of the fan club" with "the badge to prove it," and her late husband, Kim, even took the train to California to see the Riders get their star at the Western Walk of Fame in Santa Clarita. In 2010, she and Kim helped Bert set up and man the Riders' booth at the CMT Music Fest in Nashville, believing that the Riders have such loyal fans because the band members are "so approachable, friendly, and down-to-earth" and "don't act like stars." Mary Masteller and her late husband, Bob, big supporters of the Wisconsin Opry, became friendly with Richard Wiegel, guitarist and Opry house band leader for many years, and then with the Riders when they made their first appearance there in 1990. After that initial contact, she and Bob worked the Mercantile for the Riders anytime they played within driving distance. Their favorite places to do so were at the Minnesota State Fair and at the Woodstock Opera House in Woodstock, Illinois. An engaged seamstress and knitter, Mary enjoyed making Hawaiian shirts for Richard and for the Riders, especially Doug and Slim, and for their twenty-fifth anniversary, she knit each band member an afghan.[54]

Two TV science celebrities, Mr. Wizard IV and Bill Nye the Science Guy, also became passionate Riders' fans. Steve Jacobs, a.k.a. Mr. Wizard, met the Riders in Wichita not long after the band began touring, and over the past forty-five-plus years has seen them perform over two hundred times. He feels that "a Riders concert is like looking at the back of a Swiss watch, wondering how they put the puzzle of their music and humor together." Not surprisingly, he and Woody love talking physics, and Steve enjoyed creating props for their *Riders Radio Theater* performances, like an udder butter on the rope made of rubber and a custom-made hutch in which to carry Two Jaws. When the band was doing the radio show in Cincinnati, they invited Steve to read the part of the World's Smartest Man in a script they'd written with the outrageous plot that Martians planned to kidnap Shania Twain and take all the world's diamonds. He loved being on stage with them, even if Doug's yodeling, rather than the World's Smartest Man, saved the day. In the fall of 2023 Steve and the Riders traveled together to the International Science Festival in the Orkney Islands (Scotland) where he a did a "campfire science" show and the Riders performed. As "their most appreciative fan," Steve says that "what they have created and done defies scientific explanation." Bill Nye, on the other hand, discovered the Riders as late as 2016 only after he found *Classic Cowboy Corral* on Sirius XM radio, then responded to their website to tell them how much he enjoyed their show. After Slim wrote back, they established a rapport via email. Bill saw the Riders perform for the first time at Freight and Salvage in Berkeley and again five days later at Pappy and Harriet's in Yucca Valley, California, and

Jayna Henderson posing with the Riders for probably the umpteenth time. Collection of Jayna Henderson, used by permission.

Mary Masteller and Slim, wearing the University of Michigan Hawaiian shirt she made for him. Collection of Mary Masteller, used by permission.

Band of Brothers　203

Cowboy Kyle, likely the Riders' #1 fan. Collection of Susan and Butch Nelson, used by permission.

was completely captivated. He has remained an avid radio listener, telling us, "When I get a shout-out, it really makes my week!"[55]

While making Bill Nye's week is a great feat, the Riders have provided something even more valuable to "Cowboy Kyle" Nelson. Slim told us that what fans find in the Riders are the same attributes that attracted him since their group began: "We've created a place of fun, nostalgia, wit, a sense of playfulness, and beautiful and interesting music you can't hear any place else. Wrapped up in a western mythological cowboy tradition and performed by four artists who dearly love what they're doing." This assessment is especially applicable to Cowboy Kyle, probably the Riders' greatest and all-time most passionate fan. Born with a rare form of fragile X syndrome, Kyle Nelson and his parents, Susan and Butch, live in Grand Marais, Minnesota, on the northwest shore of Lake Superior. Kyle is only one of six in the world with this particular rare form of fragile X syndrome, which, as Susan explained, expresses itself in some difficult manifestations, including "developmental delays, heightened sensory feelings, longer processing time, and communication/engagement struggles." But his condition also has an upside: kindness, authenticity, humor, enthusiasm, and helpfulness. "He greets people and compliments them like they are the most important people in the world." Kyle, now in his late twenties, adores both listening to and playing music. When he was twelve, he discovered the Riders on YouTube playing "Woody's Roundup," and it was love at first sight. Susan said, "It is through music our blessings of all blessings happened: we found the Riders In The Sky."

After seeing them perform live in Rochester in about 2012, the Nelsons found that the band would be performing a little farther away, in Des Moines. Susan contacted Matt Fox, the Riders' publicist, to see if a time could be arranged for Kyle to meet them there. The Riders invited Kyle backstage before the concert since they realized that afterward, the crowd might "be too overwhelming for Kyle, and they wanted to give him all their attention. He and Slim immediately began playing their faces together," and the Riders instantly became Susan's "heroes." The Nelsons soon became "that family from Minnesota," traveling by car and RV to see the Riders whenever and wherever they were playing. They have since been to over one hundred concerts and are thrilled to see Kyle's "animation and social skills rise" when he sees the band. Susan orders the tickets two or three months before a concert and "makes a few copies ahead so Kyle can hold them and put them on his bedside table." Kyle's bedroom has a campfire, four mics, and every instrument the Riders play except the stand-up bass; the Nelsons have a dining room "tribute wall donned with posters and postcards and letters from the Riders." They have acquired nearly every item ever sold at the Mercantile, and when Kyle is in the audience—usually in the front row—he is the first to stand and shout, "Encore! Encore!" and "to have been the recipient of the 'Happy Trails' song traditional shout-out (and you, too, Cowboy Kyle)." Susan described the gratitude these encounters have brought to the family:

> We tend to not feel like we belong in a lot of this world, but when we are with the Riders, we are included, relevant, seen, heard, celebrated, engaged, and loved. I cannot thank the Riders enough for how they make Kyle feel: he thrives when he is with them in this safe, inclusive space. I find myself tearing up a lot during concerts and meet and greets. It is not lost on me that I don't need to hover, protect, shield, or worry when we are with the Riders. It's beautiful. It's like the Riders give me permission to relax and breathe knowing my son is in familiar territory. It's like my vacation from being a worried mom.

Kyle's experience succinctly encapsulates all that the Riders have given their audiences: the love they feel for their music and the fun they have with their humor continue to bring others such genuine and deep pleasure.[56]

Doug acknowledged the band's awareness of their "magnetism for those with special needs. I and we take that as a responsibility and take it seriously. To bring that kind of joy to another human is really a transcendental experience. If we have brought joy to their lives, they have enriched ours." And Fred reaffirmed the Riders' will—and creative need—to keep on keeping on. "See you soon, Saddle Pals, on this impossibly long and winding trail. You'll know us. We're the four old guys loving what they do and who have no intention of ever quitting."[57]

NOTES

Introduction

1. Such record albums included the Norman Luboff Choir, *Songs of the West*, Columbia; the Roger Wagner Chorale, *Songs of the Frontier*, Capitol; Johnny Cash, *Ballads of the True West*, Columbia; and *Bitter Tears: Ballads of the American Indian*, Columbia.
2. For information on Harry McClintock: "Harry "Haywire Mac" McClintock-Biography," *Bluegrass Messengers*, www.bluegrassmessengers.com/harry-%E2%80%9Chaywire-mac%E2%80%9D-mcclintock—1928-.aspx, accessed March 3, 2023; Harry (Haywire Mac) McClintock, *Hillbilly Music dawt com*, www.hillbilly-music.com/artists/story/index.php?id=10426, accessed March 3, 2023.
3. Don Cusic, *It's the Cowboy Way!: The Amazing True Adventures of Riders In The Sky* (Lexington: University Press of Kentucky, 2003), 5–7; and index for television cowboy references in Douglas B. Green, *Singing in the Saddle: The History of the Singing Cowboy* (Nashville: Country Music Foundation Press and Vanderbilt University Press, 2002), 386–87.
4. Julia Bricklin, *The Notorious Life of Ned Buntline: A Tale of Murder, Betrayal, and the Creation of Buffalo Bill* (Guilford, CT: TwoDot, 2020). A partial, but enormous, listing of Buntline's books is found on Wikipedia.
5. "Wild West Music of Buffalo Bill's Cowboy Band": Essays and Liner Notes from *Wild West Music of Buffalo Bill's Cowboy Band*, performed by the Americus Brass Band, 1995, https://centerofthewest.org/explore/buffalo-bill/research/buffalo-bill-band/, accessed April 4, 2022.
6. John D. Nesbitt, "Owen Wister: Inventor of the Good-Guy Cowboy," *Wyoming History* (November 8, 2014): www.wyohistory.org/encyclopedia/owen-wister-inventor-good-guy-cowboy, accessed April 4, 2022; "Owen

Wister," Theodore Roosevelt Center at Dickinson State University, www.theodorerooseveltcenter.org/Learn-About-TR/TR-Encyclopedia/Family%20and%20Friends/Owen%20Wister, accessed June 24, 2022; John I. White, *Git Along, Little Dogies: Songs and Songmakers of the American West* (Urbana: University of Illinois Press, 1975), 29–30.

7. Eric Hobsbawm, "The Myth of the Cowboy," *The Guardian*, March 20, 2013, www.theguardian.com/books/2013/mar/20/myth-of-the-cowboy, accessed July 14, 2022; Page Stegner, "How the West Was Unsettled: *It's Your Misfortune and None of My Own: A New History of the American West* by Richard White," *Los Angeles Times*, January 5, 1992, www.latimes.com/archives/la-xpm-1992-01-05-bk-2172-story.html, accessed June 29, 2022.

8. Jane Kramer, *The Last Cowboy* (London: Pimlico, 1998), 1–5, quote on 4.

9. Hobsbawm, "Myth of the Cowboy"; Green, *Singing in the Saddle*, 11. This work traces the development of the singing cowboy in beautifully researched and consummately written detail. Songster Dom Flemons's Smithsonian Folkways 2018 album, *Black Cowboys: Songs from the Trails to the Rails*, presents music to counteract the all-white image of cowboys, since "the lack of substantial images of black cowboys has limited the public's perception of these incredible pioneers of the Old West," liner notes, 5; *Dom Flemons Presents Black Cowboys: Songs from the Trails to the Rails*, Smithsonian Folkways, https://folkways.si.edu/dom-flemons/black-cowboys, accessed June 15, 2022.

10. Oscar Fox is discussed in *The Handbook of Texas*, "Fox, Oscar Julius, www.tshaonline.org/handbook/entries/fox-oscar-julius, accessed May 26, 2022; Carl Weaver, "Oscar J. Fox and His Heritage," *Junior Historian*, December 1963, www.kenfuchs42.net/kfww/Oscar%20J.%20Fox%20and%20His%20Heritage.pdf, accessed May 27, 2022. "Tex Ritter," *Country Music Hall of Fame*, https://countrymusichalloffame.org/artist/tex-ritter/, accessed June 17, 2022.

11. A good summary of David Guion's career, and his role in popularizing "Home on the Range," can be found in James Dick, "Guion, David Wendel," *Handbook of Texas*, www.tshaonline.org/handbook/entries/guion-david-wendel, accessed May 26, 2022; See also David Wendell Guion: An Inventory of His Collection in the Manuscript Collection at the Harry Ransom Humanities Research Center, https://norman.hrc.utexas.edu/fasearch/findingAid.cfm?eadid=00323, accessed May 26, 2022; both Fox and Guion are discussed in Daniel M. Raessler, "The Cowboy Song as Art Song," *Semantic Scholar*, www.semanticscholar.org/paper/The-Cowboy-Song-as-Art-Song-Raessler/cf31b7248a122ec5f79ed1ddca9cc3f7cf6752f5, 2014, accessed July 2, 2022.

12. Bill C. Malone, *Singing Cowboys and Musical Mountaineers: Southern Culture and the Roots of Country Music* (Athens: University of Georgia Press, 1993), 89; Bill C. Malone and Tracey E. W. Laird, *Country Music USA* (Austin: University of Texas Press, 2018), 163–65. For cowboy-inspired material,

see Michael A. Amundson's highly informative and beautifully illustrated *Talking Machine West: A History and Catalogue of Tin Pan Alley's Western Recordings, 1902–1918* (Norman: University of Oklahoma Press, 2017); Jim Bob Tinsley, *He Was Singin' This Song* (Orlando: University Presses of Florida, 1981) and *For a Cowboy Has to Sing* (Orlando: University of Central Florida Press, 1991), which contains sixty popular cowboy songs.

13. Malone and Laird, *Country Music USA*, 165, 321; Doug Green, email to authors, December 31, 2022.
14. Malone, *Singing Cowboys*, 91–92. The Douglas Green quote is from Malone and Judith McCulloh, eds., *Stars of Country Music: Uncle Dave Macon to Johnny Rodriguez* (Urbana: University of Illinois Press, 1975), 142–56.
15. Malone and Laird, *Country Music USA*, 176–77.
16. Authors' telephone interview with Fred Labour, April 12, 2022.
17. Patty Hall, Doug's fellow musician, friend, and oral historian at the Country Music Hall of Fame, hosted a regular night at Herr Harry. That fateful November 11, 1977, "Patty was too sick to run the evening's open mic and called her friend Doug Green to fill in. Doug got his musical pals to join him." And that's where the magic began: "Patty Hall: Native Daughter of the Golden West Comes Full Circle," *San Diego Troubadour*, September 2009, https://sandiegotroubadour.com/wp-content/pdf/2009_9_Sep.pdf, accessed September 24, 2022.
18. Doug Green, email to authors, February 23, 2022.
19. Interview with Fred Labour, April 12, 2022.

Chapter 1

1. Don Cusic, *It's the Cowboy Way: The Amazing True Adventures of Riders In The Sky* (Lexington: University of Press of Kentucky, 2003), 13; Doug Green, interview with authors, February 22, and email, February 23, 2022; John W. Rumble, "Interview with Douglas B. Green," Country Music Foundation Oral History Project, November 23, 1993, 3; Janet Hendriksen, interview with authors, June 1, 2022; Sharon Millimaki, interview with authors, May 27, 2022.
2. Doug Green, email to authors, October 10, 2022.
3. Jim Green, interview with authors, March 26, 2022.
4. Cusic, *It's the Cowboy Way*, 14; Janet Hendriksen, interview with authors, June 1, 2022; Sharon Millimaki, interview with authors, May 27, 2022; Doug Green, interview with authors, March 7, 2022.
5. Doug Green, interview with authors, February 22, email, February 23, 2022; Doug Green, email to authors, October 17, 2022; Dan Miller, "53: Bluegrass Unlimited Podcast with Ranger Doug," *Bluegrass Unlimited*, November, 2021, https://bluegrassunlimited, accessed December 20, 2024; *Doyle O'Dell.com*, www.doyeodell.com/, accessed October 23, 2022.

6. Cusic, *It's the Cowboy Way*, 14; Doug Green, email to authors, October 10, 2022.
7. Doug Green, email to authors, October 10, 2022.
8. Cusic, *It's the Cowboy Way*, 14–15; Doug Green, email to authors, October 10, 2022.
9. Jim Green, interview with authors; Sandy Peterson-Fisher, interview with authors, May 31, 2022; Janet Hendriksen, interview with authors, June 1, 2022.
10. Cusic, *It's the Cowboy Way*, 15.
11. Doug Green, email to authors, October 10 and October 17, 2022; Cusic, *It's the Cowboy Way*; Sharon Millimaki interview.
12. Doug Green, email to authors, October 10, 2022; Cusic, *It's the Cowboy Way*, 14.
13. Doug Green, email to authors, October 11, 2022; Jim Green interview with authors; Jim McQuaid, interviews with authors, April 18, 2022, and October 11, 2022.
14. Bob Chambers, interview with authors, May 12, 2022; Arch Copeland, interview with authors, May 12, 2022; Jim Green, interview with authors.
15. Jim Green, interview with authors; Doug Green, email to authors, October 11, 2022.
16. Jim McQuaid, interviews with authors; Doug Green, interview with authors, October 11, 2002.
17. Jim Green, interviews with authors; Doug Green, email to authors, October 11, 2022; Rumble, "Interview with Douglas B. Green," 4.
18. Jim Green, interviews with authors; Doug Green, email to authors, October 10, 2022; Arch Copeland, interview with authors, May 12, 2022; Connie Green, interview with authors, April 28, 2022; Sally Green Angeli, interview with authors, March 30, 2022; Liza Jane Green Parnell; interview with authors, April 21, 2022.
19. Peter Lorch, interview with authors, April 26, 2022; Doug Green, interviews with the authors, October 11 and November 1, 2022; Jim McQuaid, interviews with authors.
20. Jim McQuaid, interviews with authors; Rumble, "Interview with Douglas B. Green," 6, 9; Doug Green, interview with authors, March 7, 2022; email to authors, October 11, 2022.
21. Jim McQuaid, interviews with authors; Bill Ivey, interview with authors, April 5, 2022; Doug Green, interview with authors, October 11 and November 1, 2022.
22. Doug Green, email to authors, December 24, 2022; Jim McQuaid, interviews with authors; Nolan Faulkner, interview with authors, April 5, 2022; Rumble, "Interview with Douglas B. Green," 7; Doug Green, interview with authors, October 11, 2022; Dan Miller, "53: Bluegrass Unlimited Podcast with Ranger Doug."

23. Jim McQuaid interviews with authors; Cusic, *It's the Cowboy Way*, 16; Rumble, "Interview with Douglas B. Green," 12; Doug Green, interview with authors, March 3, 2022, and email to authors, October 11, 2022.
24. Doug Green, interview with authors, March 7, 2022; Jim McQuaid, interviews with authors; Nolan Faulkner, interview with authors; Cusic, *It's the Cowboy Way*, 16; Tom Ewing, *Bill Monroe: The Life and Music of the Blue Grass Man* (Urbana: University of Illinois Press, 2018), 293; Bill Ivey claimed that he had taped Peter Rowan's song, "Walls of Time," at an earlier Bean Blossom festival when Rowan was still with Bill Monroe. Then Bill Ivey taught it to Doug. Bill Ivey, interview with authors, April 5, 2022.
25. Rumble, "Interview with Douglas B. Green," 14, 18; Ewing, *Bill Monroe: The Life and Music of the Blue Grass Man*, 293–94; Doug Green, interview with authors, October 11, 2022.
26. "My History with Doug Green," Rodney Moag, email attachment to authors, April 18, 2022.
27. Doug Green, email to authors, October 11, 2022; Jim Green, interview with authors.
28. Doug Green, interview with authors, March 3, 2022; Dan Miller, "53: Bluegrass Unlimited Podcast with Ranger Doug;" Rumble, "Interview with Douglas B. Green," 36.
29. Doug Green, email to authors, November 10 and November 14, 2022; Liza Jane Green Parnell, interview with authors, April 21, 2022.
30. Dan Miller, "53: Bluegrass Unlimited Podcast with Ranger Doug," Doug Green, interview with authors, March 3, 2022; Rumble, "Interview with Douglas B. Green," 36–37; Ewing, *Bill Monroe: The Life and Music of the Blue Grass Man*, 308; Doug Green, conversation with authors, December 9, 2022, and email to authors, December 24, 2022.
31. Doug Green, email to authors, February 15, 2023.
32. Doug Green, interview with authors, March 3, 2022.
33. Jeff Makos, "Would You Buy a Used Guitar from This Man?" *University of Chicago Magazine*, August 1996, https://magazine.uchicago.edu/9608/9608Gruhn.html, accessed November 17, 2022; "Gruhn Guitars and the King of Vintage Guitar Collecting," *Attic Capita.com*, https://atticcapital.com/gruhn-guitars-and-the-king-of-vintage-guitar-collecting/, undated, accessed November 17, 2022; George Gruhn, interview with authors, June 20, 2022; Doug Green, interview with authors, March 3, 2022; Douglas B. Green and George Gruhn, *Roy Acuff's Musical Collection at Opryland* (Nashville: WSM, 1982). Unfortunately, much of Roy Acuff's collection was destroyed in the terrible Nashville flood of 2010.
34. Doug Green, interview with authors, March 7, 2022; Liza Jane Green Parnell, interview with authors.
35. Doug Green, interview with authors, February 22 and March 3, 2022; Bill Ivey, interview with authors; email from Bill Ivey, August 16, 2023; William

"Bill" Ivey, biography, *Country Music Hall of Fame*, www.countrymusichalloffame.org/about/collections/oral-history/william-bill-ivey-5, accessed November 23, 2022.

36. Doug Green, interview with authors, February 22 and March 3, 2022, emails to authors, December 29, 2022, and February 6, 2023; Dan Miller, "53: Bluegrass Unlimited Podcast with Ranger Doug;" Cusic, *It's the Cowboy Way*, 19.
37. Douglas B. Green, *Country Roots: The Origins of Country Music* (New York: Hawthorn Books, 1976), 107–8.
38. Doug Green, interview with authors, February 22 and March 3, 2022; Dan Miller, "53: Bluegrass Unlimited Podcast with Ranger Doug;" Cusic, *It's the Cowboy Way*, 19–20; "About Bob Pinson," *Country Music Hall of Fame*, www.countrymusichalloffame.org/about/collections/about-bob-pinson, accessed November 26, 2022; Guy William Logsdon obituary, Butler-Sumpff & Dyer Funeral Home, www.butler-stumpff.com/obituaries/guy-william-logsdon/, accessed November 28, 2022; preface, Ranger Doug, *Songs of the Sage* (Anaheim Hills, CA: Centerstream Publishing, 1997).
39. Doug Green, interview with authors, February 22, and email, February 23, 2022.

Chapter 2

1. "Facts and History," *City of Grand Rapids*, www.grandrapidsmi.gov/Government/About/City-of-Grand-Rapids-Facts-and-History#section-2, accessed December 20, 2022; Fred LaBour, interview with authors, March 18, 2022; Fred LaBour, email to authors, December 20, 2022.
2. "Frank Gotch," *WWE*, www.wwe.com/superstars/frank-gotch, accessed December 30, 2022; Fred LaBour, email to authors, December 20, 2022.
3. Fred LaBour, email to authors, December 20, 2022.
4. Fred LaBour, interview with authors, March 18, 2022; Chris LaBour, interview with authors, May 9, 2022: Mike DeVriendt, interview with authors, November 21, 2022.
5. Marcie LaBour Merritt, interview with authors, May 17, 2022; Chris LaBour, interview with authors; Fred LaBour, interview with authors, March 18, 2022, and email to authors, December 20, 2022.
6. Fred LaBour, email to authors, December 20, 2022.
7. Fred LaBour, interview with authors, March 18, 2022, and email to authors, December 20, 2022.
8. Fred LaBour, interview with authors, March 18, 2022; Don Cusic, *It's the Cowboy Way: The Amazing True Adventures of Riders In The Sky* (Lexington: University Press of Kentucky, 2003), 25–26; "Pat Boyd," *Hillbilly-Music dawt com*, www.hillbilly-music.com/artists/story/index.php?id=13142, accessed on October 30, 2022.

9. Fred LaBour, interview with authors, March 18, 2022; "Hey, Buckaroos, Do You Remember the Buckaroo Radio?" *100.5 The River*, https://rivergrand rapids.com/hey-buckaroos-do-you-remember-the-buckaroo-rodeo/, accessed December 6, 2022.
10. Fred LaBour, interview with authors, March 18, 2022, and email, January 5, 2023; Cusic, *It's the Cowboy Way*, 26, 245.
11. Marcie Merritt interview; Chris LaBour interview; Fred LaBour, email to authors, October 17, 2022.
12. Marcie Merritt interview; Chris LaBour interview; Fred LaBour, email to authors, October 17, 2022, and December 20, 2022.
13. Fred LaBour, email to authors, October 17, 2022; Mike DeVriendt interview.
14. Fred LaBour, interview with authors, October 14, 2022, and emails to authors, October 17 and October 19, 2022; Mike DeVriendt interview; "Rem Wall and the Green Valley Boys," *hillbilly music dawt com*, www.hillbilly-music.com/artists/story/index.php?id=12681, accessed December 19, 2022; Cusic, *It's the Cowboy Way*, 245.
15. Fred LaBour, interview with authors, April 5, 2022.
16. "Chocolate Festival Cowboy: Five Questions with Fred LaBour," *Anniston-Gadsden Real-Time News*, April 1, 2014, www.al.com/news/anniston-gadsden/2014/04/chocolate_festival_cowboy_five.html, accessed December 19, 2022.
17. *St. Mark's*, www.stmarksgr.org/, accessed December 22, 2022; Fred LaBour, email to authors, December 20, 2022.
18. Cusic, *It's the Cowboy Way*, 24; Fred LaBour, email to authors, June 16, 2022.
19. Fred LaBour, interview with authors, October 14, 2022; Fred LaBour, "What History Has Taught Me," *True West Magazine*, August 1, 2008, https://true westmagazine.com/article/fred-labour/, accessed on November 4, 2022.
20. Fred LaBour, email to authors, November 2, 2022.
21. Jay Cassidy, interview with authors, May 19, 2022.
22. Fred LaBour, email to authors, October 13, 2022; Freddy LaBour, "McCartney Dead; New Evidence Brought to Light," a single released in 2014, *fandom.com*, https://riders-in-the-sky.fandom.com/wiki/McCartney_Dead;_New_Evidence_Brought_to_Light, accessed December 23, 2022; Richard J. Tofel, "Misinformation and the Saga of 'Paul Is Dead,'" *Columbia Journalism Review*, December 20, 2021, www.cjr.org/analysis/misinformation-paul-mccartney-dead.php, accessed December 23, 2022; "Gary James' Interview with the Man Who Started the 'Paul Is Dead' Rumor: Fred LaBour," *classicbands.com*, www.classicbands.com/FredLaBourInterview.html, accessed December 23, 2022.
23. Jay Cassidy, interview with authors; Fred LaBour, interview with authors, June 1, 2022; Andy Sacks, interview with authors, November 29, 2022.
24. Andy Sacks interview; Fred LaBour, email to authors, June 6, 2022.
25. Lisa Silver, interview with authors, October 15, 2022; Herschel Freeman, interview with authors, December 6, 2022; Fred LaBour interview, March 18, 2022.

26. Lisa Silver, interview; Herschel Freeman, interview; Fred LaBour, interview with authors, November 1, 2022, and emails to authors, November 10, 2022, and January 5, 2023.
27. Lisa Silver interview; the biography on Lisa's website had more information on her career, Lisa Silver Songs, https://lisasilversong.com/bio/, accessed December 25, 2022; Herschel Freeman interview; his agency can be seen at http://herschelfreemanagency.com; Fred La Bour, interview with authors, November 1, 2022.
28. Doug Green, interview with authors, March 3, 2022; Fred LaBour, interview with authors, October 14, 2022; Cusic, *It's the Cowboy Way*, 29–30; Don Cusic, interview with authors, December 14, 2022.
29. Fred LaBour, interviews with authors, March 18, 2022, May 24, 2022, October 14, 2022; email to authors, January 12, 2023.
30. Fred LaBour, interviews with authors, March 18, 2022, May 24, 2022, October 14, 2022; email to authors, January 12, 2023.
31. Fred LaBour, email to authors, November 9, 2022; "Larry Ballard—Honky Tonk Heaven Is a Hell of a Place to Be," *If That Ain't Country*, https://ifthataintcountry.net/listen-again/blog/larry-ballard-honky-tonk-heaven-is-a-hell-of-a-place-to-be, accessed December 25, 2022.
32. Fred LaBour, email to authors, May 24, 2022, and December 20, 2022.
33. Dickey Lee, interview with authors, December 6, 2022; Fred LaBour, email to authors, December 20, 2022; Laura Eipper, "Green Sings of Home (on the Range)," March 28, 1978 [no newspaper source cited], scrapbook, Box 14, Douglas Green Collection, Country Music Hall of Fame and Museum Archives.
34. Conrad Fisher, "Interview with Dickey Lee, One of Country's Greatest Living Songwriters," *Saving Country Music*, June 30, 2022, www.savingcountrymusic.com/tag/dickey-lee/, accessed October 13, 2022; Dickey Lee, interview with authors, December 6, 2022; Fred LaBour, email to authors, December 20, 2022; Cusic, *It's the Cowboy Way*, 31.
35. Fred LaBour, email to authors, December 20, 2022.
36. Fred LaBour, interview with authors, September 30, 2022, and email to authors, December 20, 2022; see *Patty Hall: Native Daughter of the Golden West*, www.patriciahall.org/index.shtml, accessed on November 10, 2022; "Where Do We Come In? A Highly Subjective History of Riders In The Sky," in *Riders In The Sky* (Salt Lake City: Gibbs Smith, 1992), 6; Cusic, *It's the Cowboy Way*, 31.
37. *Nashville Musical History Tour*, June 17, 2020, https://ptbr.facebook.com/nashvillemusicalhistorytour/posts/172543304287975, accessed November 10, 2022; Tracy Moore, "Hot Bands, Big Deals, a Buzzing Music Scene," *Nashville Scene*, August 10, 2006, www.nashvillescene.com/news/hot-bands-big-deals-a-buzzing-music-scene-nashvilles-80s-rock-scene-had

-it-all/article_82b25deb-9626-582f-b8fe-cd96baff0db0.html, accessed December 27, 2022; Cusic, *It's the Cowboy Way*, 11, 31; Fred LaBour, email to authors, November 11, 2022.

Chapter 3

1. Fred LaBour, interview with authors, March 18, 2022; Don Cusic, *It's the Cowboy Way: The Amazing True Adventures of Riders In The Sky* (Lexington: University Press of Kentucky, 2003), 32–33; "Riders In The Sky, 1977–1998" [list of dates], collection of Fred LaBour.
2. Doug Green, interview with authors, March 3, 2022; Fred LaBour, interviews with authors, April 5, 2022, and May 24, 2022; Cusic, *It's the Cowboy Way*, 33–34; *Billboard*, April 14, 1978.
3. Cusic, *It's the Cowboy Way*, 45–46; Don Cusic, interview with authors, December 14, 2022; "Dear Fellow Music Lover," promotional letter from New Horizon Management Company, undated, inviting industry folks to see the Riders perform at the Exit/In on March 28, 1978, Doug Green scrapbook, Box 14, Doug Green Collection, Country Music Hall of Fame Archives.
4. "Riders In The Sky, 1977–1998" [list of dates], collection of Fred LaBour; for more information on Ralph Emery, see "Ralph Emery Biography," Ken Burns's *Country Music*, www.pbs.org/kenburns/country-music/ralph-emery-biography (accessed on December 6, 2022); Ray Benson quote from authors' conversation with the Riders backstage at the Opry, December 10, 2022.
5. "Riders In The Sky, 1977–1998" [list of dates], collection of Fred LaBour; Cusic, *It's the Cowboy Way*, 34–36.
6. Tommy Goldsmith, interview with authors, April 21, 2022; Fred Labour, interview with authors, March 22, 2022; Cusic, *It's the Cowboy Way*, 37.
7. David Walsh, "Obituary: Minnie Katherine Chrisman," *The News* (Williamson County), April 5, 2015, www.williamsonhomepage.com/obituaries/obituary-minnie-katherine-chrisman/article_35e3246c-f1ee-5ff1-827b-c1d192ca970c.html, accessed January 11, 2023; Paul Woodrow Chrisman, *Family Search*, https://ancestors.familysearch.org/en/LVSC-HS3/paul-woodrow-chrisman-sr.-1918-2007, accessed January 11, 2023; Robert K. Oermann, "Riders In The Sky: Nashville's Home Grown," *Nashville Gazette*, April, 1980; Woody Paul Chrisman, interview with authors, May 17, 2022; Allen McNeely, interview with authors, June 28, 2022; Jamie Amos, interview with authors, May 13, 2022; for a discussion of the migration south from Pennsylvania, see "The Great Wagon Road: From Northern Colonies to North Carolina," originally published in *The Way We Lived in North Carolina* (Chapel Hill: University of North Carolina Press, 2003); see R. Jackson Marshall III, "The Great Wagon Road," Encyclopedia of North

Carolina, 2006, www.ncpedia.org/great-wagon-road#:~:text=The%20route%20that%20became%20the,of%20land%20for%20new%20homes, accessed January 11, 2022.

8. Woody Paul Chrisman, interviews with authors, March 23 and May 17, 2022; email to authors from Fred LaBour, January 26, 2023.
9. Chrisman, interviews with authors; Billy Maxwell, interview with authors, April 7, 2022; Cusic, *It's the Cowboy Way*, 38.
10. Cusic, *It's the Cowboy Way*, 39.
11. Chrisman, interview with authors, March 23, 2022.
12. Cusic, *It's the Cowboy Way*, 41.
13. Chrisman, interview with authors, March 23, 2022.
14. Marshall Chapman, *Goodbye, Little Rock and Roller* (New York: St. Martin's Press, 2003), 60.
15. Chrisman, interview with authors, March 23, 2022; Cusic, *It's the Cowboy Way*, 41; Chapman, interview with authors and *Goodbye, Little Rock and Roller*, 59–62. Marshall has written a host of chart-making songs such as "Somewhere South of Macon" and "Betty's Bein' Bad," and for a time had a musical partnership with Jimmy Buffett. The books that she wrote in the ensuing years provide not only a searing and refreshingly honest account of her own life and career but also give us a revealing account of Nashville during the 1970s and 1980s. Paul Kingsbury has written the best profile of Marshall Chapman: "The Girl Can't Help It," *Vanderbilt Magazine*, summer 2004: https://cdn.vanderbilt.edu/vu-news/vanderbiltmagazine/archives/girlcanthelpit.pdf, accessed December 25, 2022.
16. Chrisman, interviews with authors; Cusic, *It's the Cowboy Way*, 42–43; Jay London, "Paul Chrisman, PhD '76, Nuclear Engineer Becomes Hall of Fame Fiddler," *MIT Technology Review*, February 20, 2013, www.technologyreview.com/2013/02/20/179889/paul-chrisman-phd-76-aka-woody-paul/, accessed on December 15, 2022.
17. Cusic, *It's the Cowboy Way*, 43; Fred LaBour, email to authors, January 26, 2023.
18. Cusic, *It's the Cowboy Way*, 47–48.
19. Goldsmith, interview with authors; Doug Green, interview with authors, March 19, 2022.
20. Fred LaBour, interview with authors, March 22, 2022 and April 12, 2022, email to authors, November 14, 2022; Tommy Goldsmith, interview; "Riders In The Sky, 1977–1998" [list of dates], collection of Fred LaBour; "History of Wind in the Willows Mansion," www.midtnlawyers.com/history-of-the-wind-in-the-willows-mansion/, accessed January 10, 2023.
21. Cusic, *It's the Cowboy Way*, 50–51; Doug Green, interviews with authors, March 7, 2022, and March 19, 2022.
22. Fred LaBour, interview with authors, March 22 and April 12, 2022, email to authors, November 14, 2022.

23. Fred LaBour, interview with authors, January 6, 2023, January 23, 2023; Tommy Goldsmith interview.
24. Fred LaBour, email to authors, November 14, 2022.
25. Fred LaBour, interview with authors, March 22 and email to authors, April 12, 2022, and December 20, 2022; Tina Walker, interview with authors, January 31, 2023.
26. Dr. Tom John, interview with authors, June 5, 2023.
27. Bill Ivey, interview with authors, April 5, 2022; Doug Green, letter of resignation to the board of the Country Music Foundation, November 6, 1978, scrapbook, Box 14, Douglas Green Collection, Country Music Hall of Fame and Museum Archives; "Green to Leave CMF Press Post," *The Tennessean*, November 10, 1978, scrapbook, Box 14, Douglas Green Collection, Country Music Hall of Fame and Museum Archives; Fred LaBour, email to authors, January 5, 2023.
28. Cusic, *It's the Cowboy Way*, 52; Tommy Goldsmith interview; Doug Green, email to authors, December 24, 2022, and interview with authors, January 20, 2023.
29. "Riders In The Sky, 1977–1998" [list of dates], collection of Fred LaBour; Townsend Miller, "Riders In The Sky Breathe New Life into Cowboy Music," *Country Music, Austin American Statesman*, February 22, 1979; Miller, "Weekend Starts Early with Riders and Conway Twitty," *Country Music, Austin American Statesman*, November 29, 1979; Cusic, *It's the Cowboy Way*, 53.
30. David Symington, interview with authors, November 23, 2022; authors' conversation with members of Riders In The Sky backstage at the Grand Ole Opry, December 20, 2022; Fred LaBour, interviews with authors, March 22 and April 12, 2022.
31. Cusic, *It's the Cowboy Way*, 55–56; Tommy Goldsmith, interview with authors.
32. Doug Green, interview with authors, March 19, 2022.
33. "Riders In The Sky, 1977–1998" [list of dates], collection of Fred LaBour; Dr. Michael Lichtenstein and Mary Flanagan, interview with authors, April 9, 2022; Doug Green, interview with authors, April 9, 2022.
34. Katherine Flynn, "Springwater Supper Club and Lounge in Nashville, Tennessee," *SavingPlaces*, National Trust for Historic Preservation, January 5, 2017, https://savingplaces.org/stories/the-springwater-supper-club-and-lounge-in-nashville-tennessee#:~:text=Although%20it%27s%20only%20been%20known,into%20a%20speakeasy%20during%20Prohibition, accessed January 20, 2023; Fred LaBour, email to authors, January 9, 2022.
35. Fred LaBour, email to authors, February 2, 2023. "Riders In The Sky on the *Larry King Show*," June 9, 1979, www.youtube.com/watch?v=EBmfFx9ipOk, accessed February 1, 2023.
36. Fred LaBour, email to authors, February 2, 2023.
37. Doug Green, interview with authors, March 19, 2022; Fred LaBour, interview with authors, March 22, 2022, email to authors, February 3, 2023; "About Rounder Records," *Rounder.com*, https://rounder.com/

about/#:~:text=Rounder%20began%20in%201970,music%20and%20its%20 contemporary%20offshoots, accessed January 21, 2023; Ken Irwin, interview with authors, October 17, 2022; Cusic, *It's the Cowboy Way*, 54–55.

38. Fred LaBour, interview with authors, March 22, 2022, email to authors, February 3, 2023; Cusic, *It's the Cowboy Way*, 54–55; Ken Irwin, interview with authors, October 17, 2022.

39. Doug Green, email to authors, February 22, 2023; Melissa Schorr, "Riders In The Sky Saddle Up to Soar at Gold Coast," *Las Vegas Sun*, July 18, 1997, https://lasvegassun.com/news/1997/jul/18/riders-in-the-sky-saddle-up-to-soar-at-gold-coast/, accessed on March 1, 2023.

40. Fred LaBour, email to authors, May 14, 2023; Doug Green, with Suze Spencer Marshall, *Rhythm Guitar the Ranger Doug Way* (Anaheim Hills, CA: Centerstream Publications, 2006). For an in-depth analysis of the Freddie Green style, see *Freddie Green: Master of the Rhythm Guitar*, www.freddiegreen.org, accessed February 28, 2023.

Chapter 4

1. Fred LaBour, interview with authors, March 22, 2022.
2. Fred LaBour, email to authors, November 14, 2022; Cusic, *It's the Cowboy Way*, 57–62.
3. Cusic, *It's the Cowboy Way*, 64–65; Fred LaBour, email to authors, February 3, 2023.
4. Cusic, *It's the Cowboy Way*, 61–62; Doug Green, interview with authors, April 12, 2022; Fred LaBour, email to authors, February 3, 2023.
5. Doug Green, email to authors, March 22, 2022; Fred LaBour, email to authors, February 3, 2023; Linda Cain, review of *Three on the Trail*, *Country Style*, December 1980; Stephen F. Davis, review of *Three on the Trail*, *Walnut Valley Occasional*, April 1981; Michael Bane, review of *Three on the Trail*, Rounder Records 0102," *Country Music*, December 1980; Robert K. Oermann, "The Inquirer's Special Album Review: *Three on the Trail*," *Music City Inquirer*, undated, all found in scrapbook 3, Box 14.
6. Robert K. Oermann, "Fresh Faces: Riders In The Sky," *Country Rhythms*, undated, collection of Robert K. Oermann.
7. "What's New Ranger Doug?" *Riders' Roundup*, October,1984; Jerry West scrapbooks, Doug Green Collection, Country Music Hall of Fame and Museum Archives.
8. Fred LaBour, interviews with authors, March 22, 2022, and January 9, 2023; Jamie Amos, "Ranger Doug: The Idol/The Man," *Riders' Roundup*, November 1986, Jerry West scrapbook collection.
9. Carin Joy Condon, "Hard Ridin', Trail Drivin', Hide Splittin' Cowboy Comedy," unpublished essay, 2022; Peter Applebome, "Singing Cowboys Ride the Range Again," *New York Times*, November 2, 1983.

10. Condon, "Hard Ridin'"; Fred LaBour, email to authors, March 2, 2023; Mike Rotch posted "Riders In The Sky—Woody Paul's Rope Tricks (1986)" on YouTube, www.youtube.com/watch?v=97egjdBwy60, for which he gives credit to Sonora Dale for the video from the Riders' performance at the Labor Day weekend Strawberry Music Festival in 1986, which can be seen in full at www.youtube.com/watch?v=PKi6UOnXjBE, both accessed February 5, 2023.
11. Doug Green, interview with authors, March 19, 2022, and email to authors, February 6, 2023; "Riders In The Sky Personal Appearances," November 1977–January 2023; Cusic, *It's the Cowboy Way*, 65; Robert K. Oermann, "Riders In The Sky," October 14, 1997, typescript, collection of Robert K. Oermann.
12. Programs for the Kennedy Center and preinaugural party performances, Scrapbook 3, Box 14, Doug Green Collection, Country Music Hall of Fame and Museum Archives; Fred LaBour, interview with authors, April 26, 2022.
13. Doug Green, email to authors, February 8, 2023; Cusic, *It's the Cowboy Way*, 73.
14. "Riders In The Sky Personal Appearances," November 1977–January 2023; Fred LaBour, interview with authors, April 6, 2022.
15. Fred LaBour, interview with authors, April 6, 2022.
16. Fred LaBour, interview with authors, April 6, 2022.
17. Fred LaBour, interview with authors, April 6, 2022, and "Roberta LaBour Obituary," February 2–3, 2018, www.legacy.com/us/obituaries/tennessean/name/roberta-labour-obituary?id=11308133, accessed February 20, 2023; Sandy Samet Wilkerson, interview with authors, May 20, 2023.
18. Cusic, *It's the Cowboy Way*, 245; Fred LaBour, email to authors, April 12, 2022, and February 3, 2023.
19. Fred LaBour, email to authors, January 15, 2023; Teena Camp, interview with authors, March 20, 2023.
20. Fred LaBour, email to authors, January 15, 2023; Carin Joy Condon, email to authors, March 10, 2022; Teena Camp, interview with authors, March 20, 2023.
21. "Riders In The Sky Personal Appearances," November 1977–January 2023; Cusic, *It's the Cowboy Way*, 75–77; Steve Webb, "Riders In The Sky Give the Fairgoers Something Different," *Post-Bulletin*, Rochester, Minnesota, September 2, 1982, Scrapbook 3, Box 14, Doug Green Collection, Country Music Hall of Fame and Museum Archives.
22. "Riders In The Sky Personal Appearances," November 1977–January 2023; Mike Mahaney, interview with authors, May 14, 2022.
23. "Riders In The Sky Personal Appearances," November 1977–January 2023; Hadley Meares, "The Palomino Club: North Hollywood's Grand Ole Opry West," KCET, February 28, 2014, www.kcet.org/history-society/the-palomino-club-north-hollywoods-grand-ole-opry-west, accessed March 1, 2023.
24. "Manuel, The Rhinestone Rembrandt," *Country Music Hall of Fame*, https://countrymusichalloffame.org/exhibit/suiting-the-sound/manuel/, accessed

March 1, 2023; Manuel Cuevas, interview with authors, June 13, 2022. For more information on Manuel Cuevas, see Michelle Freedman and Holly George-Warren, *How the West Was Worn: A Complete History of Western Wear* (New York: Harry N. Abrams, 2001); Bradley Hanson, "Manuel Cuevas: Rodeo Tailor," *National Endowment for the Arts*, on the occasion of his being named a National Heritage Fellow: www.arts.gov/honors/heritage/manuel-cuevas, accessed December 27, 2022.

25. Fred LaBour, interviews with authors, April 19, 2022, and June 16, 2022; Manuel Cuevas, interview with authors, June 13, 2022; Doug Green, interview with authors, June 23, 2022; Woody Paul Chrisman, interview with authors, January 26, 2023; see Maxwell equation shirt on page 75.

26. Fred LaBour, interviews with authors, April 19, 2022, and June 16, 2022; Manuel Cuevas, interview with authors, June 13, 2022.

27. Cusic, *It's the Cowboy Way*, 85; Doug Green, interview with authors, March 19, 2022.

28. Woody Paul Chrisman, interview with authors, May 17, 2022, and June 8, 2023; Doug Green, interview with authors, March 19, 2022.

29. "Riders In The Sky Personal Appearances," November 1977–January 2023; Jerry West, interview with authors, March 1, 2023.

30. Doug Green, interview with authors, March 19, 2022; Robert K. Oermann, "Riders In The Sky Round Up Fans," *Nashville Tennessean*, November 26, 1982, Robert K. Oermann collection.

31. Doug Green, Fred LaBour, and Joey Miskulin, interview with authors, May 17, 2022; Virgil Dickinson, interview with authors, June 2, 2023.

32. Doug Green, email to authors, March 26, 2023; Fred LaBour, email to authors, March 26, 2023.

33. Fred LaBour, interview with authors, April 26, 2022; "Riders In The Sky Personal Appearances," November 1977–January 2023.

34. Mike Breen, Steve Wozniak's "'US Festival': The Biggest Music Fest You Never Heard Of," *Totally Rad Times*, www.totallyradtimes.com/steve-wozniak-us-festival-1982-1983/2/, accessed April 2, 2023; Peter Larsen, "The '83 US Festival had a country day, and this unlikely band rode in between Willie Nelson and Waylon Jennings," *Post-Enterprise*, June 8, 2020, www.pressenterprise.com/2020/06/08/the-83-us-festival-had-a-country-day-and-this-unlikely-band-rode-in-between-willie-nelson-and-waylon-jennings/, accessed April 1, 2023.

35. Mike Mahaney, interview with authors, May 28, 2022; Fred LaBour, interview with authors, April 26, 2022.

36. Ned Ramage, interview with authors, April 3, 2022; Steve Arwood, interview with the authors, April 22, 2022; Fred LaBour, email to authors, April 10, 2023; Cusic, *It's the Cowboy Way*, 96–97.

37. Steve Arwood interview; Fred La Bour email, April 10, 2023.

38. Fred LaBour, email to authors, January 6, 2023.

39. Fred LaBour, email to authors, January 6, 2023.
40. Fred LaBour, interviews with authors, April 5, 2022, April 12, 2022, April 5, 2023; email to authors, January 6, 2023.
41. Fred LaBour, email to authors, April 10, 2023.
42. Cusic, *It's the Cowboy Way*, 66–67; Gloria Gene Moore, interview with authors, April 14, 2023; Fred LaBour, email to authors, January 23, 2023. For more on Fegan, see "In Loving Memory of Bill Fegan," *KTRN Radio*, February 4, 2021, https://krtnradio.com/2021/02/04/in-loving-memory-of-bill-fegan/, accessed on March 31, 2023; *Rider's Roundup*, November 15, 1994, Jerry West scrapbook, Doug Green Collection, Country Music Hall of Fame and Museum Archives.
43. Doug Green, email to authors, March 26, 2023.
44. Fred LaBour, interview with authors, April 26, 2022.
45. Ned Ramage, email to authors, April 25, 2022; Doug Green, interview with authors, March 7, 2022; Fred LaBour, email to authors, January 23, 2023; Stacy Harris, email to authors, April 13, 2022; George Vecsey, "My Friend Died on 9?11—Pumping Gas," *Medium*, September 10, 2017, https://medium.com/@georgevecsey/my-friend-died-on-9-11-pumping-gas-ac246d531420, accessed September 8, 2024; see Cusic, *It's the Cowboy Way*, 111, for Skepner's early career with the Riders.
46. Fred LaBour, email to authors, January 23, 2023; Paul Lohr, interview with authors, March 25, 2022. Paul left Buddy Lee in 2003 after nineteen years and worked briefly for the Agency Group. When they left Nashville two years later, Paul formed his own company, New Frontier Management, with New Frontier Touring as a division; see Tina Amendola, "Executive Profile: Paul Lohr," *Pollstar*, May 9, 2014, https://news.pollstar.com/2014/05/09/executive-profile-paul-lohr/, accessed May 5, 2023.
47. Jamie Amos, interview with authors, May 13, 2022; email to authors, April 16, 2023; Cusic, *It's the Cowboy Way*, 103–4; *Riders' Roundup*, October 1982, Scrapbook 3, Box 14, Doug Green Collection, Country Music Hall of Fame and Museum Archives.
48. Doug Green, email to authors, April 19, 2023; Doug's quote from the liner notes to their tribute album, *Riders In The Sky Salute Roy Rogers: King of the Cowboys* (Riders Radio Records, 2015).

Chapter 5

1. Hal Cannon, interview with authors, July 5, 2022.
2. Alex Williams, "Larry Mahan, Who Was Called the Elvis of Rodeo, Is Dead at 79," *New York Times*, A21, May 10, 2023.
3. "What Is the National Cowboy Poetry Gathering?" *National Cowboy Poetry Gathering*, www.nationalcowboypoetrygathering.org/gathering-frequently-asked-questions, accessed April 19, 2023. For an account of how the Gathering

broadened its vision to encompass the multiracial nature of cowboy culture, see K. T. Sparks, "The National Cowboy Poetry Gathering Is Rewriting the Typical Image of the Cowboy," *Electric Lit*, February 19, 2021, https://electric literature.com/the-national-cowboy-poetry-gathering-is-rewriting-the -typical-image-of-the-cowboy/, accessed April 19, 2023; Terrell Williams, *Magic Valley Agricultural Weekly*, Twin Falls, Idaho, February 19, 1994, Doug Green Collection, Country Music Foundation and Museum Archives; Doug Green, interview with authors, April 27, 2022; Fred LaBour, interview with authors, June 1, 2022, email to authors, May 15, 2023.

4. Katie Chicklinsk-Cahill, "Cy Scarborough, Co-Founder of Bar D Chuckwagon, Dies at 93," *Durango Herald*, May 19, 2020, www.durangoherald.com/articles /cy-scarborough-co-founder-of-bar-d-chuckwagon-dies-at-93/, accessed, April 28, 2023.

5. "Chris Ledoux," *National Rodeo Hall of Fame*, https://nationalcowboy museum.org/collections/awards/rodeo-hall-of-fame/inductees/5320/, accessed September 9, 2024; "Chris Ledoux," Alan Cackett, https:// alancackett.com/chris-ledoux-biography, accessed September 9, 2024.

6. Gary McMahan, interview with authors, January 19, 2023.

7. Brian Downes, "The Wild West Rides Again at WestFest," *Chicago Tribune*, May 28, 1995, www.chicagotribune.com/news/ct-xpm-1995-05-28-9505280066 -story.html, accessed April 29, 2023; see also *American Westfest*, www.american westfest.com/artist-lineup, for a brief biography of Michael Martin Murphey's career, accessed April 29, 2023.

8. Doug Green, email to authors, April 20, 2023; Fred LaBour, email to authors, 2023; Doug Green, interview with authors, June 4, 2022. At some point, the WMA established the *Western Way* as its official publication, published quarterly in Coppell, Texas. It contained news, poems, songs, and brief essays. Don Cusic was its editor in the early 2000s and wrote *The Cowboy in Country Music: A Historical Survey with Artist Profiles* (Jefferson, NC: McFarland, 2011); Doug Green, interview with authors, December 9, 2022.

9. *Songs of the Sage*, Warner Western, 1997; Doug Green, email to authors, May 10, 2023.

10. Karen Gogolick and Rick Roltgen, interview with the authors, August 2, 2022; Karen Gogolick, email to authors, August 8, 2022; *KG & The Ranger's Trading Post*, www.kgandtheranger.com/tradingPost.html, accessed, April 29, 2023.

11. Joey Miskulin, interview with authors, March 21, 2022; Cusic, *It's the Cowboy Way*, 125–26.

12. Miskulin interview; Cusic, *It's the Cowboy Way*, 126–31, quote, 129; "Roman Possedi," *National Cleveland Style Polka Hall of Fame and Museum*, www .clevelandstyle.com/roman~possedi.html, accessed April 21, 2023; Frank Smodic Jr., "Frank Yankovic . . . America's Polka King," *Polkas.org*, https:// polkas.org/nparts/yankovic/yankbio.htm, accessed April 21, 2023.

13. "Online Interview with Joey Miskulin," The NAAC (North American Accordion Collaborative), June 29, 2017, www.google.com/search?q=joey+miskulin%2C+interview+&source/, accessed April 25, 2023.
14. Bill Friskits-Warren, "Cowboy Jack Clement," *Country Music Hall of Fame and Museum*, www.countrymusichalloffame.org/hall-of-fame/cowboy-jack-clement, accessed April 27, 2023; Peter Cooper, "Accordion Master Joey Miskulin Finds His Place in Guitar Town," *The Tennessean*, November 16, 2014, www.tennessean.com/story/entertainment/music/peter-cooper/2014/11/16/accordion-master-joey-miskulin-finds-place-guitar-town/18994323/, accessed, January 2, 2023; Joey Miskulin, interview with authors; Cusic, *It's the Cowboy Way*, 132–33; Patti Miskulin, interview with authors, May 24, 2023.
15. Peter Cooper, host, "Nashville Cats: Salute to Accordion Player, Joey Miskulin," *Country Music Foundation*, April 24, 2018, www.facebook.com/watch/live/?ref=watch_permalink&v=10156039951234550, accessed April 25, 2023; Joey Miskulin, interview with authors; Cusic, *It's the Cowboy Way*, 132–33.
16. Carin Joy Condon, "Hard Ridin', Trail Drivin', Hide Splittin' Cowboy Comedy," unpublished essay sent to the authors.
17. Steve Arwood, interview with authors, April 22, 2022.
18. Steve Arwood, interview with authors, April 22, 2022; Bruce Nemerov, interview with authors, April 19, 2022; Thomas Goldsmith, "Riders Hit Radio Waves This Fall," *Nashville Tennessean*, July 22, 1988.
19. Cusic, *It's the Cowboy Way*, 135; Fred LaBour, interview with authors, April 12, 2022; Steve Arwood interview; Goldsmith interview; Johnny Western, interview with authors, May 31, 2023; Joey Miskulin, interview with authors, March 21, 2022.
20. Doug Green, interview with authors, April 27, 2022.
21. Linda Pender, "Urban Cowboys," *Cincinnati Magazine*, August, 1990, https://books.google.com/books?id=KOsCAAAAMBAJ&pg=PA76&lpg=PA76&dq=riders+radio+theater+cincinnati, accessed April 27, 2023; a continuing "history" of *Riders Radio Theater* serials, issued in successive chronological editions, is found at https://riders-in-the-sky.fandom.com/wiki/Riders_Radio_Theater_(series), accessed, April 27, 2023; one can also listen to episodes on the *Internet Archive*, https://archive.org/details/riders-radio-theater, accessed, April 27, 2023; Allen McNeely, interview with authors, June 29, 2022.
22. Joey Miskulin interview, March 21, 2022; Cusic, *It's the Cowboy Way*, 157–58: Doug Green, interview with authors, March 19, 2022; Cusic, "Riders In The Sky: 25 Years on the Musical Range," *Western Way* (Fall 2002): 8.
23. *Riders In The Sky* (Salt Lake City: Gibbs Smith Publisher, Peregrine Smith Books, 2023); Doug Green, email to authors, May 9, 2023; Joe Rhodes, "Riders In The Sky," *Entertainment*, September 20, 1991, https://ew.com/article/1991/09/20/riders-sky/, accessed, April 27, 2023.

24. Alan Sacks, interview with authors, April 12, 2022; Steve Dougherty and Jane Sanderson, "Riders In The Sky Lasso Listeners by Poking Fun at Cowpokes While Singing Sweetly of the Prairie," *People Weekly*, February 27, 1989.
25. *The Oakwood Apartments: Seeing Stars*, www.seeing-stars.com/Hotels/Oakwood.shtml, accessed April 30, 2023.
26. Doug Green, interview with authors, April 13, 2022; Cusic, *It's the Cowboy Way*, 168–69.
27. Mike Mahaney, interview with authors, May 14, 2022; Johnny Caps, "The Flashback Interview: George McGrath," *PopGeeks*, July 13, 2020, https://popgeeks.com/the-flashback-interview-george-mcgrath/, accessed May 2, 2023.
28. Roberta Samet LaBour obituary, *Nashville Tennessean*, February 2–3, 2018, www.legacy.com/us/obituaries/tennessean/name/roberta-labour-obituary?id=11308133, accessed May 2, 2023; Chuck Dauphin, "Riders In The Sky Look Back on 40 Years," *Billboard*, April 12, 2018, www.billboard.com/music/country/riders-in-the-sky-interview-8308248/, accessed May 2, 2023; Doug Green, interview with authors, April 13, 2022.
29. Joey Miskulin interview, March 21, 2022.
30. Tom Cole, "Encounter with Riders In The Sky," Fall 1998, www.tomhascallcole.com/encounterwithriders.html, accessed May 4, 2023; Cusic, *It's the Cowboy Way*, 188; Doug Green, interview with authors, March 7, 2022; *Rider's Roundup*, November 15, 1994; Jerry West scrapbook, Doug Green Collection, Country Music Hall of Fame and Museum Archives.
31. Jim Bessman, "Rounder Records Ropes Back Riders In The Sky," *Billboard*, September 2, 1995, 32, 34; Wrangler Awards of 1995, *National Cowboy & Western Heritage Museum*, https://nationalcowboymuseum.org/collections/awards/wha/283no-title/, accessed May 5, 2023.
32. O. J. Sikes, CD review, *Public Cowboy #1: A Centennial Salute to the Music of Gene Autry*, *Western Way* 17, no. 4 (Fall 2007): 31; Brent Truett, interview with authors, January 28, 2023.
33. A clip from *Barney and Friends* featuring the Riders, with Doug singing "How Does He Yodel," can be found on YouTube, www.youtube.com/watch?v=bEW517_Y-wA, accessed May 4, 2023; Jim Bessman, "'Rider Radio' Hits the Road," *Billboard*, July 25, 1998, 11, 85, https://books.google.com/books?id=9gkEAAAAMBAJ&pg=PA11&lpg=PA11&dq=Riders+in+the+sky,+barney+and+friends,+Billboard&source=bl&ots=Q16FYq_IpG&sig=ACfU3U3Wu4lTqegUA9_V7r65rejtZu-XSA&hl=en&sa=X&ved=2ahUKEwiAqMP3nd3-AhX8nGoFHY6rCpc4FBDoAXoECAMQAw#v=onepage&q=Riders%20in%20the%20sky%2C%20barney%20and%20friends%2C%20Billboard&f=false, accessed May 4, 2023. Jim Brown, "Twenty Years in the Sky," *American Cowboy*, May–June 1998, and *The Tenneseean*, February 27, 1998; Doug Green, email to authors, May 9, 2023; Fred LaBour, interview with authors, April 26, 2022.

34. Joe Bob Briggs, "The Vegas Guy: John Ascuaga's Nugget," *UPI Archives*, July 17, 2001, www.upi.com/Archives/2001/07/17/The-Vegas-Guy-John-Ascuagas-Nugget/6809995342400/, accessed May 5, 2023; for more information about John Ascuaga, see Howard Stutz, "Northern Nevada 'Pillar' Dies at Age 96," *Nevada Independent*, June 28, 2021, https://thenevadaindependent.com/article/northern-nevada-gaming-pillar-john-ascuaga-dies-at-age-96, accessed May 5, 2023.
35. Jon Johnson, "Ranger Doug Tells of Singing the Cowboy Way," *Country Standard Time*, November, 2002, www.countrystandardtime.com/d/article.asp?xid=751, accessed, May 5, 2023; Doug Green, interview with authors, June 23, 2022; Travis Stimeling, "Stimeling on Green, 'Singing in the Saddle: The History of the Singing Cowboy,'" H-Net, https://networks.h-net.org/node/21668/reviews/21970/stimeling-green-singing-saddle-history-singing-cowboy, accessed, May 22, 2023.
36. Jim Bessman, "'Rider Radio' Hits the Road"; David Templeton, "Happy Trails," *Sonoma County Independent*, March 19–25, 1998, www.metroactive.com/papers/sonoma/03.19.98/riders-9811.html, accessed May 5, 2023; *BPI Entertainment Newswire*, July 20, 1998, Doug Green Collection, Country Music Hall of Fame and Museum Archives; Jim Bessman, "Rounder Ropes Back Riders In The Sky," *Billboard*, September 2, 1995, 32, 34, https://worldradiohistory.com/hd2/IDX-Business/Music/Billboard-Index/IDX/1995/1995-09-02-Billboard-Page-0030.pdf, accessed May 5, 2023; "Riders In The Sky Personal Appearances," November, 1977–January, 2023; "Riders' Mail," September 10, 1999, Jerry West scrapbook, Doug Green Collection, Country Music Hall of Fame and Museum Archives.
37. Fred LaBour, email to authors, May 22, 2023.
38. Deborah Evans Price, "Riders Deliver 'Toy Story'-Inspired Set," *Billboard*, July 29, 2000, 35, https://books.google.com/books?id=kxEEAAAAMBAJ&pg=PA35&lpg=PA35&dq=Deborah+Evans+Price,+Riders+Deliver+Toy+Story-Inspired+Set,+Billboard,+July+29,+2000&source=bl&ots=HTcxQ3QmjI&sig=ACfU3U1zVcxgDyJCwdMzEJ_cMgtuHiJgPw&hl=en&sa=X&ved=2ahUKEwjoq8_-1t_-AhUWkWoFHexkArk4ChD0AX0ECAIQAw#v=onepage&q=Deborah%20Evans%20Price%2,C%20Riders%20Deliver%20Toy%20Story-Inspired%20Set%2C%20Billboard%2C%20July%2029%2C%202000&f=false, accessed May 5, 2023; Chuck Dauphin, "Riders In The Sky Look Back on Forty Years," *Billboard*, April 12, 2018, www.billboard.com/music/country/riders-in-the-sky-interview-8308248/, accessed May 5, 2023; Doug Green, interview with authors, April 12, 2022.
39. Price, "Riders Deliver 'Toy Story'-Inspired Set"; Doug Green, email to authors, August 7, 2022.
40. "Riders In The Sky Personal Appearances," November, 1977–January, 2023; Jerry West, interview with authors, March 20, 2023; Devon Dawson,

interview with authors, March 24, 2023; Joey Miskulin, interview with authors, March 21, 2022.

41. "News from Harmony Ranch," March 25, 2002, Jerry West scrapbook, Doug Green Collection, Country Music Hall of Fame and Archives.
42. Mike Mahaney, interview with authors, May 28, 2022, Fred LaBour, interview with authors; Cusic, *It's the Cowboy Way*, 221; Doug Green, interview with authors, April 27, 2022; Joey Miskulin, interview with authors, March 21, 2022.

Chapter 6

1. Fred LaBour, quoted in Don Cusic, "Riders In The Sky: 30 Years on the Trail," *Western Way* 17, no. 4 (Fall 2007).
2. Fred LaBour, email to authors, May 15, 2023.
3. Paul Lohr, email to authors, June 3, 2023.
4. Jay Peterson, interview with authors, May 1, 2023.
5. Don Cusic, *It's the Cowboy Way: The Amazing Adventures of Riders In The Sky* (Lexington: University Press of Kentucky, 2003), 119–20; Billy Maxwell, interview with authors, April 7, 2022.
6. Fred LaBour, email to authors, June 6, 2023; Ken Jones, interview with authors, June 6, 2023.
7. Fred LaBour, email to authors, June 6, 2023; Lou and Peter Berryman, "Dem Deer," on their album *Some Days*, 2005.
8. Fred LaBour, email to authors, June 6, 2023; Doug Green, interview with authors, May 16, 2022.
9. Fred LaBour, email to authors, June 6, 2023.
10. Fred LaBour, email to authors, June 22, 2023.
11. Sally Ann Green Angeli, interview with authors, March 30, 2022; Sandy Wilkerson, interview with authors, May 20, 2023; Patti Miskulin, interview with authors, May 24, 2023; Fred LaBour, email to authors, May 15, 2023.
12. Woody Paul Chrisman and Fred LaBour, interview with authors, June 8, 2023; Chrisman, interview with authors, May 17, 2022; Cusic, *It's the Cowboy Way*, 23.
13. Alice LaBour Fair, interview with authors, April 5, 2022; Liza Green Parnell, interview with authors, April 21, 2022; George LaBour, interview with authors, June 1, 2022; Doug Green, interview with authors, April 27, 2022; Annie Green and James Green, interview with authors, May 6, 2022.
14. Alice LaBour Fair, interview with authors; Liza Green Parnell, interview with authors, April 21, 2022; Sally Green Angeli interview; Lily LaBour Catalano, interview with authors, April 27, 2022; Annie Green and James Green, interview with authors; Grace Green, interview with authors, April 19, 2022; George LaBour, interview with authors.
15. Val Maiewskij-Hay, "Engine of Change: Before Its Reinvention as an Amusement Park Ride, Tweetsie Railroad Transformed Boone from an

Isolated Mountain Hamlet into a Boomtown," *WNC Magazine,* July, 2011, https://wncmagazine.com/feature/engine_change, accessed May 19, 2023; "History of Tweetsie Railroad," https://tweetsie.com/assets/documents/History-of-Tweetsie-Railroad.pdf, accessed, May 19, 2023; "Fred Kirby," *History South,* www.historysouth.org/kirby/, accessed, May 19, 2023; Doug Green, email to authors, May 19, 2023; Lily LaBour Fair interview; Sally Green Angeli interview.

16. Donna and Ed Jagodzinski, interview with authors, June 3, 2023.
17. Deborah Evans Price, "Riders, Club Each Win Two Trophies at WMA Music Awards," *Billboard,* November 23, 2002, https://books.google.com/books?id=SA0EAAAAMBAJ&pg=PA29&lpg=PA29&dq=Riders+in+the+Sky,+roast,+WMA&source, accessed, January 24, 2023; "Riders In The Sky Silver Jubilee Tribute & Roast," program, November 15, 2002, Jerry West scrapbook, Doug Green Collection, Country Music Hall of Fame and Museum Archives.
18. "Riders In The Sky Cruise to Hawaii, November 17–24, 2022," brochure, Jerry West scrapbook, Doug Green Collection, Country Music Hall of Fame and Museum Archives; "Riders In The Sky Personal Appearances," November 1977–January 2023.
19. Steven Stone, "Riders In The Sky: Silver Jubilee," *Enjoy the Music.com,* www.enjoythemusic.com/magazine/music/0905/folk/riders.htm, accessed on January 24, 2023; "Walk of Western Stars Inductees," *SCV History.com,* https://scvhistory.com/scvhistory/lw2102.htm, accessed May 20, 2023.
20. "Walk of Western Stars," *Oldtown Newhall,* https://oldtownnewhall.com/walk_of_the_western_stars/, accessed September 10, 2024; "Walk of Western Stars: Riders In The Sky, 2003," *SCV History.com,* https://scvhistory.com/scvhistory/sg032903bc.html, accessed September 10, 2024.
21. Craig Havighurst, "The Time Jumpers Beat the Time Clock," *All Things Considered,* January 5, 2009, www.npr.org/2009/01/05/99009077/the-time-jumpers-beat-the-time-clock, accessed, May 17, 2023; Andy Riess, interview with authors, May 2, 2022.
22. Craig Havighurst, "The Time Jumpers Beat the Time Clock," *All Things Considered,* January 5, 2009; Doug Green, interview with authors, March 7, 2022; Andy Riess, interview with authors, May 2, 2022; "Asleep at the Wheel," *Handbook of Texas Special Projects, Texas State Historical Association,* www.tshaonline.org/handbook/entries/asleep-at-the-wheel, accessed May 17, 2023.
23. Jewly Hight, "Who Knew Jamming on Western Swing Could Get the Time Jumpers Where Every Band Wants to Be?" *Nashville Scene,* September 6, 2012, www.nashvillescene.com/music/who-knew-jamming-on-western-swing-could-get-the-time-jumpers-where-every-band-wants/article_e819c367-7b7e-5800-93e6-48802e468a94.html, accessed April 30, 2023; Chip Chandler,

"Ranger Doug Green on Western Swing, the Time Jumpers and Being the 'Beautiful Heartbeat' of a Band," *Panhandle PBS*, July 11, 2016, www.pan handlepbs.org/blogs/play-here/ranger-doug-green-on-western-swing-the -time-jumpers-and-being-the-beautiful-heartbeat-of-a-band/, accessed May 21, 2023.

24. Jewly Hight, "Who Knew Jamming on Western Swing Could Get the Time Jumpers Where Every Band Wants to Be?"; Chip Chandler, "Ranger Doug Green on Western Swing, the Time Jumpers and Being the 'Beautiful Heartbeat' of a Band"; for a good short account of the Time Jumpers, see John Lupton, "The Time Jumpers," *Country Standard Time*, November, 2012, https://countrystandardtime.com/d/article.asp?xid=1139, accessed, January 21, 2003.

25. Tony Gonzales, "Read 1,001 Books? Ranger Doug Did It on a Tour Bus," *Tennessean*, August 25, 2014, www.tennessean.com/story/news/2014/08/25 /read-books-ranger-doug-tour-bus/14461493/, accessed, May 22, 2023.

26. "Utah Symphony Will Back Nashville's Riders In The Sky," *Deseret News*, July 15, 2001, www.deseret.com/2001/7/15/19596373/utah-symphony-will -back-nashville-s-riders-in-the-sky?_amp=true, accessed, May 22, 2023.

27. "Hollywood Bowl Annual July 4th Fireworks Spectacular Goes Western with Riders In The Sky," *The Ford*, July 2, 2007, www.theford.com/press /releases/653, accessed May 22, 2023.

28. Landmark studies in new interpretations of the West include Patricia Limerick, *The Legacy of Conquest: The Unbroken Past of the American West*, 1987, and Richard White, *"It's Your Misfortune and None of My Own": A History of the American West*, 1991; Kaylee Brister, *"Eight Seconds*: A Photo Book about Black Cowboys," *Cowboys & Indians*, February/March, 2022, www.cowboysindians.com/2022/01/eight-seconds-a-photo-book-about -black-cowboys/, accessed June 20, 2023; Steve Hochman, "Riders In The Sky: Genuine Songs, the Cowboy Way," *Bluegrass Situation*, July 3, 2018, https:// thebluegrasssituation.com/read/riders-in-the-sky-genuine-songs-the -cowboy-way/, accessed June 11, 2023.

29. Addie Moore, "Flashback: Wilford Brimley Cut an Album with Riders in the Sky," *Wide Open Country*, August 3, 2020, www.wideopencountry.com /wilford-brimley-riders-in-the-sky/, accessed, May 21, 2023.

30. Doug Green, interview with authors, April 12, 2022; Fred LaBour, interview with authors, April 19, 2022.

31. David Wolfe in *American Cowboy*, February 14, 2017, https://american cowboy.com/lifestyle/riders-sky-0/, accessed May 1, 2023; Don Rhodes, "A Riders In The Sky Discovery: Their Music Is Out of This World," *Augusta Chronicle*, March 16, 2011, www.augustachronicle.com/story/opinion /columns/guest/2011/03/16/riders-sky-discovery-their-music-out-world /14551915007/, accessed May 24, 2023.

32. "Dude Ranches: A Typically American Vacation in the Glorious West," *Environment and Society Portal*, www.environmentandsociety.org/exhibitions/cbq-railroad/dude-ranches-typically-american-vacation-glorious-west, accessed May 26, 2023; Doug Green, interview with authors, April 27, 2022, and May 26, 2023; Ken Jones, interview with authors, June 3, 2023.
33. Gary McMahan, interview with authors, January 19, 2023; Doug Green, interview with authors, April 20, 2022, and May 26, 2023.
34. Chuck Aaland, "Fifty Years of Fiddling Around," *Durango Telegraph*, June 28, 2018, www.durangotelegraph.com/second-section/features/50-years-of-fiddling-around/, accessed June 6, 2023; Doug Green, email to authors, April 27, 2022; Gary Cook, interview with authors, June 4, 2023.
35. Fred LaBour, email to authors, May 25, 2023.
36. Orin Friesen, interview with authors, May 27, 2023; "Riders In The Sky Personal Appearances," November 1977–January 2023; Doug Green, email to authors, June 25, 2022; May 26, 2023; June 3, 2023; Johnny Western, interview with authors, May 31, 2023; Fred LaBour, email to authors, June 4, 2023.
37. Woody Paul Chrisman and Fred LaBour, interview with authors, June 8, 2023; Fred LaBour, email to authors, June 29, 2023.
38. Norton Dill, interview with authors, July 13, 2022; email, September 12, 2024.
39. Norton Dill interview. Rane, from Abbeville, Alabama, was described in 2016 as the richest man in Alabama. For more on Yella Fella, see "The Story behind the Creation of YellaWood's Iconic Yella Fella Character and Campaign," *Yellow Hammer*, https://yellowhammernews.com/the-story-behind-the-creation-of-yellawoods-iconic-yella-fella-character-and-campaign/, March 25, 2020, accessed June 7, 2023. The Riders' commercials can be found on YouTube.
40. Katie Chicklinski-Cahill, "Riders In The Sky Moseying to Durango," *Durango Herald*, August 16, 2018, www.durangoherald.com/articles/riders-in-the-sky-moseying-to-durango-2/, accessed, June 12, 2023.
41. Fred LaBour, interview with authors, May 15, 2022, and June 16, 2022; Sandy Wilkerson interview; one can read Roberta's full obituary at "Roberta Lynn Barnet LaBour," *The Tennessean*, www.legacy.com/us/obituaries/tennessean/name/roberta-labour-obituary?id=11308133, accessed June 12, 2023.
42. Jennifer Robinson, "Country Music: Live at the Ryman, a Concert Celebrating the Film of Ken Burns," *KPBS*, September 5, 2019, www.kpbs.org/news/arts-culture/2019/09/05/country-music-live-ryman-concert-celebrating-film, accessed June 15, 2023; Terry Gross, "Western Music Expert Doug Green Revisits the Era of the Singing Cowboy," NPR, September 25, 2019, www.npr.org/2019/09/25/764227667/western-music-expert-doug-green-revisits-the-era-of-the-singing-cowboy, accessed June 15, 2023.

43. Wayne Bledsoe, "The Birth of Bonnaroo," *Our Tennessee*, https://our.tennessee.edu/2012/the-birth-of-bonnaroo/, accessed June 16, 2023; Katie Chicklinski-Cahill, "Riders In The Sky Moseying to Durango," *Durango Herald*, August 16, 2018, www.durangoherald.com/articles/riders-in-the-sky-moseying-to-durango-2/, accessed on June 16, 2023; Joe Reinartz, " A Few Minutes of the Trail with Ranger Doug," *Celebrity Access*, June 10, 2019, https://celebrityaccess.com/2019/06/10/a-few-minutes-on-the-trail-with-ranger-doug/, accessed June 16, 2023.

44. Fred LaBour, email to authors, May 13, 2023; Jeff Taylor, interview with authors, April 8, 2022.

45. Paul Lohr email; "Riders In The Sky Personal Appearances," November 1977–January, 2023; Fred LaBour, email to authors, May 13, 2023; "Nashville Spotlight: Riders In The Sky," *SAG-AFTRA*, March 2, 2021, www.sagaftra.org/nashville-spotlight-riders-sky, accessed June 18, 2023.

46. Doug Green, interviews with authors, March 19 and June 23, 2022.

47. Desi Green, interview with authors, May 12, 2022; Doug Green, interviews with authors, March 3, March 11, email to authors, May 11, 2022; "Nashville Spotlight: Riders In The Sky."

48. Woody Paul Chrisman, interview with authors, May 17, 2022; Lisa Reed Chrisman, interview with authors, March 20, 2023; "Nashville Spotlight: Riders In The Sky."

49. Fred LaBour, email to authors, May 13, 2022; Doug Green, email to authors, May 19, 2023; Paul Lohr email.

50. Doug Green, email to authors, May 2, 2023.

51. The Riders' forty-fifth anniversary show can be heard on YouTube, www.google.com/search?q=riders+in+the+sky+45th+anniversary&source, accessed June 12, 2023; Ollie Reed Jr., "Western Music Icon to Speak at IWMA Convention," *Albuquerque Journal*, November 4, 2022, www.abqjournal.com/2546401/western-music-icon-to-speak-at-iwma-convention.html, accessed, June 14, 2023.

52. Paul Lohr, interview with authors, June 2, 2023; Pete Fisher, interview with authors, April 6, 2022; Doug Green, email to authors, February 20, 2023.

53. Doug Green, liner notes, *Throw a Saddle on a Star*, Riders In The Sky, 2023; Doug Green, email to authors, May 14, 2024, "The Shelter of the Wildwood," Western Heritage Award Winner," *National Cowboy and Western Heritage Museum*, https://nationalcowboymuseum.org/collections/awards/wha/the-shelter-of-the-wildwood/, accessed September 12, 2024.

54. Jayna Henderson, interview with authors, June 5, 2023; Richard Wiegel, interview with authors, February 23, 2023; Mary Masteller, interview with authors, February 24, 2023.

55. Steve Jacobs, interview with authors, May 28, 2023; Bill Nye, interview with authors, March 22, 2023.

56. Fred LaBour, email to authors, February 24, 2023; Susan Nelson, interview with authors, May 30, 2022; Susan, Butch, and Kyle Nelson, FaceTime with authors, May 30, 2022; Susan Nelson, email to authors, May 30, 2022, and June 20, 2023.
57. Doug Green, email to authors, June 22, 2023; Fred LaBour, post on the Riders In The Sky Facebook page, November 11, 2022, https://m.facebook.com/Saddlepals/posts/682343659914897/, accessed June 22, 2023.

DISCOGRAPHY

Three on the Trail: Rounder Records, 1980
Cowboy Jubilee: Rounder Records, 1981
Prairie Serenade: Rounder Records, 1982
Weeds & Water: Rounder Records, 1983
Riders In The Sky, Live: Rounder Records, 1984
Saddle Pals: Rounder Records, 1985
New Trails: Rounder Records, 1986
Best of the West: Rounder Records, 1987
The Cowboy Way: MCA, 1987
Riders Radio Theater: MCA, 1988
Riders Go Commercial: MCA, 1989
Best of the West Rides Again: Rounder Records, 1990
Horse Opera: MCA, 1990
Harmony Ranch: CBS, 1991
Merry Christmas from Harmony Ranch: CBS, 1992
Saturday Morning with the Riders: MCA, 1992
Cowboys in Love: Epic Records, 1994
Always Drink Upstream from the Herd: Rounder Records, 1995
Cowboy Songs: Rounder Records, 1996
Public Cowboy #1: The Music of Gene Autry: Rounder Records, 1996
Ranger Doug: Songs of the Sage: Warner Western, 1997
Yodel the Cowboy Way: Rounder Records, 1998
A Great Big Western Howdy! Rounder Records, 1998
Christmas the Cowboy Way: Rounder Records, 1999
Woody's Roundup: A Rootin' Tootin' Collection of Woody's Favorite Songs: Disney, 2000

A Pair of Kings: Oh Boy Records: Oh Boy Records, 2002
Ridin' the Tweetsie Railroad: Self-released, 2002
Monsters, Inc. Scream Factory Favorites: Disney, 2002
Silver Jubilee: Acoustic Disc, 2003
Riders In The Sky Present Davy Crockett, King of the Wild Frontier: Rounder Records, 2004
Riders In The Sky from the Golden Age of Riders Radio Theater: Riders Radio Records, 2006
Riders In The Sky "Lassoed Live" at the Schermerhorn with the Nashville Symphony: Nashville Symphony, 2009
The Land Beyond the Sun: Riders Radio Records, 2011
America's Favorite Cowboy Songs: Cracker Barrel, 2012
Home on the Range (with Wilford Brimley): Riders Radio Records, 2013
Riders In The Sky Salute Roy Rogers: King of the Cowboys: Riders Radio Records/Too Slim's Mercantile, 2016
Songs of the Frontier (Ranger Doug: With a Lot of Help from Riders In the Sky): Rural Rhythm, 2018
Riders In The Sky: Throw a Saddle on a Star: Riders Radio Records, 2023

GENERAL INDEX

Page numbers in italics refer to illustrations

1874 Steamboat Springs, 85

Abbott, Mark, 192
Ace and the Gay Tones, 25
Acuff, Roy, 73
Albion College, 22–23, 25
Allen, Jules Verne, 7
Allen, Red (Henry James), 29
Allen, Rex, 1
Allen, Rosalie, 36, 91
Alley, Elmer, 120
Amos, Jamie, 99, 128, 201
Amram, David, 189
Angeli, Sally Green, 25
Arwood, Steve (Texas Bix Bender), 120, 121, 145, 178
Ashlock, Jesse, 12
Asleep at the Wheel (band), 12, 67, 180
Ascuaga, John, 157
Atcher, Bob, 142
Austin City Limits, 85; Riders' first appearance, 104
Austin, Texas: musical scene, 12; clubs in, 85
Autry, Gene, 1, 3, 9–10, 151, 152

Bailey, F. Lee, 53
Ball, Bentley, 6
Ballard, Bobby (Hartz Mountain Travelers), 58
Ballard, Larry (Ballards), 58
Bar D Chuckwagon, 134, 187
Bar D Wranglers, 187
Barney and Friends, 155
Barry, Buck (Chester Burry), 45
Bartenstein, Fred, 26
Baskovic, Frank and Mary, 139
Battleground Academy, Franklin, Tennessee, 71
Bayers, Eddie, 95
Beck, Dan, 66, 67, 78, 79
Benson, Ray (Ray Benson Seifert), 12, 67, 178, 180
Berryman, Lou and Peter, 171
Bierstadt, Albert, 3
Big Sandy Boys, 27–28
The Big Show, 10
Billboard, 66
Birchmere Restaurant, 77
Black, Baxter, 133, 134, 135
Black cowboys, 5–6
Blanton, Big Jim, 187
Blanton, Henry, 5

bluegrass, 57, 58
Bonanza, 2
Bond, Johnny, 36
Bonnaroo Music and Arts Festival, 194–195
Boyd, Pat, 44–45
Brannon, Ash, 161
Brimley, Wilford, 184–185
Britt, Elton (James Britt Baker), 91
Broderson, Jay, 142
Brooks, Garth, 158
Brown, Milton, 92
Bruce, Ed and Patsy, 2
Bruner, Cliff, 12
Bryan, James, 58
Buchanan, Frank, 27
The Buckaroo Rodeo, 45
Buddy Lee Attractions, 127
Buffalo Bill Cody, 4
Buffalo Bill Cowboy Band, 4
Buffalo Bill: The King of Border Men, 4
Buffalo Soldiers, 6
Buntline, Ned (Edward Zane Carroll Judson), 4
Burnette, Smiley (Lester Alvin), 11
Burns, Ken, 192, 194
Burton, Michael, 3
Byrds, 9

"Cac-ties," 110
Cain's Ballroom, 189
Candeleria, Cynthia, 72, 73, 74
Cannon, Hal, 132–134
Carolina Chocolate Drops, 183
Carolina Cotton, 10
Cartwright Brothers (Bernard and Jack), 7
Cash, Johnny, 2, 44, 112, 145
Cassidy, Jay, 52, 53
Cat's Cradle, 77, 102
cattle drives, 4, 5
CBS, 148, 149, 150, 151, 152, 159, 161
Cellar Door, 77
Chambers, Bob, 23

Chapman, Marshall, 72–73, 74–76
Chapman, Snake (Owen Chapman), 28
Chicks (formerly, Dixie Chicks), 147
Chopper, Alex, 25
Chrisman, Lisa Reed, 173, 197–198
Chrisman, Minnie Katherine Douglas (Mama Kat), 69, 72, 76, 197
Chrisman, Paul Woodrow (Old Man), 69–71, 72
Chrisman, Paul Woodrow, Jr. (Woody Paul), 3, 12, 69–77, 75, 117; birth and childhood, 69–70; introduction to and early aptitude for fiddling, 70–72; early musical influences, 72; Battleground Academy, 71; interest in physics, 72; at Vanderbilt, 72–73; marriage to Cynthia Candaleria, 72; birth of Paul David, 72, birth of Joseph, 74; divorce, 74; at MIT, 74–75; dissertation, 74–75; with Marshall Chapman, 72–73, 74–76; PhD, 76; songwriting, 75, 94, 95; work at Atomic Energy Commission, 76; returns to Nashville, 76; meets Fred LaBour, 76–77; work with Loggins and Messina, 77; marriage to Liza Ramage, 77; births of Rebecca and Jacob, 77; work with Wilma Lee Cooper, 77; joins Riders In The Sky as Woody Paul, King of the Cowboy Fiddlers, 13, 68, 81, 92; songwriting, 93; trick roping, 102, 122; eccentricities and problems, 68, 98, 114; divorce from Liza, 174; marriage to and divorce from Teresa Goicoechea, 174; birth of Katherine (Kaitlyn) and Casey, 174; mechanical expertise, 172–173; induction into the National Fiddlers Hall of Fame, 189; marriage to Lisa Reed, 173, 197–198.
Clement, Cowboy Jack, 60, 142
Cohn, Nudie (Nuta Kotlyarenko), 1, 112
Collins, Bill (Windy Bill), 11, 12, 59–60, 61, 65, 66, 67, 110

Condon, Carin Joy, 99, 102–103, 143, 154, 201
Continentals, 54
Cook, Gary, 187–188
Cooper, James Fennimore, 4
Cooper, Wilma Lee, 77
Copeland, Arch, 23
Cotton, Carolina, 10
Count Basie Band, 92, 105
Country Music (magazine), 66
Country Music (PBS series), 194
Country Music Foundation, 35–36, 78, 84, 96, 157
Country Music Hall of Fame and Museum, 35, 59, 63, 66, 89, 110, 117, 145, 157
Country Roots: The Origins of Country Music, 36, 37
Covid pandemic, 169, 195–198
"The Cowboy Who Hated Christmas," 80, 143
Cowboy Poetry Gathering, 133–134, 135, 138, 157
"The Cowboy Way," 99
Cranbrook School, 22–24
Crouch, Dennis, 179
Cuevas, Manuel (Manuel Arturo José Cuevas Martinez), 98, 112–113, 119
Curtis, Ken, 98
Cusic, Don, 38, 46, 49, 62, 66, 71, 85, 89, 90, 93, 95, 140; as manager for Riders, 67, 68, 78, 79, 174

David, Herb, 26, 27, 28, 30, 31
Dawson, Devon, 163, 164
Dean, Eddie, 36
Deseret String Band, 133
DeVriendt, Mike, 42, 48, 50, 51
Dickens, Hazel, 89
Dickinson, Virgil, 116
Dill, Norton, 190
dime novelists, 4
Discovery (NASA space shuttle), 186
Dobie, J. Frank, 6

Doug Green Band, 38, 57
Duncan, Dayton, 194
Durham, Hal, 114, 117
Dusty Roads Tavern, 31
Dylan, Bob (Robert Zimmerman), 51

Edwards, Don, 134
Eight Seconds (book), 183
Emery, Ralph, 67, 79, 84
Etheredge, Thomas, 188–189
Evans, Dale, 158
Ewing, Tom, 30
Exit/ In, 77

Farr, Hugh and Karl, 10–11, 92
Faulkner, Nolan, 27–28, 29
Fegan, Bill, 125
Fisher, Pete, 200
Fisher, Sandy Peterson, 20
Flanagan, Mary, 87
Flatt and Scruggs (Lester Flatt and Earl Scruggs), 26
Flemons, Dom, 183
Flores, Ann Marie, 173
Ford, Davis, 85, 105
Ford, Glenn, 5
Forester, Howdy (Howard Wilson), 12
Forster, Nick, 12
For the Birds, 165
Fowler, Bob, 58
Fox, Matt, 205
Fox, Oscar, 6
Fraser, Paul, 3
Freeman, Herschel, 54–56
Friedman, Kinky (Richard S.), 149
Friesen, Orin, 188–189

Gann, Carolyn, 173
General Sam's, 85
Gibb, Russ, 52, 53
Gill, Vince, 180
Goble, Pete, 28
Goicoechea, Teresa, 174
Goldsmith, Tommy (Thomas), 12, 68, 79, 80, 86; as Tumbleweed Tommy, 81

Goodbye, Little Rock and Roller, 73
Gotch, Frank, 41
Grand Ole Opry, 72, 73, 75, 200; Riders' first appearance, 84 84, Riders' induction, 113–114, 116–117, performances, 131, 184–185, 198
Great American Cowboy Concert, 188–189
Green, Annie, 35, 153, 174, 175, 187
Green, Connie (Constance), 22, 24–25
Green, Desi (Dezarria Donzella Smith), 173, 196, 197
Green, Douglas B., 10, 12, 15–38, 61, 117, 129, 192, 199; birth, 15; childhood, 16, 17, 18; in California, 18–19; in Boston, 19–20; return to Michigan, 20; Finnish family in Upper Michigan, 16, 18, 20–21; first experiences with guitar, 18, 21; yodeling, 18, 91; interest in cowboy music, 18–19; harmony singing, 23; at Cranbrook, 22–24; first guitars, 22–23; first public performances, 23; bluegrass, 23, 25–30, 32; first radio appearance, 30; and religion, 24; at Albion College, 22–23, 25; at University of Michigan, 26–27, 30; and Mary Greenman, 26, 29, 30; and Bill Monroe, 26, 28–30, 32; playing with Jimmy Martin, 32; at Vanderbilt, 31, 33; birth of Liza Jane, 31; early albums, 33; work at the Hermitage, 33; birth of Sally Anne, 33; work at GTR, 33–34; and archtop guitars, 34; divorce from Mary, 35; marriage to Cindy Turner, 35; birth of Annie Laurie and James, 35; oral historian for Country Music Foundation, 35–36, and western music, 36, meets Sons of the Pioneers, 37; organizes what becomes Riders In The Sky, 64–65, Riders fulltime, 78, as Ranger Doug, Idol of American youth 3, 11, 13, 80, as songwriter, 13, 27, 36, 93, 95, 128,

200–201; as author, 34, 36, *Singing in the Saddle*, 157–158; as scholar, 84, 157, 189; records *Songs of the Sage*, 137; divorce from Cindy, 149; rhythm guitar, 13, Freddie Green style, 92, 180–181; marriage to Dianne Rau, 150, birth of Grace, 150; subsequent two marriages and divorces, 174; *Ranger Doug's Classic Cowboy Corral*, 124; marriage to Desi Smith, 173, 196, 197; as yodeling lifeguard, 196; Time Jumpers, 179–181; health issues, 153–154, 198–199; Terry Gross interview, 194; Western Heritage Award, 200–201
Green, Freddie, 92, 105, 180
Green Grow the Lilacs, 7
Green, Hilda Maria Peterson, 15–16, 17, 21; emotional issues, divorce, and suicide, 25
Green, James Donald, 15–16, 17; professional education, 19–20; divorce and remarriage, 25
Green, James Donald, Jr. (Jim), 17–18, 22–23
Green, James Douglas, 35, 113, 174, 175, 187
Greenman, Mary, 26, 29, 30–31
Grigas, Rich, 51
Gross, Terry, 194
Gruhn, George, 33–34
GTR (later George Gruhn Guitars), 33–34
Guion, David, 6
Gunsmoke, 2

Haggard, Merle, 180
Hale, Randy, 120
Hall, Patty, 61
Haney, Carlton: bluegrass festivals, 26
Happy Chappies (Fred Howard and Nat Vincent), 9
Hargrove, Linda, 66
Harmony Ranch, 81

238 GENERAL INDEX

Hartford, John, 110
Harris, Emmylou, 119, 136
Harris, Stacy, 127
Hartz Mountain Travelers, 59
Hassinger, Jane, 54
Have Gun—Will Travel, 2
Hayes, Gabby (George Francis), 11, 49
Hedgecoth, John, 38
Hee Haw, 129, 130
Henderson, Jayna and Kim, 201–202, 203
Hendrickson, Janet Peterson, 18
Herb David Guitar Studio, 26, 27
Hester, Hoot (Hubert Dwane), 179
Herr Harry's Phranks 'n' Steins, 11, 61–62
Hill, Billy (William Joseph), 9
Hillis, Ron, 34
Hlebak, Patti, 141, 142, 173, 176
Hobsbawn, Eric, 5, 6
Hollywood Bowl performances, 182–183
Home Ranch, 186–187
Honky Tonk Angels, 54–55
Hopkins, Jerry, 54
Hospital Hospitality House, 129, 155
Hot Rize, 12
Hoyle, Peter, 57

Irwin, Ken, 89–90, 95
Ivey, Bill, 27, 35–36, 84, 93

Jackson, Tommy, 71
Jagodzinski, Donna and Ed, 176–177, 201
Jeffries, Herb, 10
Joey the Cowpolka King. *See* Miskulin, Joey (Joseph Michael)
John, Dr. Tom, 83,
Jones, Ken, 186–187, 201
Jones, Spike (Lindley Armstrong), 22
Jordan, Vic, 31
Journal of Country Music, 36, 158

Kale's Waterfall Supper Club, 54
Kay, Ron, 28
KBSU (Boise, Idaho), 147
KCRW (Santa Monica, California), 111
Kennedy Center, 104
Kennison, Warren, 23, 27
Kentucky State Fair, 78
KFRC (San Francisco), 2
KG and the Ranger (Karen Gogolick and Rick Roltgen), 138
kiddie cowboy shows, 2, 3
Kilroy, Eddie (Alva Dave Moore), 185
Keillor, Garrison, 12
King, Larry, 88–89
Kirby, Fred, 176
Klein, Jill, 83
Knottsberry Farm, 19
Kramer, Jane, 5
Krauss, Alison, 89, 147, 154
Krulwich, Sarah, 53
Kushner, Lynn, 56

LaBour, Alice Stuart, 44
LaBour, Chris (Christine), 40, 47
LaBour, Fred, 39–63, 93, 95, 96, 97, 117, 203; birth and childhood in Grand Rapids, 39–40, love of outdoors and country living, 40, 42–43; early adventures in the West, 43, 47; humor and performance, 41, 45, 46, 49, including face-slapping, 45–46, 100; cowboy sidekicks, 49; music, 44, 50; entrepreneurship, 46; as Episcopalian, 24, 50; early displays of musical talent, 50, 51, at University of Michigan, 51–54; "Paul is Dead" hoax, 52–53, films and filmmaking interest, 53; as electric bass player, 54–56, Honky Tonk Angels, 54–56; early Nashville musical experiences, 55–56; meeting and first playing with Doug Green, 56–57, 61; songwriting, 57, 93, 129; playing acoustic bass 57; playing with the Ballards, 58–59; non-musical

work in Nashville, 59, 61, at Nashville Public Library, 82–83; marriage to Peggy Young, 59; births of Frank and Lily, 59; playing with Dickey Lee Band, 59–61; meets Woody Paul Chrisman, 76–77; beginning of Riders, 64–65; as Too Slim, 3, 11, 13, 80, rabbit dancing, 87, 116; varmint dancing, 88, 102, writing scripts, 80, 81, 83, 121, 144–145, as Side Meat, 49, 123–124, 146, 185; Mercantile, 107, 108–*109*, 110; and Roberta Samet, 106–107, *125*; marriage to Roberta Samet, 134; birth of Alice, 151; birth of George, 159; *Say No More, It's Freddy LaBour*, 168; *The Sidekick Handbook*, 168; *Ranger Doug's Classic Cowboy Corral*, 124, 185

LaBour, Hazel Fredricka Gotch, 39–40, 41, 43–44, 47–48

LaBour, George F., 39, 41

LaBour, George F., Jr., 39, 40, 41–42, 51

LaBour, George F., III (Jeffy), sudden death, 39

LaBour, George Harold, 159

LaBour, Robert (Uncle Bob), 48

LaBour, Roberta Samet (Bert), 112, *125*, 127; meeting Fred, 106–107; costume design, 107, 124; work with Manuel Cuevas, 113; Mercantile, 107, 110; marriage to Fred, 134, 173; birth of Alice, 151; birth of George, 159; Daytime Emmy award, 151; sickness and death, 191–192

Landers, Jay, 161

Lasseter, John, 161, *164*, 178

The Last Cowboy, 5

LeDoux, Chris, 134–135

Lee, Dickey (Royden Dickey Lipscomb), 59–61

Lee, Ronnie, 139

Leroy, Lance, 91

Levy, Marian Leighton, 89

Lichtenstein, Dr. Michael, 87

Lickona, Tony, 85

Loggins and Messina, 77

Logsdon, Guy, 37

Lohr, Paul, 127–128, 159, *160*, 168–169, 196

Lorch, Peter, 25

Lomax, John, 6

Lone Star Café, 79–80, 105

Lucky U Ranch, 79

Lynn, Loretta, 127

Macon, Uncle Dave, 72

Mad Magazine, 11, 49

Mahan, Larry, 133

Mahaney, Mike, 111–112, 119, 150–151, 165, 201

Mainer, Wade and Julia, 28

Making It with Music: Kenny Rogers' Guide to the Music Business, 86

Malone, Bill C., 10

Mandrell, Barbara, 112, 147

Martin, Jimmy, 32

Marvin, Frankie, 36

Masteller, Mary and Bob, 202, *203*

Mattea, Kathy, 147, 158, 194

Maxwell, Billy, 69, 71, 169–170, 201

May, Elaine, 11

McAuliffe, Leon, 12

McCabe's, 111, 149

McClellan, Ivan, 183

McClintock, Harry, 2, 7

McEntire, Reba, 158

McEuen, Bill, 125

McGee, Sam and Kirk, 71–72

McGrath, George, 160, 161

McMahan, Gary, 134, 135, 200

McNeely, Allen, 70, 147, 201

McQuaid, Jim, 22, 23–24, 26, 27, 29

McRae, Wally (Wallace D.), 134

Melody Ranch, 79, 81, 160

Meier, Carl, 109–110

Melton, James, 8

Mercer, Johnny, 9

Merritt, Marcie LaBour, 39–40, 42–43, 44, 46–47, 53

The Michigan Daily, 52, 53
Mike Nichols and Elaine May, 11
Miller, Roger, 2
Miller, Russ, 95
Miller, Townsend, 85
Milloch, Gretchen, 54
Miskulin, Joseph John, 139
Miskulin, Joey (Joseph Michael), 12, 92, 134, *140*, *193*; birth and childhood, 139; first accordion, 139; early musical influences, 139; influence of clarinet players, 142; early professional performances, 139; playing with Frank Yankovic, 139–140, *141*; with Hawaii International Review, 140; first marriage and divorce, 141; move to Cleveland, 141; marriage to Patty Hlebak, 141, children, 142; Miskulin's Lounge, 141; *Polka Time USA*, 142; association with Cowboy Jack Clement, 142; producer of four Grammy award-nominated albums, 141; move to Nashville, 142; meeting up and playing with the Riders, 142–143, 146; difficulties with David Skepner, 147; touring with Michael Martin Murphey, 147–148; retuning to the Riders and becoming Joey the Cowpolka King, 152; music maven and record producer for band, 152, 154, 165; Pixar and Disney experiences, 164–165; health issues, 195; as producer of *Ranger Doug's Classic Cowboy Corral*, 124
Miskulin's Lounge, 141
Miskulin, Mary Ann Baskovic, 139
Mississippi Whiskers, 64, 77
Mitchell, Waddie, 133
Moag, Rod, 30
Monroe, Bill, 26, 28–30, 104
Monroe, Carolyn, 28–29
Monroe, James, 32
Monsters, Inc., 164–165
Montana Slim (Wilf Carter), 91

Moore, Gloria Jean, 125
Morris, John W., 30
Mr. Whitekeys, 118
Mr. Wizard IV (Steve Jacobs), 202
Murphey, Michael Martin, 135–136

Nashville Public Library, 82–83
National Barn Dance, 1
Natty Bumpo, 4
Nelson, Butch, 205
Nelson, Kyle (Cowboy Kyle), 204–206
Nelson, Susan, 205–206
Nelson, Willie, 2–3, 12
Nemerov, Bruce, 58; as Big Zeno Clinker, 144
Newhart, Bob, 21
Newman, Randy, 161, 164
Nicholls, Mike, 11
No Fish Today, 106
Nolan, Bob (Robert Nobles), 10–11, 57, 95
Norman Luboff Choir, 1
Nowlin, Bill, 89
Nudie costumes, 1, 112
Nugget Casino (Sparks, Nevada), 157
Nye, Bill (The Science Guy), 202, 204

O'Brien, Tim, 12
O'Dell, Doye (*Western Varieties*), 19
Oermann, Robert K. (Bob), 69, 97, 103, 116, 201
Ohrlin, Glenn, 2
Oklahoma!, 7
Old Crow Medicine Show, 74
Old Homestead Records, 30, 33
Old Joe Clark's Music Store, 74
Old Time Pickin' Parlor, 64, 66, 68, 77
Outlaw movement in Country Music, 76
Owens, Tex, 143

Palindrome skits, 145–146
Palomino Club, 112
Parker, Andy, 185

Parnell, Liza Jane Green, 25
Patrick, Shorty, 28
Paul, Brad, 158
"Paul is Dead" hoax, 52–53
Perryman, Lloyd, 38
Peterson, Arvid, 16, 21
Peterson, Hank, 16, 21
Peterson, Jay, 169
Phantom Empire, 146
Phantom Stallion, 1
Pinson, Bob, 37
Poor David's Pub, 77
Porter, Cole, 9
Posedi, Roman, 139
Prairie Home Companion, 12
Prairie Rose Wranglers, 188

Ramage, Ned, 120, 126, 128
Rane, Jimmy (Yella Fella), 190, 191
Ranger Doug. *See* Green, Douglas B.
Ranger Doug's Classic Cowboy Corral, 124
Raney, Wayne, 35
Rawhide, 2
Record Bar, 125
Red Knuckles and the Trailblazers, 12
Red River, 5
Reed, Lisa, 173, 197–198
"Reincarnation," 134
Remington, Fredric, 3
Riders In The Sky, 3, *130*, *155*, *160*; organizing and first gigs, 62–64; at Wind in the Willows, 77, 78–79; state fairs, 78; World's Fair, 157; festivals, 103, 111, 118–120, 177, 194–195, 200; appeal to children, 78, *100*; stage props and costumes, 6, 62, 79, 98, 112–113; skits and wacky commercials, 80–82, 145–146; humor, 81–82, 88, 98–99, 144, 145–146; development of stage act, 82–83; vocal style, 91; instrumental sound, 91–92; at presidential inaugural events, 105; variety of performing venues, 138, 156; *Austin City Limits*, 85, 104; *Larry King Show* appearance, 88–89; Rounder Records, 154, 158; first recording, 91; first album, 92–93; ongoing presentation pattern, 97, 102; relationship with fans, 99, 102, 176–177, 201–206; Too Slim's Mercantile, 107, 108–*109*, 110; Grand Ole Opry first appearance, 84; Grand Ole Opry induction, 113–114, 116–*117*; Grand Ole Opry performances, 131, *184–185*, 198; Walkway of Stars induction, 117; Tumbleweed Theater, 120–124; development of radio and TV characters, 123–124; 146; booking agents and management, 125–127; community outreach, 128–129, 147, 155; popularity in the West, 131–132; appearances at Cowboy Poetry Gathering, 133, 134; Western Music Association, 137; 177–178; casino appearances, 111, 157; travels abroad, 118, 132, *159*; *Riders Radio Theater*, 144–148; CBS kiddie TV show, 148–152; with Gene Autry, 152; Joey Miskulin joins as partner, 152; *Toy Story 2*, 161–164, *162*, *164*, and Pixar/Disney connection, 164–165; Grammy awards, *163*; Hollywood Bowl performances, 165–166, *182–183*; income, 168–169, 196; strains on marriages, 173–174; Riders' children's relations, 175; vehicles, 103, 153; road stories, 115–116, 169–170; hazards of road travel, 170–171, 172–173; Tweetsie Railroad, 175–177; cruises, 178; symphony concerts, 194, 181–182, 186; Wrangler award, 154; Walk of Western Stars induction, 178–179; politics of, 183–184; dude ranches, 186–189; making commercials, 189–191; fortieth anniversary tour, 190–191; involvement with Ken Burns' *Country Music* documentary, 192, 194; response to Covid Pandemic, 196; 45th anniversary show, 199

Riders In The Sky (book), 148
Riders In The Sky (CBS kiddie TV series), 148–152
Riders In The Sky: Forty Years the Cowboy Way, 190
"Riders Radio Theater" (skit), 80
Riders Radio Theater, 141–148
Riess, Andy, 179
Ritter, Tex (Woodward Maurice), 3, 6, 9
Robbins, Marty (Martin Robinson), 2, 3, 77
Robison, Carson, 8
Roger Wagner Chorale, 1
Rodgers, Jimmie, 7–8
Rogers, Roy (Leonard Sly), 1, 3, 9, 10, 49, 91, 130, 131, 185
Romaine, Anne, 89
Roosevelt, Franklin, 7
Roosevelt, Teddy, 4
Rose, Fred, 9
Rosenberg, Neil, 26
Rounder Records, 89–90; Riders' first recording date, 91
Roy Acuff's Musical Collection at Opryland, 34
Rumble, John, 30
Russell, Charles, 3

Sacks, Alan, 149, 178
Sacks, Andy, 53, 54
Saddle Pals, 201–206
Sawtelle, Charles, 12
Scarborough, Cy, 134, 187, 188
Scoggins, Teena, 110
Scott, Judy, 149
Seals, Troy, 56
Sears, Dawn, 180
Sears, Kenny, 179
Sebring, David, 34
Secor, Ketch, 73–74, 75
Shakey's Pizza Parlor, 38
Shaver, Billy Joe, 66
Sheriff John's Cartoon Time, 19
Shin Bone Alley All Stars, 38

Sidekick Handbook: How to Unleash Your Inner Second Banana and Find True Happiness, 168
Silver, Lisa, 54–56
Singing Cowboy, 37
Singing in the Saddle, 36, 157–158
Sirius XM radio, 124, 185, 195, 202
Skepner, Dave, 124, 127–128, 158–159
Sikes, O.J., 155
Slatkin, Felix, 72
Smothers Brothers (Dick and Tommy), 11, 21, 49
Smothers, Tommy, 178
Sneakers (band), 51
Sons of the Pioneers, 3, 10–11, 37, 57, 95
Sons of the San Joaquin, 133
South Pacific, 21
Sovine, Red, 99
Sovine, Roger, 67
Spade Cooley Show, 19
Spencer, Tim, 10–11
Spicher, Buddy (Norman Keith), 56
Sprague, Carl, 7
Springwater, 77, 87
Stafford, Terry, 3
Stars of Country Music, 10
Station Inn, 59, 180
Springwater, 77, 87, 88, 103,
Steagall, Red, 136
Steketee, Ricky, 51
Stromberg, Charles and Elmer, 180
Stromberg guitars, 180
Stuart, Marty, 112, 147, 194
Sunkel, Fred, 47
Symington, David, 85, 86

Taylor, Jeff, 195–196
Teeter, Buck, 187
Terry, Gordon, 72
Third and Lindsley, 180
Thorp, Nathan Howard, 6
Tichenor, Tom, 82
Tillman, Floyd, 12, 36
Time Jumpers, 179–181

GENERAL INDEX 243

TNN (Nashville Network), 120, 121, 124, 147, 155,
Too Slim. *See* LaBour, Fred
Toothacher, Tom, 54
Town Hall Party, 19
Toy Story 2, 161–164
Truitt, Brent, 155, 200
Tubb, Ernest, 104, 116, 117
Tumbleweed Theater, 120–124; characters, 123–124
Turner, Cindy (Cynthia), 35, 84
Tuttle, Marilyn and Wesley, 131, 163
Tweetsie Railroad, 175–177
Two-Jaws, 98, 121
Tyson, Ian, 3, 134, 135–136

University of Michigan, 15, 22, 23, 26, 28, 30, 39, 41, 47, 51, 52, 54, 57, 203
US Festival, 118–120

Vanderbilt, 31, 32, 33, 35, 57, 59, 72–73, 77, 85, 87, 153
The Virginian, 4–5

Wagonmasters (band), 19
Wakely, Jimmy, 9–10, 36
Walker, Cindy, 9
Walker, Tina, 82–83
Walkway of Stars, 117
Wall, Rem, 48
Warren, Paul, 71
Wayne, John, 49, 179, 182, 186, 190
WCKY (Cincinnati), 35
Wernick, Pete, 12
West, Jerry and Diane, 114–116, 163, 201
Western, Johnny (Johnny Westerlund), 145
Western Folklife Center, 132
Western Music Association, 135, 136, 137, 177, 186

western swing, 12, 92
Western Varieties (Doye O'Dell), 19
WestFest, 136
White, Buck, 33
White, Roland, 30, 31, 32
Whitley, Ray, 36
WHVU (Cincinnati), 146
Wiegel, Richard, 202
Wikle, Jeff, 55
Wild West Shows, 4
Wiley, Bill, 114, 136
Willing, Foy, 36
Willis, Vic, 142
Wills, Bob, 37, 92, 179, 180
Wind in the Willows, 77, 78–79, 109
Wisconsin Opry, 116
Wister, Owen, 4
WJEF (Grand Rapids, Michigan), 44
WKNR FM (Detroit, Michigan), 52
WKZO (Kalamazoo, Michigan), 48
WLS (Chicago), 21
WMAX (Grand Rapids, Michigan), 44–45
Wolf, Rod, 28, 29
Wood, Del, 36
Woody Paul. *See* Chrisman, Paul Woodrow, Jr. (Woody Paul)
WPLN (Nashville), 144, 145
WSM (Nashville), 67, 200
WVXU (Cincinnati), 146
Wynette, Tammy, 56

XXX Ranch, 81, 89

Yankovic, Frank, 139–140
YellaWood, 190, 191

Zeis, Nancy, 24
Ziegfeld Follies of 1934, 9

SONG AND ALBUM INDEX

"9 Million, 999 Thousand Tears to Go," 60

"Act Naturally," 161
A Great Big Western Howdy, 146, 158
"A Tribute to Gabby Hayes," 185
"After You've Gone," 92, 154
"Along the Navajo Trail," 185
Always Drink Upstream from the Herd, 154, 187
"Amarillo by Morning," 3
"Amber Eyes," 137

"Back in the Saddle Again," 62, 91, 119, 155
"The Ballad of Paladin," 145
"The Ballad of Palindrome," 146
"Be Honest with Me," 155
"Be My Love," 21
"Big Balls in Cow Town," 104
"Big High Wire Hop," 165
Black Cowboys, 183
"Bloodshot Eyes," 181
"Bluebonnet Lady," 68, 75, 94, 145
"Blue Canadian Rockies," 9
"Blue Montana Skies," 94

"Blue Prairie," 10
"Blue Shadows on the Trail," 11, 66, 185
"Cannon Ball Yodel," 91
"Carry Me Back to the Lone Prairie," 8, 196
"Carry Me Back to the Mountains," 196
"Casey Jones," 176
"Cattle Call," 13, 91, 143, 154
"Cattle Call/Circus Train," 98, 144
"Cherokee Strip," 200
"Chime Bells," 91
"Chattanoogie Shoe Shine Boy," 62
"Cielito Lindo," 94
"Cigarettes, Whiskey, and Wild, Wild Women," 11
"Clarinet Polka," 177
"Colorado Trail," 200
"Cool Water," 11, 13, 18, 165
Cowboys in Love, 152
"The Cowboy Song," 68, 75, 94
Cowboy Songs (Michael Martin Murphey), 136

"Danny Boy," 185
"Dark Hollow," 77

"Deep River Blues," 62
"Desert Serenade," 13
"Devil's Dream," 72, 75
"Devil Woman," 62
"Don't Bite the Hand that's Feeding You," 182
"Don't Fence Me In," 9, 94
"Down the Lullaby Trail," 128
"Dueling Faces," 98
"The Dying Cowboy," 6

"El Paso," 2
"Eminem Rap," 195
"Empty Saddles," 9
"The Everlasting Hills of Oklahoma," 11

"Faded Love," 72
"Father's Day," 55
"The First Cowboy Song," 154, 187
"Fisher's Hornpipe," 72
"Forty Hour Week for a Living," 56
Forty Years the Cowboy Way, 190
"Four Strong Winds," 135
"Fraulein," 184

"Getaway Gallop," 200
"(Ghost) Riders in the Sky," 18, 94, 195, 199
"Git Along Little Dogies," 58
"The Glory of Love," 9
"Golden Lockets," 200
"Golden Slippers," 199
Gunfighter Ballads and Trail Songs, 2

"Happy Trails," 95, 185, 199, 205
"The Happy Yodeler," 200
Harmony Ranch, 151, 153
"Have I Told You Lately that I Love You," 18
"Have You Ever Been Lonely," 9
"Here Comes the Santa Fe," 13, 95
Hoedown! The Fantastic Fiddles of Felix Slatkin, 72
Home on the Range, 184

"Home on the Range," 6–7, 62, 71, 161
"Hooked on an Eight Second Ride," 135
"How Does He Yodel," 155
"How High the Moon," 177
"Hurry Sunrise," 137

"I Always Do," 153
"I'd Love to be in Texas, When They Roundup in the Spring," 184
"If I Didn't Have You," 165
"I'm an Old Cowhand," 9, 177
"I'm Gonna Leave Old Texas Now," 58
"I'm So Lonesome I Could Cry," 75
In God's Eyes, 33
"It Ain't Gonna Rain No More," 50
"I've Been Working on the Railroad," 176
"I Want to Be a Cowboy's Sweetheart," 83

"Jambalaya," 55
"Jesse," 137
"Jesse James," 6
"Jessie the Yodeling Cowgirl," 162, 164, 167
"Just Because," 140

"Kansas City Star," 2
Ken Jones: Meanwhile... Back at the Ranch, 187
Kid Sister, 181
"Kid Sister," 181

"The Lady is a Tramp," 54
"Land of My Boyhood Dreams," 8
Lassoed Live at the Schermerhorn, 186
"The Last Roundup," 9
"Laugh and Be Happy," 19
"Liberty," 199
"Life Gets Teejus," 196
"Little Green Valley," 196, 200
"Little Joe the Wrangler," 6
Liza Jane and Sally Anne, 33
"Lonely Yukon Stars," 92, 165

"Love is a Many Splendored Thing," 21
"Lovesick Blues," 55

"Maiden's Prayer," 72
"Mamas, Don't Let Your Babies Grow Up to Be Cowboys," 2
"Maybe I'll Cry over You," 91
Merry Christmas from Harmony Ranch, 187
"Midnight on the Stormy Deep," 27
Monsters, Inc.: Scream Factory Favorites, 165

"Never Go to Church on Sunday," 177
"Night Riders' Lament," 3
"Night Riding Song," 137

"O, Bury Me Not on the Lone Prairie," 6
"Ol' Cowpoke," 200
"The Old Chisholm Trail," 2, 6, 7
"The Old Double Diamond," 135
"Old Paint," 6
"The Old Spinning Wheel," 9
"On the Rhythm Range," 200
"Orange Blossom Special," 72
"Our Love is Here to Stay," 87

"Patches," 60
"Prairie Lullaby," 9
Prairie Serenade, 128
Public Cowboy Number One: The Music of Gene Autry, 155
"Put another Candle on the Birthday Cake," 19
"Put Me in Your Pocket," 184

"The Rainbow's End," 10
"Rawhide," 154
Red Headed Stranger, 3, 12
"Red River Valley," 62
"Red Wing," 7
Riders in the Sky, 64
Riders In The Sky Live, 128

Riders In The Sky Present a Pair of Kings, 177
Riders In The Sky Salute Roy Rogers: King of the Cowboys, 185
Riders In The Sky—Silver Jubilee, 178
Riders Radio Theater, 142, 143
The Riders' Roundup, 128
Ridin' on a Rainbow, 155
"Riding Down the Canyon," 155
"Riding on the Rio," 137
Ridin' on the Tweetsie Railroad, 176–177
"Rock Island Line," 176
"Roly Poly," 184
"Room Full of Roses," 11
"Running Gun," 154

Saddle 'Em Up and Go, 187
Saddle Pals, 128
"Sally Goodin," 75
"San Antonio," 7
Say No More, It's Freddy LaBour, 168
Seventy Years of Hits (Frank Yankovic), 141
"She Thinks I Still Care," 60
"The Shelter of the Wildwood," 14, 200, 201
"Shortenin' Bread," 50
"Sidekick Heaven," 123–124
"Singing in the Saddle," 137
"Skyball Paint," 94
"Snow Deer," 7
"So Long, Saddle Pals," 95
"Someday Soon," 3, 135
"Song of the Prairie," 58
Songs of the Sage, 137
"South of the Border," 155
"The Spanish Cavalier," 18
Springtime in the Rockies, 188
"Strawberry Roan," 2
"Streets of Laredo" ("Cowboy's Lament"), 6
"Summer Wages," 135
"Surfin' USA," 145

SONG AND ALBUM INDEX   247

"Take Me Back to My Boots and Saddle," 154
"Ten Thousand Cattle Straying," 5
"Texas Plains," 13, 83, 200
"Texas Sand," 177
"That Pioneer Mother of Mine," 10
"That's How the Yodel was Born," 94, 99, 116, 145
"That Silver Haired Daddy of Mine," 155, 184
"There's a Little Bit of Everything in Texas," 104
"There's a Star-Spangled Banner Waving Somewhere," 91, 199
"They Cut Down the Old Pine Tree," 9
"Three on the Trail," 94
Three on the Trail, 92–94
Throw a Saddle on a Star, 200
"Timber Trail," 11, 62, 66
The Time Jumpers, 181
"The Trail Tip Song," 154
"A Tribute to Gabby Hayes," 185
A Tribute to the Best Damn Fiddle Player in the World, 180
"Tumbling Tumbleweeds," 11, 62, 165, 182
"Turkey in the Straw," 72

"Utah Carroll," 7

"Wagon Wheels," 9
"Waiting for the Echo," 200
"Walls of Time," 29

"Waltz Across Texas," 104
"Way Out There," 11
"The Wayward Wind," 200
"Weapon of Prayer," 30
Weeds and Water, 128
"When It's Springtime in the Rockies," 7
"When the Bloom is on the Sage," 9, 145
"When the Cactus is in Bloom," 8
"When Payday Rolls Around," 83, 94, 98, 145
"When the Swallows Come Back to Capistrano," 182–183
"When the Work's All Done this Fall," 7
"Where the Silvery Colorado Wends Its Way," 7
"Won't You Ride in My Little Red Wagon," 184
"Woody's Roundup," 161, 167, 195, 205
Woody's Roundup: A Rootin,' Tootin' Collection of Woody's Songs, 161, 164
"The World's Most Broken Heart," 56
"Worried Mind," 18
"Wreck of the Number Nine," 196

"Yodel Blues," 58, 91
"The Yodeling Cowboy," 8
Yodel Songs, 91
Young Blood and Sweet Country Music, 58
"Your Cheating Heart," 54, 75
"You've Got a Friend in Me," 162

"Zeb Turney's Gal," 196